This book is dedicated
to the guardians of the elephants:
the Game Scouts, Rangers
and Park Wardens of Africa.

ELEPHANTS OF AFRICA

PAINTINGS AND DRAWINGS BY
PAUL BOSMAN
TEXT BY ANTHONY HALL-MARTIN

SAFARI PRESS
Post Office Box 3095
Long Beach, California 90803

First published in the USA in 1989 by Safari Press
A Division of The Woodbine Co.
Post Office Box 3095, Long Beach, California 90803

ISBN: 0-940143-11-9

Editors: Jennifer Still and Douglas van der Horst
Design and Typography: Wim Reinders
Jacket Design: Abdul Amien
Index: Peter Coates

Dustjacket (front)

*Shingwedzi – one of Kruger's best-known tuskers – stands aside, avoiding the bustle
of a breeding herd. He waits patiently as cool, clean water seeps into the drinking hole
he has dug with his massive foot and dextrous trunk.*
(Mphongol River, Kruger National Park, South Africa)

Dustjacket (back)

*João, one of the magnificent elephant bulls of the Kruger National Park, his skin worn
and patterned by fifty summers, contemplates the cooling mud of an autumn wallow.*
(Shingwedzi, Kruger National Park, South Africa)

Title page

*Africa burns: the grass is tinder dry and the sun a dull white orb through the pall of
smoke that shrouds the continent. Elephants then seek out the greenery of swamps and
flood plains.*
(Mbawala, Shire River, Liwonde National Park, Malaŵi)

CONTENTS

PAUL BOSMAN

FOREWORD

A. E. RUPERT

President
S.A. NATURE FOUNDATION
Vice-president
WORLD WIDE FUND FOR
NATURE

(Left) *Against a leaden sky the bull Shawu –
his long, slender, curved tusks like ivory scythes –
strides through the low shrubveld of the
Lebombo Flats.*
(Shilowa, Kruger National Park, South Africa)

The conservation of the African elephant and its habitats has been the key reason behind the creation of some of Africa's finest national parks. The elephant has thus helped to ensure the survival of many other forms of wildlife – ranging from plant, mammal and insect species to whole communities and ecosystems.

While the protection of entire ecosystems with their wildlife populations is a major priority for the long-term functioning of our living world, it is equally necessary to have a key to unlock the support of governments and people for conservation. The African elephant has often provided this key.

Some of the pages of this book make sad reading – especially the author's discussion of the threat to the African elephant posed by ivory poaching and civil disorder, and the relentless human expansion which is destroying the natural resources needed for the future survival of both man and wildlife. Africa as a continent faces many other grave economic, social and political problems. There are growing demands for health services, education, housing and food production, and many countries are hard-pressed to maintain even minimum levels of support for these essential requirements. It is therefore greatly to the credit of Africa that some of the continent's poorest countries maintain viable national parks where elephants and hundreds of other species find sanctuary.

That these parks have survived is of immense significance, as they play a vital role in the healthy functioning of a country's natural 'life-support' systems – a prerequisite for a stable nation with a happy future.

The World Wide Fund for Nature (WWF) has supported a wide range of projects in many African parks and reserves where elephants occur. The Southern African Nature Foundation, which is affiliated to the WWF, has been actively involved in conservation projects in twelve African countries. A considerable portion of S.A. Nature Foundation funds has been channelled into the creation, expansion and development of national parks. Among the areas assisted, and which are featured in this book, are Kasungu, Liwonde, the Kaokoveld, Pilanesberg, Chobe, Kruger and Maputo.

The existence of national parks is essential for man and for the survival of the African elephant. This book shows that without suitable protected areas where the elephant can find sanctuary, no other action can ensure the survival of the species in the wild.

Anton Rupert

7

ACKNOWLEDGEMENTS

In gathering material for this book we enjoyed the help, hospitality and advice of many people. The text was influenced by the ideas of the scientists, guides, game rangers and hunters who know the areas mentioned much better than we do. We cannot recall the names of all who have contributed, but would, nonetheless, like to thank them and, in particular, those most closely associated with the project.

For help in Senegal we thank André and Alexis Dupuy; Hamady Sow, S. Ndiaye and Dr J. Verschuren; our Mali chapter would have been impossible without the considerable contributions of Bruno Lamarche and Iain Douglas-Hamilton. In Côte d'Ivoire, the co-operation of Dr Harald Roth was invaluable; we were also assisted by Patrick and Glenda Ponroy, Marcello and Cathy Maio, M. Aratan, Bengt Hoppe and Knut Henschel. In Gabon, our hosts and informants were Claude Pradel and Mme Pradel, Michele and Jacky Cuminetti. Our path through Zaïre was smoothed by Helmut Reimann, Jacques Feyerick, Claude Delbol, Pat and Poppit Rogers, and we greatly appreciated the help and interest of Dr Kakiese Onfine, Mankoto ma Mbaelele, Iyhemopo Bebu, Tatala Tatika and Gregory Nicolaides.

Our knowledge of East Africa was broadened by Ian and Chris Parker, Dr Iain Douglas-Hamilton and Oria Douglas-Hamilton, Bill Woodley, Kes Hillman, Dr David Western, Cynthia Moss, Peter and Sarah Jenkins, Sam Weller and Phil Snyder.

In Zambia we were aided by Norman Carr, Dr Geoffrey Zyambo, Patrick Ansell, Vic and Pamela Guhrs, and Phil Berry; in Malaŵi by Dr Richard Bell and Cathy Bell, Max and Elizabeth Morgan-Davies, Matthew Matemba and Alfred Kombe; and in Zimbabwe by Rowan and Elizabeth Martin, Dr Dave Cumming, Russell and Lynne Taylor, Graham Hall, Kevin Dunham and Dr Colin Craig.

At Savuti in Botswana we stayed with Lloyd Wilmot and June Anthony, and in Chobe we were guests of Jonathon Gibson at the Chobe Game Lodge. Our companions on many safaris to Botswana and Namibia were Clive Walker, whose encouragement was generous, and Peter Joffe, and we have much to thank them for. Also in Namibia we enjoyed the hospitality of Colin and Ina Britz and drew freely on the experience of Slang Viljoen, Garth Owen-Smith, Professors Fritz Eloff, Koos Bothma and Guillaume Theron, Dr Hu Berry and Dr Ian Hofmeyr. We thank the National Parks Board of Bophuthatswana and the S.A. Nature Foundation for sponsoring our visit to Pilanesberg and are grateful for the friendship of Dr Jeremy Anderson and Elizabeth Anderson and the help of Pete Hancock and Randall Moore.

We thank Garnet Jackson, Herb Bouirn, Solomon Ngubane and Peter Murless for help in Maputaland; and Harold and Toni Braack for helping us at Addo. Finally, in the Kruger National Park – where it all began – we thank Dr U. de V. Pienaar, Hugo van Niekerk, Piet Otto, Bruce Bryden, Merle Whyte and Lazarus Mangane.

Our information and reference material was gathered throughout Africa, but it was in our own homes that it was polished and put together. We gratefully acknowledge the support and encouragement of our wives, Elaine Bosman and Catherina Hall-Martin. Our family and friends who contributed in many ways to our labours and lives while working on this book are Edith Bosman, Kate and Simon Bosman, Christopher and Caron Bosman, Adrian and Rosemary Bosman, Chris and Brenda Visser, Sally Antrobus, Cornelis and Helen Derksen, and Andrew and Elizabeth Embleton. Our travel arrangements were seldom conventional, and without the perseverance of Avryl Gray our itineraries might have been very different.

Our dealings with the team at the publishers have been most pleasant. We thank Pieter Struik, Gerry Struik, Peter Borchert, Wim Reinders, Jennifer Still and Douglas van der Horst for their commitment to this project. To Maryna Potgieter of Skukuza, our thanks for her typing, and to Koppes Photographic Studio in Phoenix, Arizona, our appreciation of their photo reproduction work.

We are particularly grateful to Dr Richard Bell, Ian Parker and Dr Iain Douglas-Hamilton for reading the text, for making stimulating and penetrating comments, and for concepts which have shaped our thoughts on the conservation of the African elephant.

PREFACE

We are both children of Africa – our roots nurtured in the African soil for generations. Paul grew up in the vastness and silence of the Karoo and I in the shadow of the Magaliesberg. The immense beauty and glory of this vast continent, its squalor and misery, have always been part of our lives. Both of us, in different ways, have been associated with elephants for many years – Paul as an artist and I as a scientist. We have seen elephants through different eyes – yet similarly.

It was an elephant, the great bull Mafunyane of the Kruger National Park, that brought our paths together. I had written a short magazine article on some of the big tuskers of the Kruger, including Mafunyane, which Paul had read and remembered. He concluded that his long interest in elephants would find a natural culmination in a project to study and portray in pastels this great elusive tusker – who had only ever been seen by a handful of people, all rangers or game scouts.

Permission to seek the bull was given by a sympathetic Park Warden, Dr U. de V. Pienaar, and we set out to the gently rolling mopane woodland country of the far north of the Kruger. Because Mafunyane lived in a remote part of the huge 20 000 km² park, one of the largest in Africa, we were airlifted in by helicopter and dropped off near our quarry by Chief Pilot Hugo van Niekerk. Accompanying us on that eventful day was Bruce Bryden, now Chief Ranger of the Kruger. We tracked Mafunyane for a long way and eventually in a grassy clearing we came across him, accompanied by a single askari. It was an autumn day and the mopane leaves, already golden-brown and yellow, were being gently flushed off the trees by a fickle wind. The elephants caught our scent and Mafunyane turned on us, lifting his great ivory off the ground. He charged instantly, burning his image into our minds, then veered away and hurried off into thicker cover, following his askari.

It was a moving and awesome experience. I could not believe that there was a bigger tusker in all of Africa. Paul was equally moved – and painting elephants has since been his passion.

Since that day we have spent much time together watching and studying elephants. Initially it was to gather reference material for a series of paintings of the seven largest tuskers in the park – now known as the 'Magnificent Seven'. Paul's paintings of four of these bulls have been released as limited edition prints. I wrote a short text for each, telling something about the animal.

From this beginning grew the idea of a book of paintings and text to celebrate the African elephant. To us these creatures are surpassingly magnificent. They are exciting animals to study and portray. They are never dull – their colours, tones, textures and habits, their very look and feel, are infinitely variable, as are their habitats. Where elephants survive, something of the spirit of primeval Africa is also found.

In this book we present a view of elephants in a selection of 24 different but representative environments spread across Africa. We also provide a glimpse, no more, of some of the other more interesting creatures, including man, which share these habitats. But our focus is always the elephant. We make no apology for this. Rather than present a balanced ecosystem ap-

The ostrich is the largest living bird: males stand 2 metres high and weigh 100 kilograms or more. (The Great Karoo, Cape Province, South Africa)

proach to describing Africa, we have chosen to indulge in the African elephant – to us the greatest animal of all.

Since embarking on this project we have travelled the length and breadth of Africa – as far as political exigencies allowed – and visited 15 countries, passing briefly through another five, in search of elephants in the most varied environments. We covered about 180 000 kilometres between us. In the air we travelled in wide-bodied jets, small turbo-prop passenger aircraft, light aircraft and helicopters. We made a memorable flight in a 40-year-old Douglas DC3 Dakota or 'Gooney Bird', a legendary aircraft which still flies regularly in the most remote parts of Africa. On Africa's highways, byways and rutted tracks we travelled by bus, mini-bus, car, pick-up truck and four-wheel-drive. We also journeyed by canoe and boat and traipsed many weary kilometres on foot, alone or with a guide, tracker and porters.

In Côte d'Ivoire we walked for days through the Tai rain forest, and paddled through the Azagny swamps, in search of the small West African forest elephant. We trod the white beaches of Gabon where forest elephants swim in the sea, and climbed the Virunga volcanoes in Zaïre. In pursuit of the famed desert elephants of Kaokoland, we enjoyed much good companionship. We visited many of the greater national parks of Africa and other areas – forest reserves, game reserves, hunting reserves and wilderness areas uninhabited and unspoiled.

Our odyssey has taught us much about wildlife and the land of Africa. Inevitably, it has also sharpened our perceptions of African society, politics and economics. We knew Africa before the winds of change swept over it, and we have now seen many of the blessings and burdens of independence and nationhood and have skirted around the edges, and aftermath, of revolution, insurrection and civil war.

Political systems in Africa span a wide range. Their strengths and weaknesses, indigenous attitudes to wildlife, as well as the different legacies of conservation tradition and philosophy inherited from the colonial powers, have influenced the development of national parks in Africa over the past two decades. Everything we have seen has convinced us of the necessity of parks and equivalent areas for the survival of the African elephant.

As human numbers swell and more of Africa is settled and brought under the axe and the hoe, the elephant, which is incompatible with man and his works, will disappear. Besides the physical pressures, we must realise that conservation concepts, as understood in the Western world, have little relevance for the homeless and the hungry. It is only in the refuges that are set aside for wildlife – be they national parks, safari areas or whatever – that the elephant will survive. And such sanctuaries will remain only if enough Africans decide, or can be convinced, that they want them or need them.

The national parks and other refuges must be strengthened, cared for, and cherished. If they do not function as they should, no other action can do any more than postpone the inevitable demise of the African elephant and the great assemblage of other animals and plants which know no other home.

INTRODUCTION

The African elephant

The charge of a fully-grown elephant bull may begin with no warning preliminaries. The old tusker, sensing your presence, spins around with stunning speed. The head is raised in the turn, the tusks held high, the eyes red and straining out of their sockets as the animal searches for, and then focuses on his target. The great ears fan out in the turn, like sails set. The tail is lifted up in anger, taut and tense with the long hairs streaming in the wake of this colossus. The ears might slap once against the shoulders, raising a cloud of dust; the sound of it mingles with the elephant's scream – a chilling trumpet, harsh, shrill, terrifying – or, more ominously, with no sound at all, only merciless purpose.

He begins the charge with head held high and forward, seeking you out. The ears are held tightly against the heaving body and the trunk is curled up under the jaw so that its solid muscular base, like a giant balled fist, can hit you as the elephant lowers his head at the end of the charge and knock you down, rolling, in a cloud of dust. Then the bull will drop to his knees as though at an offertory, roaring and screaming, and stab with those dull white tusks that can effortlessly transfix a man; or with the base of the trunk crush the life out of a frail human body. Sometimes the elephant might kill with less style and simply trample a man into pulp with its huge front feet.

The African elephant *Loxodonta africana*, the largest and most powerful animal on land, can kill a man as effortlessly as a man despatches an insect. Yet the elephant is threatened by puny man and in the face of man's technology and relentless procreation, the elephant must give way.

If the elephant were an entirely obnoxious creature, its passing would be universally celebrated. But it is not that – it is intelligent, has a complex social life, and plays an important but poorly understood role in the functioning of African ecosystems. Beyond that it is an emotive beast, commanding almost universal respect and admiration, and also fear and loathing from the African farmer wandering through the trampled remains of his crops. Even poachers, who so relentlessly pursue these great beasts, go in awe of their enormous quarry.

In earlier times, before man and his offspring covered the face of the continent in such demanding and overwhelming multitudes, there was room for both elephants and people. Today that is no longer so, and we are witnessing – in its most elemental form – an ecological clash between two competing species. Man, with his terrible power and his imagination, can so easily decide the fate of other creatures – and he can exterminate the African elephant. But if he so chooses, a sufficient number of elephants will be allowed to survive in those few small areas that he sets aside for the purpose or that he cannot use effectively for agriculture.

The elephant not only looks imposing – it is also a triumph of biological design. The trunk is sensitive and mobile and serves the functions of breathing, smelling, communicating, collecting and manipulating the great quantities of food and water the animal requires. It is also a formidable weapon. Among the consequences of large size in the tropics are the need to keep the body cool and a high rate of food ingestion. In the ele-

11

Found in the rain forest of West and Equatorial Africa, the relatively small forest elephant has rounded ears and thin, straight tusks.
(Petit Isle, Azagny National Park, Côte d'Ivoire)

phant, cooling is achieved by flapping the ears which cools the blood in the superficial blood vessels; by using the trunk to shower the head, ears and body with sand, mud and water; and resting in shade.

The elephant communicates intelligently and subtly by voice, posture and the movements of the ears and trunk, and by low-frequency sounds inaudible to humans. When angered, it intimidates an intruder by adopting a posture with head raised, ears spread and trunk lifted up – coiling menacingly. This body language sends an unmistakable signal: beware. In this attitude, the elephant also shows off its most obvious dental specialization in a particularly impressive way. The tusks are modified upper incisors, developed primarily as weapons, also used as tools for gathering and manipulating food, and increasingly an object of man's desire.

The family group consisting of a cow with her offspring is the basic unit of elephant society. Related cows often live together permanently, forming 'herds' of 3 - 30 animals. The matriarch – usually the oldest and most experienced animal – leads the herd. When herds become larger than about 20 animals, a younger cow and her offspring will gradually split off and form a new herd, which retains close links with its original matriarch. On her death, the herd may sometimes split up. In old age, matriarchs may be replaced by a daughter or sister who gradually takes command of the group.

When male calves reach puberty at 10 - 12 years of age they gradually sever their ties with the family group, or are forced out by the matriarch. They join up with their peers or with older bulls in ranges not occupied by breeding herds. Such 'bull areas' have long been recognized by elephant hunters. The bulls may wander alone, in pairs, or even larger, short-lived groupings of 10 - 30 animals. Unlike the breeding herds, however, there are no permanent bonds between bulls.

In human terms, life for an elephant calf is idyllic. The mother takes great care of the baby and the older calves act as nannies and companions. An elephant calf is in almost constant physical contact with its mother or members of its family group. Up to its first birthday it can walk under its mother's chest without difficulty and has only to raise its mouth to suckle from its mother or from other cows in the herd. The care taken of an elephant calf ensures the highest rate of calf survival of any of the large mammals of the bush. Apart from disease, accidents and starvation during hard times, the only threat to elephant calves is from lions which occasionally manage to take them. Not surprisingly, therefore, elephants are antagonistic towards lions. For the forest elephant, however, predation is not a problem.

Elephant society is well ordered, and there is a strict hierarchy or pecking order. In the case of males this is determined from calfhood. Youngsters play and tussle with

12

one another and as they grow older they spar more strenuously. Among cows there, is also a hierarchy, as well as between family groups. In general the female offspring of a dominant matriarch have higher status than those of a lower-ranking animal.

The advantage of this system is that the dominant or fittest animals get first choice of any resource over which individuals or herds may compete – whether it be a shady resting place, clean water, choice food or a cow in oestrus.

Elephant origins

Africa was the evolutionary cradle of both elephant and man. A recent interpretation of fossils from East Africa, by Vincent Maglio, provides a plausible theory of the evolution of elephants. A single ancestral form gave rise via numerous intermediaries to the three modern elephant genera *Loxodonta* (African elephants), *Elephas* (Asian elephants) and *Mammuthus* (the European mammoths).

The mammoths were larger than the two surviving elephant forms and were hunted by prehistoric man. Primitive artists adorned the walls of their caves with exquisite paintings of these great hairy beasts. Mammoth tusks, which were three to four metres in length, were like sweeping, curved scythes. One of the oldest ivory carvings – a stylized female form – is at least 25 000 years old. This indicates how far back into antiquity man has been fascinated by ivory. A few thousand years ago, at the end of the last ice age, the mammoths died out. The remains of entire mammoths, frozen in the Siberian ice, have been found, some with flesh preserved so perfectly that it was edible. Throughout the eighteenth and nineteenth centuries

Though superficially alike, African elephants in different environments have distinctive features. Body size, tusk form and length, and ear shape serve to distinguish, in a general way, the different types of elephant, depicted here as a series of adult bulls. In the rain forest of West Africa the small, round-eared forest elephant (1) is found – this might be the so-called pygmy elephant with a shoulder height of about 2,2 metres. The forest elephant (2) of Gabon and Zaïre has typically long and slender tusks. The West African savanna elephant (3) seems to be smaller than the East African savanna elephant (4). The Moçambique or Kruger elephant (5) is large and generally carries heavy ivory. The elephant of the Kaokoveld and adjoining arid areas (6) is the tallest elephant on record with a shoulder height of 3,5 metres or more in adult bulls.

mammoth ivory kept Russia in the forefront of the ivory trading nations and even today it is still a valuable source of ivory.

The ancestors of the Asian elephant, of the genus *Elephas*, migrated from Africa to colonize much of Europe and Asia while other forms remained behind. *Elephas recki* flourished for about three million years, and was the dominant elephant in Africa throughout the Pleistocene period – it was apparently a woodland and savanna inhabitant. *E. iolensis*, the most advanced descendant of *E. recki*, was still present in East Africa as recently as 40 000 years ago. Its remains have been found at Early Stone Age sites. The modern Asian elephant *E. maximus* was presumably always a forest specialist, and

survived only in the relatively stable rain forest environment. Modern man tamed the Asian elephant and since about 3 000 BC has used it both for work and war. But for many people, the elephant is not only a servant, it is also a deity, and is revered as Ganesha, the Hindu God of wisdom. However, as the twentieth century draws to a close the Asian elephant has been eliminated from most of its former range by man's ever increasing numbers and expanding technology.

The African elephant, *Loxodonta africana*, is known from the fossil record to have existed for little more than half a million years. It arose in Africa, and never left. The immediate ancestor was most likely an animal called *L. adaurora*, which flourished

13

The bond between elephant mother and calf is strong and long-lasting – as the bonds between man and elephant must be if this magnificent species is to survive as the dominant animal of the African fauna.
(Tweelingsvlei, Addo Elephant National Park, South Africa)

grew larger than the ancestral stock which remained in the forest. And so it is only within the last 30 000 years – a mere instant in the history of the world – that *L. a. africana*, the magnificent African savanna elephant emerged, flourished, and began to decline.

Taxonomy

The taxonomy of the African elephant is still not settled. Most modern authorities recognize one species, whose scientific name is *Loxodonta africana*. This is divided into two subspecies – the savanna or bush elephant *L. a. africana*, and the forest elephant *L. a. cyclotis*. A minority still recognize a pygmy elephant, *L. a. pumilio*, and others distinguish subspecies in East, West and Southern Africa.

At various times many other subspecies were described – one based on evidence no more substantial than a dried ear! These are no longer considered valid. What must be recognized, however, is that elephants are variable; it is possible to distinguish, for example, an Etosha elephant from an Amboseli elephant. The features which differ are body and tusk size and shape, ivory colour and hardness, and ear shape.

The main differences between the forest and savanna elephants are given below (some intermediate forms exist):

Forest elephant	Savanna elephant
Adult bulls shoulder height 220-280 cm	Adult bulls over 300 cm
Ears rounded in outline	Ears like a map of Africa in outline

from 4,5 to 2 million years ago and then disappeared.

While the *Elephas* lineage was lording it over the drier savannas and woodlands of Africa, in the depths of the rain forest the descendants of *L. adaurora* were evolving into *L. africana*. It is interesting to note that the modern forest elephant *L. a. cyclotis* shows many of the features expected to be advantageous to life in a forest environment.

When *E. iolensis* died out – for whatever reason – the elephant niche in the savannas was left vacant. Into this void *L. africana* spread. The savanna habitat had an effect upon the immigrants – not least of which might have been food quality – and they

Basic social units of 2 - 3 animals	Basic herds of 6 - 12 animals
Tusks long, straight and pointing downwards	Tusks usually pointing forwards, curved, bowed, thick
Ivory hard and dark coloured	Ivory soft and pale coloured

The elephant problem

Elephants, like man, can modify the landscape by changing the composition and structure of the natural vegetation – mainly by de-barking and uprooting trees. The effect of elephants on their habitat – and what to do about it – has been one of the most vigorously debated topics in African wildlife conservation.

When we speak of habitat destruction by elephants we should appreciate that we are expressing an aesthetic judgement of a natural phenomenon. The morality of killing trees is in the eye of the beholder. But park managers who set themselves the goal of maintaining the landscape in a certain state with a given balance of trees, grass and animal communities – a perfectly valid objective – are concerned when one factor, such as an elephant population, can push the entire system to a condition which they find less desirable. The rationale is mostly aesthetic if it is a question of large, attractive trees dotting the landscape as opposed to dead ones or small struggling seedlings.

If the plant species can survive, there is no irreplaceable biological loss. However, things are seldom so simple in the relatively small island parks of today, and a drastic change in the vegetation may mean the loss of habitat for other animals with very spe-cialized requirements or tastes. Species which browse, such as the gerenuk in Tsavo, may not be able to survive as well in a grass-land dominated system. The opening up of woodland by elephants, and its possible replacement by grassland, can have many other effects on the ecology of a park – whether it be in the impact of predation on an antelope species, the loss of nesting sites for birds, a decrease in available browse which may detrimentally affect black rhino, or a change in the intensity or frequency of fires.

Not all the effects of elephant habitat modifications are deleterious. Some grazing animals are benefited by an opening up of woodland. The trees which are pushed over may continue to live and provide foliage closer to the ground for smaller browsing animals. When the trees are killed the nutrients and minerals locked up inside them are released by decomposition (or fire) and returned to the system. In a small zone sur-rounding an uprooted tree the ground is broken and aerated, water penetration is increased and leaves and other material are blown in. This material rots, creating a small-scale compost effect.

The vast amounts of plant material consumed by elephants (each accounts for 150 - 200 kg per day) results in the production of 140 - 180 kg of dung per animal per day. In an area like the Kruger National Park, with only 7 000 elephants, this amounts to 980 - 1 260 tons of dung per day. Much of this is taken underground by dung beetles and termites, effectively enriching the soil.

Nobody has yet drawn up a really accurate balance sheet of the ecological effects of elephant on woodlands. So, for now, conservative managers tend to the view that damage must be minimized or prevented. They achieve this by culling elephants to maintain their numbers at safe levels (as is currently done in South Africa and Zimbabwe). Else-

At Gangala-na-Bodio, in north-eastern Zaïre, there are still a few trained working elephants of the cyclotis type. They are the remnants of an unfulfilled Belgian dream – which may yet be resurrected by the Zaïrois – of domesticating the elephant.

There are several forms of black-and-white colobus monkey in Africa, and they show great variation in the amount of white around the face and shoulders.

A common adornment of trees in the southern savanna is the untidy collection of nests of the white-browed sparrow weaver.

The black-backed jackal stays paired for life. Despite being hunted for its pelt and as a stock killer, it thrives in suitable areas of isolated or protected habitat.

The flightless dung beetle of Addo lays its egg in a ball of dung which it buries. When the larva hatches it finds itself in a secure nursery and surrounded by food.

where, nature is allowed to take its course (as in Tsavo and Luangwa). In many African parks the authorities may be opposed to culling, or have no firmly held opinion, but it has been widely acknowledged that poaching has effectively controlled the elephant population (as in Uganda).

Several scientists have explained the 'elephant problem' in terms of biological cycles. Some hold that elephant numbers will build up in an area, woodland will be destroyed, the elephants will die and the woodland will recover: evidence for such cycles has been found in the age distribution of tree species in some areas. However, these hypotheses are not universally accepted. The low mortality found in elephants possibly indicates that had populations not been reduced from time to time in the past, there might have been more elephants around in the past few thousand years, and less woodland. The impact of predators such as sabre-toothed cats on elephants may also have played a greater role in the past. As primitive man was well established before the appearance of *L. africana*, he too may have contributed some form of control through hunting. The stability of populations under hunting pressure certainly indicates that predation could have kept elephant populations in balance with a mixed woodland/grassland system over large parts of Africa.

Elephant management

The management or manipulation of African elephant populations is usually an attempt to solve a conflict between elephants and agriculture, or to control elephant numbers relative to a desired state of the habitat.

This usually results in elephants being killed – one way or another.

The successful separation of elephants from man by fencing was first decisively demonstrated at Addo in 1954. Long-standing problems of elephants raiding crops and being shot were solved by confining the elephants behind an elephant-proof railway line-and-cable fence. Fences of various kinds, including electrified fences, have since been used successfully in Etosha (Namibia), Kruger Park (South Africa) and Kasungu (Malaŵi). Ditches have been used to confine elephants in the Aberdares (Kenya), and keep elephants out of plantations in Côte d'Ivoire.

In addition to controlling elephant movements by barriers and shooting, other actions taken specifically to 'manage' elephants include the provision of water supplies, attempts to control poaching and the regulation of professional ivory hunting, subsistence hunting and hunting for sport.

With the appearance of 'elephant problems' in national parks in the last two decades, the culling of excess numbers of elephants has become a further management procedure. Elephant culling was initiated in the Murchison Falls National Park (Uganda), where contractors removed a specified number of animals. To minimize the disturbance, entire family groups were shot and the operations were carried out quickly and cleanly. The same technique was later used in Kenya and Tanzania for single operations, and in Zambia (Luangwa Valley) for a few years. This method is still used in culling operations in Zimbabwe.

The shooting of entire herds of elephants from the ground is a specialist's job, and beyond the competence of the average park warden or ranger. Wherever the technique has been successfully applied, full-time professional hunters or rangers on permanent assignment to culling operations have done the job. As well as competent marksmanship (most animals falling to a single brain shot), it demands clear thinking under pressure and considerable courage. Aircraft have been an integral part of most operations – either to locate the elephants and guide the hunting party to a suitable position, or to drive the elephants towards the waiting guns. In the densely wooded areas in Zimbabwe where the operations are carried out, ground-to-air radio communication is constantly used to guide rangers to animals that might have broken away from the herd or occasional wounded 'runners'.

The shooting, as presently done in Zimbabwe, is a tense, quick, noisy, dusty operation with men having to move quickly to place their shots among the milling groups of elephants. The matriarch or lead cow of a herd has to be taken out first using a heavy calibre rifle. The rest of the herd then becomes a leaderless mob milling around the fallen cow with much screaming and crashing about. Bulls which may be with the herd may try to get away or to attack the hunters and they have to be dispatched as a second priority, also with a heavy-calibre rifle. Thereafter the younger animals are killed with military style self-loading rifles. A seasoned team of three men can take out a group of 20 elephants in about 30 seconds. The panic and terror of the elephants is short.

The carcasses are butchered where they fall, and skins, meat and ivory transported to a temporary base camp for processing.

As the waters of Lake Kariba recede in the dry season, elephants move onto the newly exposed flats in search of the greenery that soon springs up.
(Tashinga, Matusadona National Park, Zimbabwe)

In the Kruger National Park a very different technique is used. The elephants to be culled are herded by helicopter to an appropriate spot near a service road. Streamlined aluminium hypodermic darts containing succinyl choline chloride are then fired into the animals – at excessive dosage levels. Scoline works on the muscle system and within a few minutes the elephants are paralysed and fall to the ground. When the entire herd is down they are shot in the brain by a man on the ground and their throats are cut to bleed the carcasses. This method of killing is regarded as inhumane by some authorities – as scoline paralyses the respiratory muscles and causes the elephants to suffocate. It takes some minutes to administer the darts to all the animals in a herd and the stress of the animals darted first certainly lasts longer than those darted last. Nevertheless, it is an efficient method requiring a minimum of skill from the marksman as the dart is effective regardless of where it strikes, the animals can be properly bled, and the meat is safe for human consumption as scoline breaks down rapidly.

The elephants are degutted on site and trucked to the abattoir near Park headquarters at Skukuza, where total utilization of the carcasses is achieved. Meat (dried, or cooked and canned), skin and ivory are the basic products, but the bones and offal are also processed to fat and carcass meal. The veterinary and public health authorities take great pride (they are backed by legislative muscle) in ensuring that the elephant carcasses are processed under ultra-hygienic conditions. The fact that most animals killed in Africa, domestic or wild, are butchered under primitive conditions with no apparent ill-effects on the growing human population, is lost on these sanitary paragons. The field butchery, and the salting and drying of the meat in Zimbabwe is an object lesson in the application of appropriate technology for Africa.

The Zimbabwean culling operations have been linked to programmes to benefit the people living around the parks, and most of the meat is sold to them. Their immediate response has been positive and the incidence of elephant poaching has declined. Whether this will influence attitudes towards the retention of these areas for wildlife in the face of land shortage and growing human populations in the future remains to be seen. If it does, then Zimbabwe has a head start on other advocates of the idea.

Distribution and status

The African elephant, before modern man reduced its numbers and range so drastically, once ranged throughout the continent. The most extreme desert areas, such as the Namib dune sea and the Sahara, some high mountains and some other areas, including the central Kalahari and the highveld grasslands of southern Africa, probably did not support elephants in any numbers in recent times. Elsewhere in almost every type of savanna, woodland, shrub and forest community there were elephants to be found. There are 46 countries in Africa, all of which – with the possible exception of Lesotho – had elephants in historical times. Today elephants are found in only 35 countries, and in most of these their numbers are declining.

The status and distribution of the African elephant was documented by Dr Iain Douglas-Hamilton and a network of associates under the auspices of the IUCN/SSC Elephant Specialist Group in 1979. The estimates were revised by Rowan Martin of Zimbabwe in 1985. Despite limitations on reliability – sometimes the information amounted to informed guesses – Martin arrived at a minimum estimate of 1 181 900 elephants in 1985. Estimates in 1988 range as low as 450 000 elephants. The claims – regularly made by the Western news media – that the African elephant is on the verge of extinction are patently untrue. There are more elephants in Africa than a host of other species of large mammal, none of which is regarded as endangered. The Asian elephant, with numbers estimated at only 28 000 - 42 000, has not attracted nearly as much attention from the media. By contrast the southern white rhinoceros is now widely regarded as safe – yet there are only 4 000 of them.

The mean number of elephants per country, regardless of how accurate one regards the figures, is illuminating. In the 9 countries in which elephants are limited to protected areas, the mean number is 3 044 per country (ranging from 100 - 9 000), while the 11 countries with relict populations average only 1 167 elephants per country (range 40 - 2 500). The remaining 15 countries accommodate 97 per cent of Africa's elephants. The mean elephant population is 30 973 for 13 of these countries. Tanzania and Zaïre with 739 000 elephants account for 62 per cent of the total. In all countries other than Botswana, Equatorial Guinea, Gabon, Malaŵi, South Africa, Tanzania and Zimbabwe, elephant numbers are reported to be declining.

It is difficult to assess the viability of the relict and isolated elephant populations. Size is not the only criterion – as shown by the spectacular growth of the Addo elephant population from 11 to 140 in 57 years – but in most situations in Africa it is a useful guide. This is because relict or isolated populations, almost without exception, are the result of agricultural developments. When the pressure is great, as in the Karama and Rwinzoka areas of southern Rwanda in 1973, the elephants will be exterminated.

In the West African forest zone (Côte d'Ivoire and Sierra Leone), our knowledge of forest elephant distribution and status is fairly good – largely due to the exhaustive surveys undertaken by Dr Harald Roth. Forest elephants still occur in 34 localities in Côte d'Ivoire and five in Sierra Leone. The only large population (1 500 animals) is found in and around the Tai National Park in Côte d'Ivoire. The mean size of the other 33 groups in Côte d'Ivoire is only 47, while the average size of the Sierra Leone groups is only 40. Many of these relict populations are as small as 10 animals, and there can be no realistic hope of conserving them. The few scanty details available on their population dynamics indicate that most of these groups are declining at rates of up to 10 per cent a year.

The parallel with the status of the Asian elephant population is of more than passing interest. Over the past century the increase in the human population and use of new technology in Asia have resulted in an accelerated rate of forest clearing and settlement. The Asian elephant, like the forest elephant of West Africa, has been reduced to small groups living in isolated patches of forest habitat, usually in hill country which is difficult to cultivate. The conclusions are obvious. If the historical processes which have produced the present distribution pattern of elephants in both Africa and Asia are to continue – and they certainly will – then by the turn of the century there will be very few areas in Africa where elephants will still occur outside national parks or protected reserves.

Ivory and conservation

Ivory in its many forms – whether from an elephant on the dusty plains of Africa, a walrus on a frozen ice floe off Alaska or a sperm whale in the warm blue waters of the Pacific – has an irresistible attraction to man. The desire to possess ivory, as with gold, transcends ethnic, religious, cultural and ideological boundaries, not because it is a utilitarian product but because it is beautiful, sensuous, and commands a price.

Ivory is traditionally regarded throughout Africa as an ornament, a sign of wealth, a badge of rank or legal tender. Early explorers

recorded widespread trade in four commodities – ivory, gold, people and cattle. Many African rulers claimed at least one tusk of every elephant which died in their domain. Usually the tusk on the underside of the carcass was forfeit. This tradition lives on in Zaïre, where hunters are entitled to only one tusk of an elephant shot on licence – they have to pay extra for the second tusk.

The flow of ivory from the hinterland of Africa was well established in the time of the Pharaohs, and ivory was traded by the Phoenicians. The major eastern ivory routes were down the Nile; across the Ethiopian highlands to the Red Sea; or around the Horn of Africa. Further west, the ivory was carried across the Sahara in camel caravans to the Mediterranean, this route being a major source of Roman ivory. The Arab and Indian dhows which plied along the East African coast from the seventh century carried ivory to India. The problem of transporting tusks overland was eventually solved by slavery: the ivory was carried to the coastal markets such as Zanzibar and Mombasa by slaves who were then sold along with their loads, the ivory commanding the higher prices.

Ivory was incorporated in the artistic traditions of West Africa. It was inlaid in masks and jewellery, carved into bracelets, combs and head rests, and used as legal tender. From the fifteenth century onwards European traders entered the West African ivory market, as ivory had many uses in Europe. The later demand for ivory and labour in the New World resulted in a mingling of the West African ivory and slave trades.

The elephants of southern Africa were hunted to some extent by the Khoisan people, whose preferred technique was to dig

When not paired off during the breeding season, helmeted guinea fowl form large flocks which forage, travel and roost together.

pitfalls or use arrow poison. However, it was only after the advent of firearms and white hunters that the major elephant slaughter in the south got under way.

The absence of a slave trade, and the absence of tsetse fly in the interior plateau, dictated that the transport of ivory to the coast would be by ox wagon. Some enterprising hunters operated in the nineteenth century from the Portuguese domain at Delagoa Bay. One such man, João de Albasini, operated in what is today the Kruger National Park: by 1845 he was employing 400 black hunters to shoot elephant and rhinoceros. However, most of the ivory shipped from the Portuguese enclaves was acquired by trade.

The suppression of the slave trade removed the major overland transport system for ivory in both West and East Africa, and the trade declined. It was not until alternative means of transport were developed, such as porters (in employment rather than

19

as slaves), railways, steamers and roads that the export of ivory on a large scale could be resumed.

It is clear that thousands of elephants are killed illegally every year, their tusks entering the trade. However, there is also a legal trade based on officially sanctioned killing and natural mortality. This legal ivory trade has every right to be regarded as a perfectly legitimate human endeavour – and it provides revenue to African governments. The attempts which have been made to control the ivory trade, such as the Washington Convention (CITES), are apparently not achieving their objective of stopping the killing of elephants for their ivory. The reasons are many: they include corruption, the parlous state of the African economy (which makes the ivory trade so rewarding), the bureaucratic difficulties of enforcing the Cites' regulations, and the ease with which 'legalizing' documents can be forged.

Control of the ivory trade is not a simple conservation issue. Ivory has a complex psychological, monetary, diplomatic and intrinsic value. As with gold, ivory prices will rise when investors perceive a crisis. Cutting off the supply of ivory, whether by conservation action or by the dwindling of elephant numbers, will serve only to push the price upwards. The rising price will stimulate poaching by making it more profitable. Conversely, there is no evidence that a drop in prices will lower the rate of elephant killing, as many conservationists claim. Instead, we might expect that if the elephants are still available, lowered prices will result in more being killed to maintain the income of established elephant hunters.

In the long run, the success or failure of Cites in curbing elephant poaching is not likely to make much difference to the ultimate status of the African elephant. If it succeeds, it can ensure that elephants are killed legally and that the governments derive the revenue – but it is unlikely to stop the decline in the numbers of elephants. The ultimate determinant of how many elephants, if any, will be left in Africa, is not the ivory trade, but the size of the human population, and human attitudes towards elephants.

Elephant and man cannot co-exist – each seeks his own place in the sun – but the balance between the numbers of man and elephant has been ecologically determined since the dawn of the Pleistocene era, when primitive man first emerged as a serious competitor for space with the early elephant types. In Africa, rainfall and soil are the ultimate determinants of how much and what quality of food an area can produce – regardless of whether it is intended for man or elephants – and hence the density of either species which can be supported.

The human population of Africa in 1975 stood at about 399 million. In some countries, like Kenya, the population is doubling every 17 years. If Africa's human population continues to increase at the present rate, then by the year 2 000 the continent will have 814 million inhabitants. Only 28 per cent will be making a living in an urban environment; the remaining 587 million people will depend on agriculture for their subsistence and will require the land which is today occupied by elephants. The process becomes inexorable – the more humans, the fewer elephants. Every hectare brought under cultivation is of necessity a patch of land lost to wildlife – and this process will continue. Eventually only the national parks and a few areas of marginal land will be left for the elephants, as is now the case in South Africa, Rwanda, Namibia, Malaŵi, Uganda, Senegal, Niger, Mali and Mauritania. Alternatively, the elephants are completely exterminated – as in Burundi, Gambia, Swaziland and North Africa.

The deepest sincerity and the highest moral convictions of the animal welfare movements of the Western world will not prevent the demise of most of Africa's elephants. A ban on the ivory trade will not feed a single starving African. The utilization of elephants, be it for ivory, food, leather, sport hunting, tourism or even by poachers, can and does provide employment, revenue – and food. If elephants maintain a financial value to African governments, even if it is no more than the value of ivory recovered as a result of natural mortality, the chances for their survival will be greatly improved. But in the final analysis, elephants will survive only if men decide that they should.

For Western conservationists to insist that Africa's elephants, and their conservation, represent an international responsibility is an idealistic and simplistic view. If they ignore the underlying ecological conflict between elephants and man, and the motivations and ideals of Africans, they will do little to solve the conflict. In some African countries the conservation authorities are unable or unwilling to function according to Western expectations, and if national parks are not properly managed there can be no realistic hope of maintaining viable elephant populations. There is not much to show for the international money channelled into African wildlife schemes over the past two decades.

The few successful parks, and hence the most successful conservation, are home grown. Though conservation programmes may well be nurtured, and usually must be guided, by an input from the West – and may well require tourism to sustain them – their success will depend on local attitudes. Without the support of the governments and people of Africa, no conservation project for the African elephant can succeed.

Iain Douglas-Hamilton's survey showed that there were possibly as many as 250 000 elephants scattered over 90-odd national parks and game reserves of various kinds throughout Africa. If these 'protected' elephants alone survive then the species is safe. In 1931 there were 11 Addo elephants left in South Africa. They were effectively conserved behind an elephant-proof fence enclosing only 20 km² – and today they number 140. The lesson is clear: the national parks of Africa are the best hope for the elephant – if they are sensibly and effectively managed – and that is where the conservation effort should be concentrated.

The environment of the African elephant
Geographical features. Africa is the second-largest continent on earth, ranking only behind Asia. It covers an area of 30 million km².

Geological events over millions of years have formed and shaped the rocks, the backbone of the continent. Climatic and other factors have interacted with these to create diverse soils and topography. Highlands are a feature of the east of the continent, while most of the west lies below 1 000 metres. The Great Rift Valley cuts through the Ethiopian highlands and stretches all the way to the Zambezi and beyond. The western

branch skirts the Kivu highlands of Zaïre while the eastern branch cuts through Kenya and Tanzania, the two meeting in northern Malaŵi. Scattered lakes are found on the floor of the Rift, the largest being Tanganyika (west), Turkana (east) and Malaŵi. Large, shallow lakes like Lake Victoria – the second-largest lake in the world – and Lake Chad occupy extensive basins in East and West Africa respectively. The major rivers are the Nile, Zaïre (Congo), Niger and Zambezi.

Climate. In Africa the seasons are wet (rainfall) and dry (no rainfall) rather than summer and winter, and there are several climatic zones. The equatorial belt has high temperatures and rain throughout the year – a rainforest climate – with December and January being the only relatively drier months. North and south of this zone, rain falls during the hotter months on either side of the summer solstice – December in the south and June in the north (to the edge of the Sahara). The rest of the year in these areas is generally dry and cooler. The zones lying adjacent to the equatorial belt (to about 10° N and 15° S) experience higher and more reliable rainfall which gradually grades into the lower-rainfall arid zones. In part of East Africa, east of the Rift Valley, there are two clearly defined wet seasons. Around March to May are the 'long rains' and from mid-October to December, after a dry spell, the 'short rains'. At the southern tip of Africa, and on the Mediterranean coast, rainfall is centred on the winter solstice – December in the north and June in the south.

There are exceptions to these general patterns caused by topography and by ocean currents. In the south-west, the cold Ben-

guela Current has created an extremely low-rainfall zone, resulting in the Namib Desert of Namibia and Angola. On the east coast, the warm Moçambique Current creates high-rainfall conditions. An upwelling of cold water south of Ghana and Benin creates the dry zone which breaks the distribution of the rain forest, the so-called Dahomey Gap. In general, Africa is a dry continent; even its well-watered equatorial regions, with 2 000 - 2 500 millimetres of rain a year, receive less than similar latitudes in South America and Asia.

Temperatures fluctuate only slightly at low altitudes in the cloudy equatorial zones. Further away from the equator, in the dry areas where clear skies are the rule, the fluctuations are much greater. The highlands are cooler than the surrounding lowlands at all latitudes – and the equatorial mountains – Ruwenzori, Mt Kenya and Kilimanjaro (Africa's highest mountain at 5 894 metres) – have permanent snow and some glaciers. Regular winter snowfalls occur on the Atlas mountains and on the mountains of South Africa and Lesotho. On the high interior plateau of South Africa and highlands of eastern Africa, frost is also frequent; elsewhere it occurs sporadically.

A limp and mutilated trunk is not an uncommon sight in areas where elephants run the risk of being caught in snares set for lesser game.

21

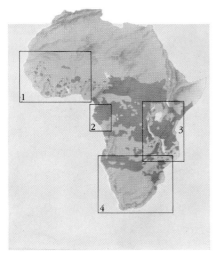

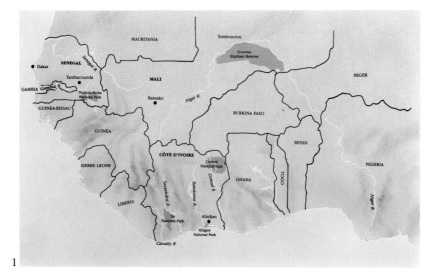

1

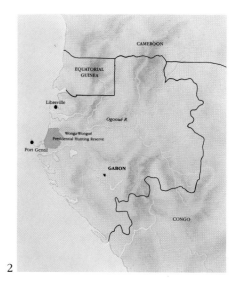

2

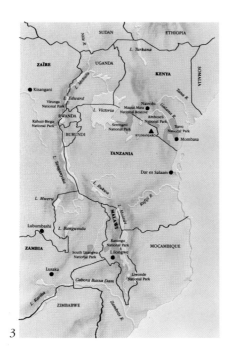

3

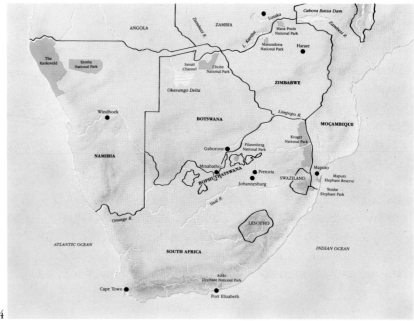

4

The map of Africa above shows the continent's relief, major lakes, the distribution of the African elephant c. 1980, and the location of the areas covered by the four detailed maps. These show the localities of the national parks, game reserves and hunting reserves featured in the text.

(1) West Africa: This shows Gourma in Mali, Niokolo-Koba in Senegal, and Tai, Azagny and Comoé in Côte d'Ivoire.

(2) Equatorial Africa: The map is centred on Gabon to show the location of Wonga-Wongué.

(3) East and Central Africa: This shows the location of Kahuzi-Biega and Virunga in eastern Zaïre, Maasai Mara, Amboseli and Tsavo in Kenya, Serengeti in Tanzania, South Luangwa in Zambia, and Kasungu and Liwonde in Malaŵi.

(4) Southern Africa: This shows the position of Mana Pools and Matusadona in Zimbabwe, Chobe (including Savuti) in Botswana, Etosha and the Kaokoveld in Namibia, Pilanesberg in Bophuthatswana, Maputo in Moçambique, and Tembe, Kruger and Addo in South Africa.

Vegetation. Rainfall, altitude and soil determine the type of vegetation to be found in most parts of Africa. On a continental scale the vegetation belts like forest, woodland, savanna, scrubland and grassland, correspond roughly with the climate. On a local scale plant communities are influenced by soil origin and type, aspect, slope, groundwater conditions, fire, elephants and man.

It is difficult to portray the major vegetation types of Africa on a continental scale. Today much of Africa is very different to its appearance 100 years ago, as the highland grasslands in South Africa have largely been converted to monocultures, and in the more densely populated territories like Nigeria, Rwanda and Malaŵi subsistence agriculture has modified the entire spectrum of plant communities. Timber exploitation in West Africa has wrought vast changes and most of the primeval rain forest has been converted to secondary forest types or destroyed completely. In general, of course, elephants do not occur in man-made habitats and so these are of little consequence to the purposes of this book.

Within each vegetation type – as is clearly illustrated in some of the paintings – there is variation. Thus in the rain forest which appears so endlessly homogenous there are gaps along river courses where the understorey is denser. In deciduous woodlands there are usually thickets of predominantly evergreen trees and shrubs covering termite mounds, the soils of which differ in nutrient and moisture status. Drainage lines – whether they carry a perennial flow of water above ground or not – are usually characterized by fringing forest or thicket. Many of the larger rivers have extensive flood plains. Other local features like lakes, swamps and isolated mountains also introduce great variety.

Frozen into immobility, ears flattened, the hunter waits for the quarry to relax its vigilance. Then the cheetah will explode across the veld to run down even the fleetest of antelope.
(Seronera, Serengeti National Park, Tanzania)

The plains of the Gourma region in Mali are flat and featureless. Sparse shrubs and patches of pale withered grasses alternate with bare areas of dark ochre-coloured lateritic gravel. Multi-stemmed spreading *Acacia* and *Commiphora* shrubs dominate the scattered dense thickets, with here and there a taller tree struggling to raise its branches above its fellows.

In this landscape a milling herd of elephants, chased for many kilometres, has turned to face its pursuers. A phalanx of bulls bursts from a clump of thicket, their ragged and tattered ears spread wide. Their trunks hang low, as though exhausted by the chase. The forehead of the leading animal is wet, from precious water regurgitated and then drawn up into his trunk and blown out over his head and ears to cool himself in the heat. His trumpet of anger is taken up by the herd and it becomes a roaring, rumbling scream of fury with even the young calves crying in terror and confusion. Dust rises from the parched skins of the animals where traces of their last mud wallow have turned to powder, more dust billows up from the crashing feet; branches shaken and snapped and dry leaves flying add to the impression of an eruption of primeval violence.

If the vehicles contain hunters, an elephant will soon be dead, and another may be wounded. If the occupants are out only for thrills, they will turn away from the charging, infuriated animals. Either way the elephants lose. The disturbance of such a chase, the stress on calves, the waste of energy and precious water all add to the pressures under which these, the last of the Sahel elephants, still live.

Elephants survive in a few small areas in

GOURMA ELEPHANT RESERVE

MALI

(Above) *The roan antelope with its horse-like mane is appropriately named* Hippotragus equinus *– the 'horse' antelope.*
(Right) *Standing tall, with head held high and ears spread, tail stiffened in alarm, the echo of a scream floating away with the dust and the egrets – an elephant in anger.*
(Benzéna, Gourma Elephant Reserve, Mali)

24

In ancient Egypt the sacred ibis symbolized Thoth, the God of learning and wisdom and the scribe of the spirit world.

Mali, but the only viable population occurs in a 30 000 km² area known as the Gourma Elephant Reserve, although it has never been formally proclaimed. This plains country is typical of much of the Sahel region with sparse *Acacia* savanna or steppe. Gourma lies south-east of Tombouctoo, between the great bend of the Niger River and the border of Burkina Faso (Upper Volta). The boundary to the west is the huge inland delta of the Niger inundation zone. In the south-west, the Gourma plains are penetrated by a low plateau and the spectacular spires and rock pillars of Hombori Tondo, an isolated mountain which rises sheer from the plains to 1 155 metres and soars above an otherwise dull, sere and monotonous landscape. The migration route of the elephants from Gourma to Burkina Faso brings them plodding past this spectacular landmark, one of the few high mountains in the entire Sahel region.

There are probably about 500 elephants in the Gourma. Apart from small groups of bulls, they are usually found in large herds, with as many as 150 animals in one aggregation. But such large groups are likely to be a seasonal rather than a permanent phenomenon. Their size might also be a consequence of disturbance, although poaching for ivory is not regarded as a major threat at present. Gourma elephants have been shot at for years by hunters from the capital Bamako. More recently – after the imposition of a hunting ban – some have been poached. Their heaviest losses to poachers take place during their stay in Burkino Faso, but even so this source of mortality in recent years has been less significant than deaths due to drought.

The Gourma elephants are the most northerly viable population left in Africa. A few stragglers are still reported in southern Mauritania but there can be little realistic hope of their survival. Apart from their intrinsic value as the last elephants living in the Sahel, on the very edge of the great Sahara, the Gourma elephants could also serve as a reservoir of animals for introduction to areas such as the Boucle du Baoulé National Park in south-western Mali, where a population of 5 animals is on the verge of extinction, and Niokolo-Koba National Park in Senegal, where a viable population of about 50 animals is rapidly being exterminated. In both cases large areas of suitable elephant habitat are available, but ivory poaching has overwhelmed the protection effort.

The elephants of Harr in the valley of the Senegal River in southern Mauritania were reported to be the same in appearance as the Niokolo-Koba and Gourma elephants. Yet those of the Affole mountains, some 160 kilometres north of the river, have been consistently referred to as small elephants by hearsay and by the few reliable observers to see them in the last 30 years. It is now unlikely that more than few if any of these Mauritanian elephants still survive. With their passing we have lost the most perfectly adapted desert elephants of north-western Africa and perhaps a link to Hannibal. If the Mauritanian elephants are small and more like forest elephants in appearance, there is the intriguing possibility that these may have been the last elephants of the subspecies *Loxodonta africana pharaohensis*, which formerly occurred in North Africa and which were captured and trained for war by the Carthaginians. Whether such speculation is fanciful we will, sadly, probably never know.

The large mammals of the Sahel region, now mostly reduced to remnant populations, including the Gourma elephants, are to a large degree nomadic and migratory. Animals move to areas where rain has fallen and food is abundant, leaving a temporarily

Where water is not freely available, elephants are adept at digging in river-beds and around springs to suck up sufficient for their needs.

dry and unproductive area for another time when rain will make it attractive. The dama and dorcas gazelle gathered in large herds, sometimes hundreds strong, and moved southwards during the dry season, returning northwards after rain. Korrigum also gathered in large herds and undertook extensive seasonal movements, as well as localized movements in search of better conditions.

Whereas the antelopes, which can generally survive for long periods without drinking, move mainly in search of grass and herbs, the elephants are dependent on water and must leave areas with adequate food reserves once the last waterholes have dried up. The extent of the elephant migration from the Gourma area to Burkino Faso encompasses a return journey of as much as 800 kilometres. This is the longest elephant migration on record, easily exceeding the 180 kilometre return movements of elephants reported in Chobe and Etosha in the similarly arid south-western part of the continent.

The Gourma elephants are typical savanna elephants. Yet they have a thick set about their bodies more reminiscent of the Addo and Etosha elephants than of those in the eastern savanna. They are classified as *Loxodonta africana oxyotis*, the West African savanna elephant. Their ivory today is usually short and thick, and curved upwards. They have massive, thick-set heads and large ears with the high shoulders and deeply wrinkled skin of the true bush elephant. Not too long ago, there would have been continuous elephant populations stretching from Gourma through Burkino Faso into Comoé in Côte d'Ivoire, a distance of only about 700 kilometres. But the elephants of

Comoé, at least the southern ones which we saw at Gansé in 1983, are a transitional form between a Gourma-type savanna elephant and the true forest elephants south of Comoé.

It is not uncommon to see typical Gourma-type bulls near Gansé and Kakpin with the smaller, more delicately proportioned Comoé cows with their slender sloping tusks, small heads, tall hindquarters and forward sloping backs. Similar areas of transition between the true forest elephant *L. a. cyclotis* and the East African savanna elephant *L. a. knochenhaueri* are found in the Budongo area of Uganda, and the Semliki Valley and Garamba area of Zaïre.

The elephants of the Gourma, like those of Kaokoland in Namibia, have adapted to a desert-like way of life. The essential difference, however, is that because of its geology and soils Kaokoland has many fountains which have never been known to dry up, but food supplies are limited. In the Gourma, food is usually available in sufficient quantities for the elephants which can survive by browsing trees and shrubs long after the grass has withered away or been eaten, but water is the critical factor.

The southern edge of the Sahara is ill-defined. The transition from desert to arid savanna or steppe of the Sahel or Sudanian zone is seldom marked by clear boundaries between landscapes, plant or animal communities. Instead, there is a gradation from the utterly barren desert, with very little life and virtually no rain, to a slightly less harsh environment where rainfall is still low, but frequent enough to nurture a sparse growth of bushes, trees and grass. The Sahel is a fairly homogenous biome stretching from

The most perfectly adapted of desert antelopes, the addax has been hunted nearly to extinction throughout most of its formerly widespread range in the Sahara.

Senegal and Mauritania across Mali, Niger, and Chad to the valley of the Nile in Sudan, and beyond to the Red Sea. The ranges of many of the plants, birds and other animals found in the Sahel region extend south to the Cape Province of South Africa.

The appearance of the Gourma, as anywhere in the Sahel, varies greatly according to both long-term and recent rainfall. Mean annual rainfall may be as low as 100 millimetres in the north, and as high as 500 millimetres in the south. Most of the rain falls during the summer months in one short season from June to September: the rest of the year is dry. In years when good rains fall, the

27

The isolated massif of Hombori Tondo stands athwart the migration route of the Gourma elephants. This route stretches from the Niger River deep into Burkino Faso.

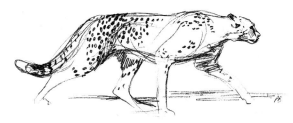

Extremely rare in Mali, it is unlikely that more than a remnant population of cheetahs still survives in the Gourma.

The honey badger shares a taste for honey and grubs with honey guides. The birds lead the way to the hive, which is opened by the badger.

Walking at a steady pace, elephants can cover 50 - 70 kilometres overnight; but they usually travel shorter distances with frequent feeding and resting along the way.

Sahel may have very good grass cover dominated by *Aristida mutabilis, Panicum turgidum* (which reaches into the Sahara) and *Cenchrus biflorus*. Many other ephemeral plants appear after rain, grow rapidly, set seed and then die. Their seeds can lie dormant for years if necessary, until sufficient rain falls for them to germinate and repeat their life cycle. During successive dry years, or years of very low rainfall, there may be little or no grass growth, and where fields of grass stood a season before, there may be nothing but bare ground and sand blown into miniature rippling dunes. The woody plants are well adapted to the arid conditions with deep or spreading root systems. Most species are widespread, such as the flat-topped *Acacia tortilis*, the smaller *A. senegal* with its spines characteristically grouped in threes, and along watercourses *A. nilotica* and the desert date *Balanites aegyptiaca*. Along larger rivers, such as the Niger, the doum palm *Hyphaene thebaica* is common. On termite mounds and other localities where conditions are favourable there may even be small patches of thicket dominated by *A. ataxacantha, Capparis lianescens* and *Maerua crassifolia*, and where rainwater pools have soaked the soil, herbs such as *Sesbania punctata* grow tall.

The characteristic ungulates of the Sahel include the scimitar-horned oryx, of the northerly steppe country and the edge of the desert, if it survives at all in the wild. In Mali the oryx was found only to the east of Gourma, near the frontier with Niger but by 1980 only six individuals remained. Like the addax, the antelope of the true desert, the scimitar-horned oryx has enlarged hooves which help it cope with running on sand.

Oryx are highly nomadic and concentrated in areas where rain had fallen. This habit made them vulnerable to motorized hunting. The dama gazelle, the largest of all the gazelles, ranged from what was Rio de Oro to the Sudan, but is now greatly reduced in numbers. This antelope occurs in a range of colour forms from pure white with a reddish neck (*rufifrons*) in the east to an animal with a dark rufous-maroon back, thighs and neck (*mhorr*) in the west. An intermediate form, *permista*, is found in the central part of the range and this probably includes a subspecies, *weidholzi*, the type specimen of which comes from Hombori. Other gazelles widely distributed in the Sahel are the much smaller dorcas and red-fronted gazelle, the ecological equivalents of the springbok of the south-west arid zone. Like the springbok, they too are the preferred prey of the fastest of all mammals, the cheetah – a small population of which may survive in the Gourma.

Conditions in the Sahel are ideal for cheetah, but not nearly so suitable for lions and leopards, although both these species still occur. As the cheetah seldom returns to a carcass after feeding, there is usually something left for the pied crow, striped hyaena and other scavengers. This scavenging habit has unfortunately made the striped hyaena and its spotted cousin vulnerable to poisoned baits, the most common means of destroying them in Mali.

The birds of the Sahel zone show many adaptations to life in a semi-desert. They also move to where food is abundant, breed there if conditions are suitable, or move on if not. The most conspicuous bird of these arid areas is the ostrich. Too heavy to fly, it depends on sharp eyesight and running to escape predators such as cheetah, which occasionally take young birds.

The people of the Gourma area are predominantly Tuareg (also known as Tamasheq) or Peul and number 100 000; they are necessarily also largely nomadic. They move with their livestock – 379 000 cattle, sheep, goats, donkeys and camels – tents and worldly goods in search of pasture and water, subject as much as the native wildlife to ecological restraints. Until recently these people had no quarrel with the wild animals. There was enough food and water for a fairly stable system to operate. In general, the livestock occupied the ranges closer to permanent water and the wild animals the more distant areas. The people watered their livestock in daylight, and at night the elephants would drink, undisturbed by the fires, sounds and smells of the encampments and settlements.

People and elephants simply avoided contact and went about their business. That system has now been changed, and is likely to undergo even more radical changes in the future. Medical and veterinary advances have ensured unprecedented increases in both human and livestock numbers. Boreholes have created permanent water, resulting in continuous grazing and over-grazing of areas previously only seasonally utilized and then rested. Droughts now have a far

more traumatic impact on the over-utilized veld and the enlarged herds – and many animals die.

During March 1983 the only water in the western Gourma was at Benzéna. Hundreds of elephants concentrated there. But there was very little open water – most was in small wells. The tolerance between man and elephant vanished in the bitter competition: the people needed all the available water for themselves and their livestock. They tried to keep the elephants away – sometimes they succeeded, at other times the elephants became stuck in the wells. At least one man was killed by a desperately thirsty elephant. By early May the water supply at Benzéna was exhausted and the area contained only mud and dead or dying elephants. Most of the elephants moved away, but not before at least 40 had perished from thirst.

Large-scale development of groundwater sources, presently planned or under way, will create a more settled way of life for the people and their livestock, but will change the ecosystem dramatically. In such systems, wildlife is more likely to be seen as a nuisance and will be gradually eliminated unless sanctuaries are set aside. If well-managed ranching schemes are introduced – taking adequate cognizance of the carrying capacity of the range – the Gourma could become a more productive area in terms of human welfare, livestock numbers and wildlife. But

The dama gazelle occurs in several distinct forms spread across the Sahara and its arid fringes; the westernmost form, the mhorr, has a rufous chestnut back and flanks.

if it is not well managed, the region could, in time, become no more than an extension of the Sahara, with vegetation destroyed, wildlife eliminated and the elephants no more than a memory.

The flightless ostrich depends on speed and stamina to escape from predators.

Paul Bosman

NIOKOLO-KOBA NATIONAL PARK

SENEGAL

(Above) *Large ears and a dewlap extending to the chest are distinguishing features of the Lord Derby eland. This is the largest of Africa's antelopes and one whose numbers are rapidly declining.*
(Left) *The few surviving elephants of Senegal still occasionally feed on the flood plains of the Gambia River, but only rarely is this done in daylight.*
(Simenti, Niokolo-Koba National Park, Senegal)

Like grains of sand slipping through one's fingers, the last elephants of Senegal are being killed, one by one. In 1974 there were about 450 in the Niokolo-Koba National Park; a scant fifteen years later there are fewer than fifty. They are poached for one reason only – their ivory. The meat is left to scavengers, the sun and the rain.

At the present rate of decline – close to 40 elephants a year – the Niokolo-Koba elephants could be gone within two years. However, we can assume that it will become increasingly more difficult to hunt the few survivors and that they may well live precariously for another decade or more. Despite the heavy poaching, the elephants of Niokolo-Koba are still a viable population. Several young calves among the survivors indicate that breeding continues, despite the harassment. These are the last elephants in Senegal. The rest have long since been eliminated. They have survived till now only because Niokolo-Koba has been a reserve since 1926. In this they illustrate the situation which must eventually prevail throughout Africa, because elephants cannot survive in competition with man outside protected areas.

In the past, the Niokolo-Koba elephants moved out of the park during the wet season between July and November when most of the country along the Gambia River and its tributaries is water-logged. They ranged south to the higher country in Guinea and east towards Mali, where a few remnant decreasing populations barely survived. Once out of the park they were hunted persistently – particularly so along the Guinea border, where poverty and unemployment were widespread and a pair of tusks represented a

31

The red-flanked duiker, which occupies a wide range of habitats along the edge of the rain forest, has less specialized needs than the other true forest duikers.

fortune. As the pressure mounted on the remaining Niokolo-Koba elephants, and numbers declined, they stopped moving across the park boundaries.

Then the hunters entered the park, and the incidence of poaching increased dramatically from 1974 onwards. The harassed elephants became shy and nervous, fleeing at the first sign of man. However, they are still dependent on the Gambia River and a few other perennial water points during the dry months of January to April, though they usually drink at night. Daybreak finds them far away in the most inaccessible, waterless terrain. Only their spoor, crossing and recrossing the roads parallel to the river, shows that they are still there.

The poaching has whittled away the

herds. It was not unusual to see herds of 20 animals ten years ago, but today groups rarely number more than seven. The old bulls, with fairly good ivory, were shot first, and today only the young bulls are left. Their ivory is typical of savanna elephants – fairly thick, curved, and usually short and sharp-pointed from much use. The tusks are quite commonly stained black, said by the guards to be due to the elephants rubbing them against the stems of borassus palms (*Borassus aethiopum*). The park warden, based at Tambacounda (some 120 kilometres from the park), has a collection of 23 tusks confiscated from poachers. The composition of this haul bears mute testimony to the state of the Niokolo-Koba population. Seven tusks are from adult bulls, four from teenage bulls and the rest from cows and calves, indicating that the poachers are taking whatever they come across. The heaviest tusks, from a bull, weigh about 20 kilograms each and show that the poachers are using military weapons, most probably the ubiquitous Soviet AK47 automatic rifle. One of the tusks took a burst of fire and was hit by three bullets. They chipped great holes into the tusk – in one of them the bullet is still lodged, a bright metallic silver message of death, embraced by the jagged shards of wounded ivory.

Our visit to Niokolo-Koba was not without sadness, for we found the carcass of a poached elephant, a stock item in far too many African parks. Being early summer the park was closed to tourists, the roads were impassable to all but fourwheel drive vehicles. In a Land Rover, loaned by the warden, Mr Ndiaye, we ploughed along the tracks through pools of water from recent rains, the heavy tyres sending miniature waves surging

over the muddy ground and the carpet of bright green new grass. We were close to the Gambia River, in the Simenti area, where the track wound through a fairly open savanna with scattered trees.

Clumps of last summer's grass still stood tall, dry and fibrous among their flattened companions, and trampled game trails criss-crossed in every direction. The heavy stench of death and decay, and a gathering of white-backed, Ruppell's and hooded vultures brought us to a stop. Spotted hyaena and lion spoor on a well-used path led us to the remains of a young elephant cow that had been dead for about ten days. She had been shot in the head and had collapsed on her brisket, legs splayed out. Her feet had been

Niokolo-Koba is a stronghold for the last viable lion population in Senegal, which numbers only about 120 animals.

In areas where they are harassed by poachers, elephants become extremely wary and are quick to test the breeze at the least hint of disturbance.

cut off, and her tusks drawn. The ground under the carcass was sodden and the scavengers had steadily eaten their way into the hollow casing of her skin. The grass around her was flattened by the flesh-eaters, and her back was streaked with long white splashes of vulture excrement.

A dead elephant is a sad sight. Because it is so easy to empathize with them, it seems as though much more life has been taken with the death of an elephant than with the killing of an antelope or an insect. Yet, biologically, the process is similar. But an elephant carcass is more emotive. The savanna elephant of West Africa is certainly in danger of extinction, except, perhaps, for those in Burkina Faso, Comoé in Côte d'Ivoire and the W National Park on the border of Niger, Benin and Burkina Faso. But even the most optimistic view must be that these populations are also threatened. However, localized extinctions, usually in the face of human pressure and development, do not necessarily make the elephant an endangered species.

Elsewhere on the continent, elephants are over-abundant; more were culled in Southern Africa in 1988 than exist in all of West Africa. The small, isolated pockets of West African elephants outside the national parks will soon be gone, and even those inside national parks, such as Niokolo-Koba, stand little chance of survival. There is enough habitat set aside within national parks to save the species, but if park authorities cannot maintain the integrity of their parks, then the elephants will disappear. Adequate police work and efficient anti-poaching forces can eliminate poaching, as shown in Malaŵi and elsewhere. The long-term survival of the parks, however, will depend on the motivation and education of the inhabitants of the countries concerned.

The national parks service of Senegal is probably the best-organized in West Africa. An education warden, Hamady Sow, is conducting an intensive campaign to promote elephants among the people of the eastern region of Senegal, where the park is situated. That the guards are dedicated to their task is shown by the many, and sometimes fatal, clashes which have taken place between them and poachers. But patrolling a park is not the most effective means of combating poachers. Experience in Malaŵi and Uganda shows that undercover intelligence work aimed at tracking down the poachers, the couriers and the dealers to their home bases produces far better results, and can virtually eliminate elephant poaching.

As one travels south from the Sahara, one passes through several zones or belts of vegetation which stretch from the Atlantic to Sudan. The rainfall, and the height and density of the trees, increase southwards. The arid fringe of the desert is known as the Sahel and is dominated by scattered small trees, mainly *Acacia* spp. This gives way to the Sudanian savanna zone (in which trees are larger and human settlement more intense), the higher rainfall Guinea woodland zone, and the rain forest belt. Each of the zones has some typical large mammals and other animals which are less commonly found elsewhere. The Sahara has addax, the Sahel gazelles and oryx, the Sudanian savanna giraffe and korrigum, and the Guinea woodlands roan antelope and Lord Derby eland.

Niokolo-Koba lies in the Guinea woodlands, with a fairly high annual rainfall of

According to Herodotus, the crocodile bird or Egyptian plover reputedly picked food from between the teeth of basking crocodiles. Like the reptiles, it has the habit of burying its eggs on sandbanks.

1 100 millimetres. Even though its elephant population is on the brink of being wiped out, it is still one of the major national parks of West Africa. With the exception of korrigum, and marginally also giraffe, all the larger mammals, including rare species, such as the African wild dog, are still found. In many respects the fauna of Niokolo-Koba shows that it lies on the transition zone from the rain forest to the Sudanian savanna as it has both lions and chimpanzees. All three of the African crocodile species – Nile, slender snouted and West African dwarf – occur here.

The 9 000 km² park is generally flat or gently undulating, well-wooded throughout and with denser riverine thickets and forest along the Gambia and its major tributaries. In the south-east, in the more varied laterite country, the Assirik plateau reaches 311 metres and its flanks are covered by tall woodland.

33

When an elephant dies, the scavengers take their fill, maggots feed, sun and rain wear down the remains, the elements are returned to the soil, and the cycle of life is completed.

Lazing away the daylight hours on a sun-drenched sandbank, the Nile hippo is still common along sections of the Gambia River.

These laterite plateaus, known locally as 'bowal', are characterized by scattered boulders in open country covered by short grasses *Danthoniopsis tuberculata* and herbs such as *Dipcadi* sp., with trees such as *Combretum etessei* and *Parkia biglobosa* growing only in pockets of deeper soil or along the edges. Rising up to 80 centimetres above the gravelly soil are clusters of large toadstool-shaped termite mounds built by *Cubitermes niokoloensis*. These must be a valuable link in soil-forming processes, for vegetation grows profusely where they have collapsed.

Most of the trees are fairly widespread in the Guinean zone, with the dominant genus being *Combretum*. Others include a tall spreading tree *Pterocarpus erinaceus, Bombax costatum, Terminalia laxiflora*, and *Cordyla africana*, and on compacted soils *Anogeissus leiocarpus*, which produces masses of pale yellow flowers in summer. Many of the genera of trees, such as *Combretum, Ficus* and *Acacia*, are found throughout Africa. Some species occur from Senegal to South Africa, such as the marula *Sclerocarya caffra, Burkea africana* and *Piliostigma thonningii*.

A characteristic component of the Niokolo-Koba woodlands is the bamboo *Oxytenanthera abyssinica*, which grows in scattered clumps or forms dense groves under which few other plants thrive, except for the occasional pale mauve-flowered *Kaempferia aethiopica*. In June 1984 large areas of bamboo were dead, so there must have been a widespread flowering the previous year. The faded straw-coloured bracts of the flowering heads showed that there had been life where now there were only dead bamboo poles, their old leaves burnt away by dry-season fires, idly rattling against one another in the breeze.

On the deeper soils along the Gambia, the borassus palms with their swollen stems tower conspicuously above the other trees. On old flood plains and oxbow lagoons, a grassland of *Vetiveria nigritana* interspersed with sedges and herbs occurs, around the edges tall *Andropogon gayanus* grasses reach up two metres or more.

Early in the summer, when the first rains transform the *Vetiveria* pastures into greenery, and rainwater pools become small lakes, these places are much sought-after feeding areas for Senegal or Buffon's kob, oribi, warthog, Sing Sing or Defassa waterbuck, buffalo and bushbuck. Cattle egrets, spurwinged plovers, sacred ibis, crowned cranes, and spurwinged geese all clamour and feed on the abundant life of the summer.

When the pools dry up, the animals must range much further for food in the savanna and woodland around Simenti. For some, however, the routine is different. The giant or Lord Derby eland are found mainly in tall woodland in the southern and eastern sections of the park. The herds are largest during the dry season presumably when they concentrate near water, and disperse when it rains. Unfortunately, these animals – like the elephants in the park – still move to the higher, drier ground along the Guinea border, and they are increasingly being poached for meat.

In addition these eland are apparently more susceptible to rinderpest than other bovids. The Lord Derby eland are spectacular beasts, larger than the Cape eland, with massive horns, dewlaps that begin under the chin and stretch down to the chest, larger rounded ears more like those of greater kudu than Cape eland, but with the same timidity and shyness, fleeing at the least sign of man. In the past these giant eland migrated in herds that were hundreds strong, but today there are scarcely more than a few hundred left. The eland of Niokolo-Koba and Baoulé in Mali are the last viable populations of the western race *derbianus* which was formerly widespread in West Africa. A different subspecies *gigas* is still found from Cameroon to Sudan, but only in isolated pockets.

Like the woodland system south of the Zaïre rain forest, the Niokolo-Koba area is characterized by high rainfall, poor soils, fire and tsetse fly. The broad-leaved trees probably have a fairly high concentration of secondary chemical compounds which make them unpalatable to ruminants, which may explain the absence of giraffe, and the carrying capacity for large game is therefore low. Predators also occur at relatively low densities, although there is a wide variety. The large male lions of Niokolo-Koba, like most West African lions, have only modestly developed manes – the spectacular black, ginger and blonde manes which are the pride and glory of East and Southern African animals are not found here. Leopards, spotted hyaena, golden and side-striped jackals still occur, but cheetah are rare, being more at home in the arid gazelle country.

The bird life of Niokolo-Koba is spectacular, and it seems as though some West African birds have outdone their eastern counterparts in the colour stakes. The Barbary shrike, with a brilliant red chest, black back and yellow-green crown, is superb. Senegal parakeets are brilliant green, and the Senegal fire finches are blood-red. Yet among all this colour, so exotic and striking, there are still the drab staples of the continental African avifauna – the laughing dove, Namaqua dove, and hadeda ibis. The red-chested cuckoo, a bird of the southern summer which calls monotonously for hours on end from October to January south of the rain forest, calls in the Niokolo-Koba woodlands during the northern summer in June and July.

Is there a chance of saving the last of the Senegalese elephants? There is, but if the basic anti-poaching patrol systems cannot beat the poachers, then there is not much

'Behold, he drinketh up a river, and hasteth not: he trusteth that he can draw up Jordan into his mouth.' The Book of Job, chapter 40, verse 23.

hope that more sophisticated, expensive methods will work. It has been suggested that several elephants be marked with radio collars, and closely and permanently followed by guards, who can take preventative action against poachers. But the level of expertise required for such an operation carries with it its own considerable logistical problems.

A more expensive alternative, with more hope of long-term success, would be to fence off a suitable area of 100 - 200 km² and maintain a breeding nucleus of elephants which can be intensively protected by saturation patrols and daily contact. The basic requirements are political support on the part of the authorities, and money. The finance might come from international fundraisers or from the government of Senegal. It may be argued, however, that the government, with pressing priorities in other fields, cannot afford such a scheme. Yet the commitment of scarce resources by a motivated leadership and officialdom would do much more than foreign aid to ensure the success of such a programme.

COMOÉ
NATIONAL
PARK

CÔTE D'IVOIRE

(Above) *Whether perched, or flashing shades of deep blue, ultramarine and cobalt as it flies, the blue-bellied roller is an avian gem.*
(Left) *While a nervous herd of kob splash by, a few elephants, dimly seen in the grey haze of the Harmattan (the annual dust storms from the Sahara), move down to the Comoé River to drink. (Gansé, Comoé National Park, Côte d'Ivoire)*

When we first saw the Comoé elephants, a heavy cloud of dust, blown south by the Harmattan storms, hung low in the sky, mingling with smoke from dry-season bush fires and making it twilight at mid-afternoon. Visibility faded into grey at about a mile. Looking downstream when the sun was low, the edge of the water was highlighted against the deep grey-green flow of the river. A flight of snow-white cattle egrets passed, floating in the half-light to land on a small outcrop of washed blue-grey rock. Some Buffon's Kob – chunky, golden-brown antelope – splashed through the shallows from a low island that was scarcely visible in the gloom. Every ripple and wave of their passing flashed silver threads of reflected light across the water. Further downstream, at the water's edge, a small herd of elephants gathered to drink, their wet backs shining a liquid silver, barely seen by the naked eye.

For three days we had searched for the elephants in the 11 500 km² wilderness of the Comoé National Park, which is situated in the north-east, close to the borders of Burkina Faso and Ghana. It is the largest sanctuary in Côte d'Ivoire, and in the whole of West Africa. It was not until we reached the Lola plains and the forest patches around Gansé in the south of the park that we found signs of elephants. We took on a local guide, of the Lobi tribe, a hunter who could follow spoor and read the signs of the bush. With his help we established that the elephants drank in the Comoé River during the late afternoon or early morning.

They moved out of the dense riverine forest at dusk, regularly tramping along the same paths, and fed in the woodlands and scattered forest patches throughout the

The Senegal or Buffon's Kob is the most abundant of the larger antelopes in the savanna and woodland zone of West Africa.

night. Dawn would find them back at the river to drink. They then either stayed in the gallery forest, or hurried across the strip of open country to disappear into one of the larger forest patches, where they spent the day. This routine was the result of persistent hunting pressure both within and outside the park. The elephants were alert, wary of any sign or scent of man.

It was only with extreme caution, and luck, that we were ever able to approach a group of Comoé elephants close enough to study them in detail. Our chance came when a herd moved out of the riverine forest late one afternoon and instead of rushing through the open country, they ambled along slowly, feeding as they moved. Leaving our timorous guide behind, Paul and I hurried after the herd, the wind in our faces, revelling in our first good view of West African elephants.

Yet these elephants are something of a puzzle. Most have the rounded ears, tall hindquarters and sloping shoulders of the true forest elephant, thin tusks and relatively small size, yet many also have a distinct savanna-elephant look about them. This is particularly so in the adult bulls. They are small by comparison with the East African savanna elephant, but decidedly more bulky than the forest elephant of Tai and Azagny. Their tusks are also sometimes slightly bowed and curving, like those of the Gourma elephants in Mali, but often straight and downward pointing. They looked so different from any other elephants that it is not surprising that they are recognized as a distinct subspecies of the African elephant, *Loxodonta africana oxyotis*. Some modern scientists ignore this taxon, but they are perhaps insensitive to the subtle differences between elephants in different parts of Africa. To one who has looked at them as living, breathing creatures, rather than as abstract measurements and statistics, or as reproductive units isolated or not, they are very different.

Moving north from the rain forest which covers the southern part of Côte d'Ivoire, one passes into regions of increasingly lower rainfall. The rain forest breaks up, the forest trees become more sparse, standing apart, and almost imperceptibly the tree species change. The tall buttressed forest giants are replaced by shorter, slim-stemmed trees. Among the scattered trees tall *Andropogon* and *Hyparrhenia* grasses take the place of the shrubbery of the forest. Then one reaches the Guinea woodland zone, which stretches across Africa from Senegal to Sudan.

In many respects it is similar to the miombo woodland which lies between the Zaïre rain forest and the savanna of Southern and East Africa. The vegetation of the Guinea zone is in places a fairly dense, semi-deciduous woodland which eventually gives way to the more open Sudanian savanna – a certain indicator that ahead lies the arid fringes of the Sahara. The changes in the vegetation are largely due to the lower precipitation and the clearly defined dry season during which no rain falls. The open nature of the tree layer also allows the introduction of one of the most important ecological influences in Africa – the bush fire. The annual fires which sweep through the savanna regions are sometimes started by summer lightning and sometimes by man. Fire helps to maintain the subtle balance between woody plants and grasses, usually tipping the balance in favour of grass and eating into the edge of the rain forest wherever man-made clearings give it a chance.

Comoé lies on the northern edge of the Guinea woodland zone and the southern edge of the Sudanian savanna. The predominant vegetation is a woodland of medium height dominated by *Isoberlinia doka*,

The whoop of the spotted hyaena – the voice of the African night – is a call whereby this hunter and scavenger signals his position to other members of his clan.

Detarium microcarpum and a tree well known as far south as the Transvaal in South Africa, *Burkea africana*. The Comoé River is fringed by dense, tall, evergreen gallery forest characterized by the smooth, grey-barked *Cynometra megalophylla*. Close to the river in the Gansé area are patches of forest, links with the rain forest to the south. As one passes northwards the forest draws closer to the lifeline of moisture along the Comoé, which provides a ribbon of habitat for many of the rain forest animals which penetrate deep into the savanna zone. Parallel to the rain forest fringe is an open, short alluvial grassland which is seasonally flooded and waterlogged, and hence virtually treeless. This grassland is replaced by woodland and savanna further away on better drained poorer soils. To the east, there are isolated domes of granite, in appearance like the inselbergs of the miombo, each with a small island of fringing denser woodland or forest. This juxtaposition of rain forest and savanna biomes creates the essence of the Comoé atmosphere – it is an area of transition.

While the inhabitants of the various biomes generally stay where they belong, there are some striking examples of animals using the ecotones, the boundary areas between different habitat types. In the short grasslands we were amazed to see Western black-and-white colobus monkeys, normally forest dwellers, foraging near territorial male Buffon's or Senegal kob. We once stood in the gallery forest, habitat of the giant forest hog, watching in the distance a tawny lioness, the epitome of the savanna, stalking a warthog. The harnessed antelope, known as the bushbuck throughout the rest of Afri-

ca, is a species which naturally crosses the divide between rain forest and the thicket-line watercourses of the savanna. Other forest dwellers, with more specialized requirements, rarely leave their habitual surroundings. Thus the chimpanzees of Comoé, the giant forest hog, bongo, several species of forest duikers, white-nosed monkeys and the elegantly coloured Diana monkeys stay well within the evergreen dappled depths of the forest.

The savanna strip has the highest concentration of animals, made possible by the higher nutrient status of its deep alluvial soils. Buffon's kob, of which there are about 50 000 in the park, are the most abundant species. The woodland, like the miombo woodlands to the south, have typical low-density, highly specialized grazing animals like roan antelope, western hartebeest and oribi. Ranging through the savanna is a strange-looking, terrestrial monkey, the red Hussar or Patas monkey. It is a gaunt, long-legged animal, at home on the ground and generally capable of a fine turn of speed.

The Patas monkey is an elusive, open country denizen, found throughout the Guinea and Sudanian savanna and northwards into the Aïr mountains of the Sahara in terrain so harsh that not even anubis baboons venture there.

In the rich rain forest along the coast there may be as many as seven species of forest duiker in one area, as in Taï. The Comoé Park alone has no fewer than six species. Three of them – the yellow-backed, bay and black – are essentially forest duikers. The red-flanked and Maxwell's duiker are most common on the ecotone between forest and savanna or woodland, and only the grey

Looking more like a greyhound than a primate, the sleek, long-limbed Patas monkey is well adapted to terrestrial life and can rely on a fine turn of speed when danger threatens.

duiker is a pure savanna form. Even so, we regularly saw black duiker in the woodlands near the forest and red-flanked ones many kilometres from the nearest forest patch. On two occasions we saw three duikers together, which was unusual for such generally solitary animals. In both cases there were two Maxwell's (presumably a pair) and a single red-flanked. When we saw them the first time, they were all feeding off the tender green leaf flush of a *Combretum molle* tree that had been felled by an elephant, yet remained alive.

We usually found duiker singly or in pairs, and regularly saw the same animals in the same locality, implying a clear link to a particular area or territory. The black and Maxwell's duiker, like the grey, were shy and usually moved off quickly. The red-flanked duiker were more tolerant and often continued foraging in the leaf litter or under shrubs while we watched them, tails regular-

39

Just launched from its waterside perch, a fish eagle rakes the air as it speeds to snatch a rising fish in its powerful talons.

Widespread throughout Africa, the warthog is abundant in the largely Islamic sub-Saharan zone, where it is seldom hunted.

The short-legged clumsy appearance of the Nile hippo on land belies the speed and agility with which it can move.

ly flicking from side to side. When alarmed they trotted away, heads held low, instead of bouncing and diving like the open-country grey duiker.

Nile hippo lay in heaps on the steep banks of the Comoé. Their deep grunting and bellowing carried far down the river, echoing against the solid wall of the gallery forest. They are found southwards usually only as far as the edge of the rain forest, for where the grasslands are covered over and replaced by the shrubbery of the forest floor, there is only silence and the muted calls of birds along the great river.

Comoé provided us with a striking image of functional beauty in animals. It was not the elephants which were so impressive, but our first view of a troop of colobus monkeys. Much to our surprise we came across them on the ground in fairly open woodland. They looked other-worldly as they fled, throwing glances back at us over their shoulders. They hopped and ran in a curious gliding motion with their long, full, silky, white tails floating and rippling behind them. The stark contrast of their sparkling white and black fur heightened the unreality of the image. They moved across the open country as gracefully as porpoises riding the surf.

But their grace and poise on the ground was almost pedestrian compared with their liquid movements when they glided into their element, the forest. They progressed from the ground to the very tops of the tallest trees in a series of effortless scrambles and leaps, exuding an air of enjoyment as they bounced up into the tree tops. Once safely above ground, they chased one another, taking spectacular leaps from tree to tree, sometimes landing on a branch then running along it to fly off over a gap, arms spread wide, legs forward for their landing and tail floating parachute-like behind them. All the while they were chattering and calling to one another, vigorous, lively, exuberant.

The birds of Comoé were a mixture of West African forms that we had not seen before and reassuringly familiar species from the southern savanna. New to us were birds such as the blue-bellied roller, Senegal wattled plover, white-headed plover, and the aptly named stone-partridge – this small francolin was commonly found around rocky outcrops and inselbergs. Among the familiar species was the helmeted guinea fowl, which has a somewhat whiter face in West Africa than in the south. Cattle egrets were common near game and hunted in the open grassland, their graceful necks zigzagging from side to side as they feinted before striking at an insect. Perhaps the quick side to side movement, allowing both eyes to see the prey, made for more accurate judgement.

All the buffalo we saw were accompanied by yellow-billed oxpeckers which clung precariously to their flanks, their heavy beaks diligently searching for ticks. Sometimes they sat nonchalantly on the heads of their hosts or clambered into their drooping ears. One evening at dusk, while we were preparing our meal in a bush camp, we watched the amazing performance of a standard-wing nightjar, which was displaying its fluttering, swooping and turning manoeuvres against the still bright but darkening sky. The ninth primary wing feathers are elongated into 25 cm-long shafts which have oval-shaped vanes on the end. These adornments float like two huge butterflies staying with the bird in perfect formation. The mingling of birds of the forest and savannas is richly illustrated in the diversity of bee-eaters, hornbills and kingfishers in Comoé – there are eight bee-eaters and ten each of the latter two species.

Although the Comoé National Park is largely a savanna region, it differs markedly from the southern savanna in the composition of its fauna. There is a paucity of savanna species, but because of the rain forest corridor along the river the total species diversity is great. Comoé has no fewer than 11 species of primates, 17 carnivores, seven duikers, eight other antelopes, buffalo, three pigs, hippo and elephant. Most species are shared with the rest of sub-Saharan Africa such as warthog, bushpig, aardvark, spotted hyaena, wild dog, leopard, lion, serval, banded mongoose, water mongoose and others. Only a few are limited to West Africa – such as the giant pangolin, western hartebeest and some of the monkeys.

The buffalo of Comoé like those of Niokolo-Koba in Senegal are recognized by many authorities as a subspecies, *Syncerus caffer brachyceros*, and indeed they differ markedly from the true forest buffalo *S. c. nanus* and the Cape buffalo *S. c. caffer.* They are extremely variable in colour and are found in various shades of dull red or yellow, brown or black. The old bulls are massive,

but not as large as Cape buffalo. They are black, but lack the heavy boss and curved bracketed horns of the southern buffalo. They have virtually no boss and their horns are short, flat, broad at the base and curled like half moons on their head. Like buffalo elsewhere the herds usually had cattle egrets moving along near them.

The Comoé elephant population is now isolated, like every other elephant population in West Africa. There is no longer any exchange of genetic material with forest elephants to the south and only a tenuous link with savanna elephants across the park border to the north in Burkina Faso. Fortunately, Comoé is large enough to support a population of elephants which will be genetically viable in the long term. It is the only protected population of savanna-type elephants in Côte d'Ivoire and, with an estimated strength of 1 500, is one of the largest savanna elephant populations in West Africa.

In one respect, the Comoé elephants were very much like the other savanna elephants – their impact on the habitat was clear to see. Trees were pushed over, branches broken and bark stripped off. Some of the small forest patches were devastated. A dense tangle of felled trees and broken branches lay on the ground, through which black duiker delicately selected a path. Above the wreckage, the forest roof seemed even higher than usual, and only the

Most Comoé elephants have the features of the forest elephant, namely small heads, rounded ears, and sloping forequarters. Others have features more suggestive of savanna elephants.

tall buttressed forest giants were immune to the onslaught of the elephants. In some areas most trees within reach of the elephants had been broken down.

Because fires are not able to penetrate the forest, as there is no grass to act as fuel, the evidence of elephant damage has accumulated, and it is not regularly reduced to ashes as in the savanna. This, of course, made the impact so much more intense. Clearly, in time, the Comoé forest will look very different unless effective security encourages the elephants to leave the forest patches and spread out into the largely under-utilized savanna and woodlands.

TAI
NATIONAL
PARK

CÔTE D'IVOIRE

A crowned eagle launches itself from its nest, a few shallow wing beats lift it, and it soars westwards towards the Cavally River and the border between Côte d'Ivoire and Liberia. To the east the forest stretches unbroken almost as far as the Sassandra River. Below the eagle the forest canopy is a solid mat of greenery – the largest tract of primary rain forest in West Africa – Tai National Park. Some trees stand higher than others, some are pale green, others dark, and here and there a tree-top is white in flower, or flushed pink with new leaves.

A splash of grey and red marks a flock of screaming African grey parrots bursting from a tree. A black-casqued hornbill throws itself clumsily from a branch, the wind soughing through its feathers. The green canopy appears to be a solid bank upon which the birds land, but beneath it lies another world. Almost 60 metres below, on the forest floor, the dark shapes of two round-eared forest elephants, a cow and a sub-adult bull, move silently, searching for fallen fruits and choice herbs.

The elephants wandered along, oblivious of our presence as we watched them. Approaching elephants in the rain forest is always tricky because there is no wind, and the animals are instantly alerted by the faintest whiff of man: they are heavily poached, and know the consequences. Their pace was slow as they stopped frequently to feed, and it was very difficult keeping them in sight in the gloomy cathedral of the primary forest. Eventually we saw light ahead; it was the Hana River. Where the canopy was broken, the sunlight streamed down to the forest floor, pale and smoky in the haze of the dry-season dust storms, or Harmattan,

43

Behind the slate-grey eyes of the golden cat lurks a forest predator whose habits and behaviour are largely unknown.

which reach from the Sahara to the Atlantic early in the year.

The elephants suddenly hurried ahead and burst on to a white sandy beach, bellow-

By whistling against the edge of a leaf, a hunter of the Bété tribe produces an eerie wail that brings monkeys to within range of his shotgun.

ing and roaring with delight as they dashed into the shallow, cool water. They drank and splashed around and then, perhaps having caught our scent, or having heard an incautious sound, they tore through the water and disappeared into the dense greenery on the far bank. There was not a sound to mark their passage through the forest; like ghosts they were gone, and the heat and the haze and our elated spirits were left behind. These were the only forest elephants that we saw close up. But after four days of tramping through the undergrowth, living on rice and fish and the clean forest water, it would not have mattered if we saw none, for the richness and fascination of the rain forest was constantly rewarding.

The small forest elephant of West Africa seems perfectly *en rapport* with its environment: unlike its large savanna relative, it does not destroy its habitat. Perhaps it is better adapted – fossil evidence indicates that elephants have spent much longer in the forest than the savanna. Perhaps the seeming inability of the bush elephant to live in harmo-

Jentink's duiker, the largest of the duikers, is extremely rare, seldom seen, and occurs only in a small area of Liberia and Côte d'Ivoire.

ny with its environment is attributable to the fact that it is a relative newcomer. On the other hand, the role of the savanna elephant is not yet fully understood, and its destruction of woodlands, far from being a symptom of a newly evolved and incompletely adapted species, could be a vital part of the functioning of savanna systems. For the present, we can only weigh up the scanty evidence and speculate. Throughout the Tai forest, and several other areas in Côte d'Ivoire where forest elephants are fairly numerous, there are no reports of damage to the vegetation that are in any sense comparable with that found in the savanna.

The African lowland rain forest extends from Sierra Leone in the west to the Ruwenzoris, the Mountains of the Moon, in the east. The western unit, known as the Upper Guinea Forest, stretches as far as Ghana where it is cut off from the rest of the forest by the Dahomey Gap, a 300 km-wide corridor of dry savanna vegetation reaching to the sea. To the east, in Nigeria, the rain forest begins again. This Nigerian block is sometimes regarded as a unit distinct from the rest of the Lower Guinea (or Congo) Forest block, which stretches as far as the border of Uganda and Tanzania and south to Angola, but mostly it lies in Zaïre, the heart of the continent.

The rain forest interior, like the depths of the ocean, does not know sun and wind. Here it is always twilight and calm, save when a giant tree, heavy with age and rot, and mantled by epiphytes and ferns, crashes down. Its fall tears limbs from its neighbours and crushes many lesser trees, creating a huge gash in the otherwise even green canopy. The shock of its fall is short, soon seedlings, of fast growing pioneer species and younger trees that have been patiently waiting for light send up their slender stems. The first tree to reach the canopy wins the prize – space – and draws a curtain of shade over the scene again. But while the rare patch of sunshine lasts, shrubs and herbs proliferate as they also do along stream banks, acting as a magnet to the forest elephants and other animals.

The rain forest from its impoverished soil to the top of the canopy is home to many diverse creatures – their lives finely tuned to the rhythms of the forest plants, to the twilight, the rain and the steaming heat. This is the most complex and intricate natural system on earth.

Of the numerous animals using the plant material, the most important of all are those constantly recycling the litter of leaves, twigs and fruit, putting back into the soil the minerals and nutrients that are essential for the life cycles of the forest. Because the Tai soils receive 2 000 - 3 000 millimetres of rain a year, they are leached and relatively infertile, most of the nutrients being locked up in plant tissue. The insects, tiny anthropods and bacteria are therefore the major elements keeping the nutrients moving within the system, and preventing their loss via the rivers to the sea.

The generally stable climate of the forest, with virtually no drought or cold spells, ensures that food is available evenly throughout the seasons. There are, nevertheless, changes in the relative abundance of various food types, such as the availability of fruits from certain trees in some locations at different times of the year. To take advantage of this spatial distribution of food, larger mammals, including the chimpanzee and forest elephant, move around according to what is available. Chimpanzees, for example, may return to the same tree daily for as long as it has fruit.

Forest elephants eat a great amount of fruit and this is important to some trees, for the seeds of many species will only germinate, or germinate more rapidly, after having passed through their gut. The elephants also serve as dispersal agents, carrying seeds to other areas of the forest and of the 71 tree species in Tai whose seed dispersal mechanisms are known, 21 are dependent on elephants. While many animals eat fruit, only elephants can swallow very large seeds and deposit them intact; most of the droppings that we examined contained large seeds, and sometimes whole fruits as well. Elephant dung also fertilizes the poor forest soil.

Food resources for ground dwellers in the forest are simply not as abundant as in the grassland or savanna where ungulates can live in large herds, and the relatively sparse distribution of food has had at least one consequence for all large forest mammals – they are solitary. Even the highly social and intelligent elephant lives in a basic unit of cow and calf here, rather than in a family herd. The bulls are solitary, though sometimes two are seen together and, of course, they do associate briefly with cows from time to time. But not all forest mammals are placed under the same restrictions of group size. Monkeys, for example, can exploit the full spectrum of plant material available in the rain forest, from ground level to the canopy. Bands of monkeys may frolic above the solitary bongo.

In the rain forest the small elephant

In the shadowy undergrowth which the zebra duiker prefers, stripes break up its outline, probably making it less conspicuous to predators.

groups can satisfy most of their requirements in relatively small areas. Consequently they do not move over large ranges and Günter Merz, a German ecologist who has done the only intensive study on the forest elephant, has found their average daily movements to be no more than about five kilometres. The elephants do, however, undertake seasonal movements, probably within some kind of clan range.

The forest elephants, like their savanna cousins, make use of the occasional pool of rainwater, especially during the short dry season from January to March when the Harmattan wind blows hot and dry from the Sahara, covering the forest with a fine layer of powder-like dust. They wallow and shower in these pools, and it is not unusual to find them being used by pygmy hippos and bushpigs. Near such wallows, trees may be coated in mud up to about two metres – an indication that the forest elephants enjoy a scratch against a tree and that they are much smaller that savanna elephants. The largest

45

From the buttressed bases of the forest giants of Tai, the trunks sweep up to disappear into the canopy almost 60 metres above the forest floor.

The velvety pod of a large legume curls up when dry, expelling the seeds, and then provides a shelter for insects on the forest floor.

During the wet season, which is most of the year in Tai, poachers build shelters, complete with raised beds made of saplings, to keep themselves dry.

footprint that Merz measured in Tai had a circumference of only 1,1 metres, implying a shoulder height of about 2,2 metres. By comparison large savanna bulls may have a forefoot circumference of 1,5 metres, with a shoulder height of 3,4 - 3,5 metres.

Rivers such as the Hana which flow through Tai have steep banks and sandy beds littered with fallen trees, branches and driftwood. Their waters are cool and clear, but tea-coloured from the tannins contained in the leaves of forest trees. Banks are favoured as feeding areas because of the more lush groundcover in these sunny spots. Flood waters undercut the banks ensuring a more regular fall of trees there than further away from the river. This promotes secondary plant growth, as well as providing convenient log bridges.

The rain forest teems with animals, but many remain hidden and silent, either busy deep beneath the ground like the subterranean termites, or high above in the trees. The forest termites build small termitaria, with structural features designed to cope with rainfall (such as toadstool shapes and overhanging roofs) rather than with temperature fluctuations, which are the concern of savanna termites. These ground-dwelling termites of Tai have to contend with a specialist predator, the giant pangolin, while those that have fled to the treetops, where they build arboreal nests, have to cope with two climbing species, the tree pangolin and the long-tailed pangolin.

Unexpectedly, birds are scarce in the African rain forest, and the absence of birdsong is striking; only in the early morning and for a brief evening period did we hear much calling. The African lowland forest block has only 266 forest bird species, fewer than in a five-square-kilometre patch of Central American rain forest in Costa Rica. The Upper Guinea forest has only 182 forest species, many of which are fruit-eaters such as hornbills, touracos and parrots, or flycatchers, bee-eaters and other insect-eaters. There are very few water birds apart from Hartlaub's duck, which is restricted to forest, and also few ground-dwelling birds, the most widespread of which is the crested guinea-fowl.

Rich as it is, the rain forest is a demanding environment and it seems, superficially at least, that most of the animals that occupy it are highly specialized. There appear to be fewer generalists than in the savanna, where many species occupy a wide range of habitats. Perhaps in the forest niches are more rigidly defined and competition greater.

The nature of the forest limits the extent to which certain animals, such as large birds, can operate, and few raptors use it regularly. The exception is the crowned eagle, the most powerful eagle in Africa. Its short, rounded wings and long tail are designed for speed and tight turns under forest conditions. It waits patiently on a perch overlooking a forest path or stream bank, and from this vantage it dives like a thunderbolt, killing animals far heavier than itself in the crushing grip of its powerful talons. Monkeys, tree hyrax and small antelope such as duikers, Royal antelope and chevrotains are its main prey.

There are seven species of duiker in the West African forests, all found in Tai. These range from the tiny Maxwell's duiker weighing between four and eight kilograms to the large, smoky-grey Jentink's duiker, which may weigh as much as 70 kilograms. Jentink's and the zebra duiker, with its conspicuous transverse blackish stripes across the back and rump, are known only from a small area of Liberia and the adjoining Tai region of Côte d'Ivoire. Others – such as the yellow-backed duiker – occur throughout the African forest zone.

Few carnivores stalk the Tai forest – but they are nevertheless sufficient to make life hazardous for the weak and careless. The largest is the leopard, the ubiquitous cat which is equally at home in the desert or rain forest. Leopards spend much of their time on the ground hunting duiker, bushpigs and the like, but a study of their food habits in Tai – based on an analysis of their droppings – revealed that monkeys made up 35 per cent of their diet and duikers only 25 per cent. How else could the leopards catch monkeys if not at night in the trees when they are roosting?

Two forms of the mysterious golden cat are found in the forest, one 'golden' or reddish-brown with brown spots and the other greyish or blackish with black spotting. These beautiful, stockily built medium-sized cats are secretive and almost nothing is known of their habits – other than that they are solitary, elusive and feed on rodents, birds and hyrax.

The West African forest covers about 1 500 kilometres from east to west and averages about 250 kilometres in width. Over this huge area the forest has been cut, burnt, cultivated and settled, except for isolated patches. In Côte d'Ivoire alone more than 90 per cent of the original rain forest has been changed or destroyed. The only exception is the 350 000 hectare Tai National Park which is the largest, and last, piece of intact primary rain forest in the Upper Guinea block. Despite large scale poaching, illegal logging and the encroachment of settlements along its borders, now fortunately demarcated by a WWF project, Tai still had about 1 500 forest elephants in 1980, the only large population remaining in West Africa. But the Tai elephants are particularly hunted for 'rose' ivory, a form of ivory which commands premium prices, and numbers are rapidly declining. No less than 47 of the 52 larger mammal species known from the Upper Guinea Forest occur in Tai. Its botanical assets alone make it important – at least 10 per cent of the more than 1 500 plant species in the park are found nowhere else.

The size of the park, its biological complexity and completeness make Tai a vitally important conservation area, especially in view of the status of African rain forest else-

At dawn and sunset, raucously calling flocks of African grey parrots flew high over our bivouacs along the Hana River, heading for feeding and roosting sites.

where. The recognition of this unique area under the World Heritage Convention by UNESCO is fully justified. Tai is also recognized by IUCN as one of the world's most threatened reserves. This recognition unfortunately does little to maintain its integrity. Only the efficient protection of the Tai forest as a functioning national park can do that.

On the Ebrie Lagoon, which stretches along the Atlantic shore of Côte d'Ivoire, lies Abidjan, the thriving, sophisticated capital of the republic. Dual motorways cross the lagoon, and the gleaming white tower of the Hotel Ivoire reaches to the sky. Everywhere there is noise and bustle and activity. At the western end of the lagoon, scarcely 90 kilometres away, lies the Azagny National Park where forest elephants feed in the swamps, red forest buffalo contentedly chew the cud and pygmy hippos silently plod along under cover of the night.

Azagny occupies the low-lying land which stretches between the Ebrie Lagoon and the Bandama River. It is a small park, only 200 km², a mere 16 kilometres from east to west. Its southern boundary is the mangrove-lined canal which links the Ebrie to the Bandama; its northern boundary lies only 14 kilometres away. Most of the park is swamp, swamp forest, thicket and seasonally flooded marsh. The rest is more or less evenly divided between tall primary rain forest, secondary forest and a tropical coastal savanna. Within the secondary forest areas, only recently incorporated within the park, are fairly extensive cultivated sites where coffee, cacao and oil palms are still tended. The people had been re-settled, but on the understanding that they could still harvest these crops for three years. This ensured that the extension of the park boundaries, necessary for its viability, could be accomplished with less trauma for the affected people than has usually been the case elsewhere in Africa.

Like many other reserves in Africa, Azagny owes its existence to the penchant of colonial administrators to seek relaxation in the rig-

AZAGNY NATIONAL PARK

CÔTE D'IVOIRE

(Above) *Forest elephants are usually found alone, or in small groups of two or three animals.*
(Right) Islands of Pandanus *rise out of the lush and soggy greenery of a shallow tropical swamp where forest elephants feed, wading belly-deep through the matted vegetation.*
(Grand Isle, Azagny National Park, Côte d'Ivoire

Brightly coloured Diana monkeys are common in the Côte d'Ivoire rain forest, and also occur in the thickets and woodlands along its northern edges.

ours of the chase. It was set aside as a hunting zone, particularly for buffalo and elephants. Because it lies so close to Abidjan, it has potential for tourist development, more so than the other parks in the rain forest zone. This is simply because game-viewing as practised in the open savanna parks is not feasible in the forest. A silent walk along a forest path, a patient wait at a lookout point or hide, often not rewarded, or a low level flight over the swamps, are the only options for the development of game-viewing.

Though it was the height of the dry season when we visited Azagny, the *Cyclosurus* swamps were waterlogged and the elephant paths nothing more than muddy channels, the dark brown mud and swamp water trails criss-crossing the deep green of the vegetation. Elephants seemed to be especially fond of these areas and were mostly seen wading up to their bellies, cattle egrets on their backs or flapping around precariously on the floating mat of sedges, ferns and water grasses. The birds used the elephants as moving islands or platforms from which to hunt in-

sects disturbed by their steady passage. Forest buffalo were also seen wading along and feeding in the swamps. Others, more in the fashion of Asian water buffalo, lazed in the muddy water, occasionally with egrets clambering over them. Those who preferred to remain dry would seek out the small dry short grass islands and rest through the heat of the afternoon.

The Azagny elephant population of about 50 animals is isolated. Their nearest neighbours, also a relict population, are in the forest of Go, about 20 kilometres to the north-west across the Bandama River. There was contact in the past, and a village headman near Nzi-Nda described how as a young man he often saw elephants swimming across the Bandama, a wide, deep river. Today they no longer leave the park; if they did, they would enter densely settled and developed areas. The Azagny elephants spend most of their time in the secondary forest, swamp forest and coastal savanna in the south-western corner of the park. They follow a fairly regular routine, and can be found feeding in the *Cyclosurus* swamp most afternoons, or in the raffia swamps, where because of the density of trees they are not as easily spotted.

They are usually in small groups of two or three animals, and occasionally herds of as many as seven or eight, but the bulls are generally solitary. There are also reports from Azagny of gatherings of as many as 30 or 40 elephants – a phenomenon seen on a much larger scale among savanna elephants, where hundreds of animals gather for a day or two and then disperse. Because of the nature of the swamp and the difficulty of access, the only sure way to see the elephants is from the air. Being buzzed by light aircraft does

Clumps of wild date palms (Phoenix reclinata) *grow on small hummocks in the seasonally waterlogged grasslands that occur around the edge of the Azagny swamp.*

Some termite mounds in the forest are built with large eaves, which are worn away by the high rainfall. New roofs are built on top of the old, giving the termitarium a stacked appearance.

With practised ease an Ivoirean fisherman casts his net from a canoe in the Bandama estuary.

not appear to disturb the animals at all. Aerial game-viewing is therefore considered the most likely means of developing tourist activity in the park. The buffalo, however, are not as tolerant of the aircraft and often run for cover.

The Azagny elephants are typical *cyclotis* animals. They appear to be a little larger than the elephants of Tai, perhaps because of the considerably better nutrition in the humus-rich swamp soils. The largest bulls we saw were perhaps 2,4 metres at the shoulder. They have the typical rounded ears of the forest elephant which do not meet on the top of the head, and have high hindquarters, but differ from other forest elephants in that they have somewhat thicker tusks. We followed spoor through the primary forest of Petit Isle and found that they wallowed in muddy pools, very rarely dug a tusk into the bark of a tree, and their droppings were much smaller, finer textured and darker coloured than savanna elephant droppings.

The reproduction rate seems to be good in the Azagny population as there is a high proportion of young calves. Of the 29 forest elephant we saw there, three (10,3 per cent) were calves which we estimated to be three years or younger. All our elephants were seen in the swamp. As the babies apparently have great difficulty moving through the swamp, it seems likely that cows with small calves keep to the edges of the swamp on firmer soil. The forest cover is better, which is probably why we did not see any babies. Other surveys have recorded up to 10 per cent of calves aged less than one year. As the population has not increased markedly in the past few years, it seems possible that numbers are being kept stable by poaching.

The predominant colours of Azagny are shades of green – the grassy swampland is pale green, the *Cyclosurus* swamp dark green, the *Pandanus* thickets a blue-green, and the forest patches olive green. Splashes of colour are seen in the rain forest of Grande Isle, one of the two forested islands in the swamp, where trees with reddish and golden leaves, pale white and pink flowers break the dark variegated green mosaic of the forest canopy. The *Phoenix reclinata* and raffia palms also offer a tinge of darkness, with always a splash of black and white where a palm nut vulture perches in solitary splendour. True to their common name, these birds are usually found around dense stands of palms.

The swamps boast a wide variety of different plant communities. At one end of the scale is open seasonally flooded grassland with *Echinochloa pyramidalis* and *Paspalum vaginatum*; there is swamp dominated by the fern *Cyclosurus oppositifolius*, dense *Raphia palmapinus* palm swamp; a mixed swamp forest composed of *Raphia* palms and *Syzigium guineense* trees, and then various forms of swamp forest dominated by broad-leaved *Uapaca paludosa* and *Mitragyna ciliata*. Closer to the sea and the lagoon are large areas of dense mangrove forest dominated by *Rhizophora racemosa*.

The open swamplands are dotted about by dense clumps or islands of screwpines *Pandanus candelabrum*. This strange tree, which looks like a palm, grows in circular colonies or thickets. The oldest and tallest trees are at the centre with ever younger and smaller trees growing around them. The outlines of these thickets show a smooth rounded hump when seen from ground lev-

Dense groves of raffia palms (Raphia palmapinus), *with dead and fallen leaves protruding at all angles, form an almost impenetrable barrier to man.*

el. In places where elephants had forced open a path into the *Pandanus* thickets the pale white stems of the trees were exposed, each with a series of prop roots growing out of the stem to give support in the soft, swampy ooze. The raffia palms have the largest leaves in the plant kingdom; these can be up to 18 metres long, the fronds radiating out from the stem with almost geometric precision. The raffia swamp is almost impenetrable, except by elephants and pygmy hippo, and monkeys which keep to the trees. The water is dark chocolate-brown and muddy.

Under every palm lies a tangle of dead and fallen, rotting fronds, scattered in all directions. On the rotting hummocks formed by dead trees grow sedges, ferns, delicate orchids and a beautiful white-flowered amaryllis *Crinum jagus*. On the rare patches of open water, the dark green pads of water lilies *Nymphaea lotus* battle for space against the ferns. The water lily blooms are white with brilliant yellow stamens. They open at night. During the heat of the day they are

51

closed, presumably depending on nocturnal moths for pollination.

Moving through West African rain forest on foot is not difficult as the understorey is usually fairly open and the shrubs are remarkably free of thorns or spines, lending credence to the theory that it is only the savanna shrubs which require thorns as a defence against browsing animals. However, the swamp forest is a different matter entirely. Throughout the length and breadth of Africa we had never encountered any plant quite as noxious as the *Calamus deeratus* palm. *Calamus* is a horrible climbing palm with sharp, hooked spines on stems, leaves and petioles. It sends out long whiplike tendrils which are armed with clusters of three-hooked spines at regular intervals. These tendrils droop down from above, grow up from below and are maddeningly effective at catching and tearing any careless arm, leg or ear. Their function is to aid the palm to scramble upwards towards the light, but they form a devilish barrier which can be breached only by patience and laborious hacking away with a machete.

In the eastern reaches of the swamp, there are areas of open water which vary in colour from dark muddy brown to fairly clear

The pygmy hippo is a solitary species, spending most of its time away from water but wallowing regularly in forest pools.

pools. Some are completely covered by water lilies and other floating plants. The lily leaves are dark green, and when turned over by the gusting sea breeze, they show a deep reddish or purple hue.

The water birds of the swamp, like those from wetlands elsewhere in Africa, are very different from the forest avifauna. Pygmy goose, jacana, purple heron, black crake, moor hen, and many other species that are widely distributed in Africa feed on the small lakes and scatter into the tussocky sedges and grasses when disturbed. The pygmy geese, which feed largely on water lily seeds, take to the wing in groups, their metallic grey upperparts and white wing patches blurred with the speed of their flight. The white faces, and the neck patches of the males, emerald green shot through with violet, flash across the dull surface of the water. Their co-ordinated landings raise a shower of silver drops and long trailing ripples as their tight little bodies settle down in the water.

Well-used trails of buffalo and elephant wander from one pool to another. These paths are a blessing to the lighter-bodied western sitatunga, which otherwise struggle to travel through some of the dense swamp vegetation. Small islands of dry, close-cropped grass attest to the frequent presence of red buffalo in these areas. In these pools large Nile crocodiles slide away into deeper water, while in the swamp forest the smaller *Osteolaemus tetraspis* retires into a burrow.

Though we spent most of our time in Azagny in the swamp areas, looking for elephants, our base camp was situated in a lush stand of untouched primary rain forest opposite Petit Isle. This camp was built by Dr

Harald Roth, whom Paul and I were fortunate to have as our guide and companion during our visit to Azagny. He has worked in Côte d'Ivoire for many years and co-ordinated the first ecological surveys of the three parks we visited. Azagny is his particular interest and he ran a special management unit, staffed by Ivoireans and funded by the World Bank, which was developing the park.

We found that troops of lesser white-nosed and Mona monkeys sometimes moved out into the swamp forest to forage during the day, but in the late afternoon they would hurry back to the tall primary forest to spend the night. Chimpanzees were occasionally heard hooting, and their distant drumming on the plank buttresses of the forest trees also carried far. This habit is said to be a unique feature of the West African chimps. They pound the resonant buttresses as a form of magnified chest thumping behaviour, and the sound has obvious social communication value. Another 'cultural' feature of the West African chimps which we were told about is their habit of nut cracking – they collect nuts, place them on large flat stones and crack them by hammering on them with a smaller stone. Some of these nut-cracking stones have a distinct hollow in the middle, much like the hollowed-out stones used by African women for grinding grain. These reports attest to a fairly sophisticated form of tool use by the chimpanzee.

Azagny is presently the eastern-most point where the pygmy hippo is found. It is extinct in the Niger River delta where an isolated population may have occurred. This animal, no bigger than a large pig, lives alone or in groups of mother and young. Unlike the huge Nile hippo the pygmy does not spend much time in rivers, and it will flee away from water when harried.

The zoogeography, or distribution of animals, of the rain forest biome is fascinating. Several duikers are found only to the west of the Dahomey Gap; other animals, such as the gorilla, are found only to the east; yet others, such as the chimpanzee, are found on both sides in the forest, but not in the savanna country of the Gap. Within the Upper Guinea Forest there are situations interpreted as recent or active speciation, which illustrate the isolating effects of natural barriers. Thus in Côte d'Ivoire one finds three races or subspecies of the Western black-and-white colobus monkey. One of these *Colobus polykomos polykomos* occurs from Senegal in the west to the Sassandra River. On the east bank it is replaced by *C. p. dollmani* which occurs as far as the west bank of the Bandama River. East of this river as far as Nigeria, a third subspecies *C. p. vellerosus* is found. Many similar puzzles will never be solved, because many of the species, especially of the lesser animals such as the invertebrates, will probably be extinct before they are discovered by scientists.

The abiding impression of Azagny is the swampland, green and wet, with the dark bodies of forest elephants churning through the dense vegetation, and in the distance the forest looming up on the high ground. Fur-

Colonies of Pandanus candelabrum *form island thickets in the otherwise featureless swamp where elephant paths cut channels through the vegetation.*

ther away the forest breaks up into a mosaic of cultivation with here and there palm-thatched huts and coffee drying mats out in the sun. Near every village the smoke of burning forest trees curls lazily into the air, the whitened skeletons of the dead trees, the pathetic grey, dead, hanging cords of the lianas, and then the miles and miles of straight lines of oil palms and rubber trees. The past, present and future of the forests of West Africa are all seen in one sweep within a few short kilometres.

A herd of elephants strolling along a sandy tropical beach and splashing into the Atlantic surf is one of the more unusual sights of Africa. This intriguing activity is witnessed regularly on the coast of Gabon. Forest elephants in small groups of two or three, and sometimes as many as a dozen, amble out of the forest and gather on the sparkling white beach. Some rush into the sea; others, such as the small calves and their anxious mothers, are hesitant and splash only in the breaking waves. The adult bulls move out, beyond the breakers, which are small and close together on this coast, and there they roll, frolic and bellow with every indication of enjoyment.

There are two reserves in Gabon which reach to the seashore. Just to the south of Libreville is the Presidential Hunting Reserve of Wonga-Wongué, and south of Port Gentil, Gabon's second city, is the Petit Loanga National Park. In both these areas the elephants have taken to spending time on the beach and bathing in the sea. The beach at Wonga-Wongué is narrow, as the continent shelf slopes only gradually to the west. The sea is, therefore, shallow with hardly any surf on a calm day, only gentle waves breaking in a flurry of white on the shore.

The vegetation along the coast of Wonga-Wongué is patchy – sometimes the rain forest reaches to the shore; elsewhere there are groves of trees such as *Syzigium*, which can apparently stand the effects of salt spray, set in open grassland; there are also swamps, broad coastal lagoons and estuaries which are home to manatees and the princely game fish, the tarpon. The beaches are littered by thousands of logs which have drifted away from the timber pools at Port Gentil and

WONGA-WONGUÉ PRESIDENTIAL HUNTING RESERVE

GABON

(Above) *The brilliantly coloured face of the adult male mandrill is striking even in the poorly lit depths of the forest, and possibly serves to signal his status to his fellows.*
(Right) *Escaping for a while from their dark haunts, forest elephants splash in the gentle Atlantic surf on Gabon's placid equatorial coast.*
(Sangatanga, Wonga-Wongué Presidential Hunting Reserve, Gabon)

54

The forest or dwarf buffalo is much smaller than the Cape buffalo of the savanna, with small, flattened, curved horns and long, hairy tassles on the ears.

Calling up duikers, by making a miauwing sound that is modulated by pinching the nostrils, is part of the skill of the forest hunters.

The black-casqued hornbill is one of several species of large hornbills that have a wide range throughout the rain forest zone of West Africa.

Isolated forest patches in the grasslands indicate that fire may also play a role in maintaining this characteristic feature of the Wonga-Wongué landscape.

elsewhere. Most of them are valuable hardwoods, others are the semi-deciduous softwood known as okoumé (*Aucoumea klaineana*), which grows only in Gabon. The forest giants are felled in the seemingly endless forests of the interior and the logs are floated down the rivers to the sea. One such river is the wide Ogooué which flows past Lambarene, site of the famous mission hospital founded by Albert Schweitzer in 1926.

Wonga-Wongúe lies to the west of Lambarene and covers 3 800 km². It has been a hunting reserve for many years, and this has ensured its protection. Few animals are ever hunted in the area and there is very little human activity. Most of the reserve is rain forest, but in the central zone, about 30 kilometres from the sea, there is a stretch of largely open grasslands with scattered small lakes and isolated patches of forest. But the solid wall of dark green primary forest is always on the skyline. It is gently undulating country, lying on ancient coastal dunes and sand ridges. In places there are eroded limestone cliffs, such as Petit Bam Bam where the reserve headquarters are located. The grasslands have a good road network, laid out and maintained by Claude Pradel, warden of the reserve and our genial host. These provide easy access to most of Wonga-Wongúe. Closer to the coast they are linked to a network of roads cut through the forest for oil exploration. For Paul and me, it was indeed a rare treat to drive through superb rain forest and see forest elephants from an air-conditioned safari car – a far cry from our days of foot-slogging, drenched with sweat, through the forests of Go and Tai in Côte d'Ivoire.

The Gabon elephants are usually grey, but

may also be reddish or red-grey in colour, for like other elephants, they sometimes take on the colour of the local soil from wallowing and showering in mud and dirt. One impressive bull that we saw on the edge of the forest near Petit Bam Bam had long, stained, yellow, almost amber-coloured tusks that reached almost to the ground – impressive trophies, but slender. This animal had a badly torn ear, a common feature in savanna elephants, but seldom noticed in forest elephants. The ears of forest elephants, apart from usually being in better repair than those of the savanna, do not have the distinctive lappet at the bottom corner of the ear and the turned-over upper edges of the savanna animals. Apart from the physical differences between the forest and savanna elephants, there was a different quality about them which we could not describe objectively. The smaller forest animals simply have a different bearing and movement, somehow quicker, almost furtive, and lacking the slow, majestic grace of the savanna elephants.

The elephants of Wonga-Wongúe, as others elsewhere, are creatures of habit, and they move out into the grasslands every afternoon. They sometimes spend the night out in the open, feeding, but in the early morning move back into the forest. While we were moving slowly along a track, as a dense pre-dawn mist still wafted low on the ground, reminiscent of the coastal fog of the Namib areas, two dark shapes loomed up ahead of us. An elephant cow, with a calf about five years old, were hurrying along towards the cover of the forest ahead of us.

They were agitated and their tails were high up on their backs in tight curls, more like those of rhinos than elephants. Their heads were stretched out as they hurried, the calf moving ahead and then swinging around as if to make sure the mother was following. They crossed the road in that deceptive shuffle which is no more than a fast walk for an elephant, but with which a human would find it hard to keep pace.

The grasslands around Petit Bam Bam, so unexpected in the midst of the dense equatorial forest, are perennial, and coarse tussock grasses are dominant. Various *Hyparrhenia* species and *Imperata cylindrica* are common, and sedges are abundant in the deep sandy soil. Fire is one factor maintaining these grasslands, and in places annual fires are slowly eating into the smaller forest patches. Whether fire played a role in the genesis of these grasslands, or whether soil factors are more important, is not clear.

Part of the management strategy adopted by Claude Pradel is to burn the grasslands regularly. This removes moribund grass, as under the high rainfall conditions growth and the build-up of old material is rapid. In some areas the forest patches are restricted to drainage lines, sheltered amphitheatres, and ravines in the sand dunes and limestone ridges. The bottomlands are sometimes marshy, but true swamps are found only inside the forested areas.

About 85 per cent of Gabon is still covered by rain forest. In this area of 267 667 km², inhabited by only 1 230 000 people, very little human impact is seen, except in the inland savanna areas and the recently logged swathes of forest. Where logging has taken place, and on old cultivation sites, secondary forest soon establishes itself. This is a more productive habitat for most of the

Normally the inhabitants of swamps and marshes, the western sitatunga of Wonga-Wongué make good use of the open grasslands.

mammals and birds than the undisturbed primary forest. Many of the people, such as the hunting Pygmy tribes and the Okande 'piroguiers' are still living in traditional style within the forest environment. The Okande carve twelve-man canoes out of huge trees and then in full cry, singing the songs of their ancestors, launch them like flashing spears through the boiling rapids of the forest rivers. The Gabonese have, of course, been influenced by the West, and among other things the headlamp and the twelve-bore shotgun is having its effect on duiker and monkey populations, but the reduction in their numbers is nothing like the scale of havoc wrought in West Africa. Like the other

forest peoples of the Equatorial and West African regions, the Gabonese hunters know the forest intimately. Not only is their hunting and tracking skill outstanding, but their knowledge of animals and their habits is highly developed. In Gabon the calling of monkeys and duikers to within shotgun range has been developed to a fine art. We saw the same techniques demonstrated in the Tai forest of Côte d'Ivoire. For duiker-calling, the hunter's nostrils are pinched closed with two fingers and a strange mi-auwing sound is made. The call is repeated for some moments and then followed by a blowing or sneezing sound; the caller pauses and then starts again. The sounds which imi-

57

The palm nut vulture is widespread and abundant in West Africa, being especially common where oil palms occur.

tate the distress calls of duikers seldom fail to bring one trotting up. Forest duikers are territorial beasts, and presumably they are drawn to the sound to see off an intruder rather than to render aid to a stricken fellow, as has been suggested.

The rain forest of Wonga-Wongué, evergreen, hot and humid with a mean annual rainfall of about 2 300 millimetres, is typical of the lowland forest, which stretches all the way through West and Equatorial Africa. The forest is dominated by huge trees which reach up 60 metres and more to form a solid roof or canopy, each occupying just as much space as it can wrest from its neighbours.

The canopy trees have straight, clean boles, with never a branch until right up near the top. They are supported by plank buttresses which reach out around the base, sometimes as much as 10 metres in all directions.

Below the canopy is a secondary layer of trees, between 10 and 20 metres high, composed of seedlings of the canopy species or other species which can tolerate low light conditions. The undergrowth, in half-darkness, is composed of a layer of shrubs mostly with dark waxy-green leaves with conspicuous points or drip-tips from where drops of moisture collect and fall to the ground. On the sandy forest floor herbs are scattered on the dense carpet of dead leaves. The filtered light slants down from the canopy in beams, like the light let in by the high arched windows of a Gothic cathedral. If one stands in the silence, for there is little bird song or insect noise, all that one hears is the gentle rain of falling leaves on the forest floor.

Where the sun is unobstructed by the canopy, the lesser vegetation runs riot, such as along stream banks, around the edges of forest pools and patches of forest such as are found near Petit Bam Bam, or along tracks and clearings where the giants have been felled and secondary forest has developed. Here there is a dense growth of shrubs, small trees, seedlings, ferns, sedges, and all manner of climbers and lianas scrambling for the light. Many of these plants have medicinal value, or are used as food by the forest people. Others, such as the wild ginger *Aframomum*, is used to make a refreshing cordial.

The high rainfall and sandy soils result in a typical low-nutrient system. The many small lakes have white, sandy beaches with little plant or bird life. Presumably the aquatic systems are also low in productivity. At one of the larger lakes we found a few reed cormorants and two black-headed herons – indications of at least some aquatic life.

We never went far in the grassland without seeing forest buffalo. Sometimes they were in small groups, on their own or in pairs, grazing on the new flush of burnt grasslands, or on the most attractive patches in groups of up to 40 animals. When these large groups were disturbed they did not run off in a compact mass as savanna buffalo would, but quickly split up into their smaller constituent groups as they raced for the cover of the forest. These buffalo, also known as dwarf buffalo, are smaller than their large black cousins, the Cape buffalo. The forest buffalo, which occurs throughout the forest zone, is a bright reddish-brown to chestnut colour with a yellowish to orange-coloured belly and inner parts of the legs, and with long tassles of brownish hair on the tips of its ears. The horns of the forest buffalo are rather small and half-moon-shaped, as might be expected in an animal that lives in fairly dense vegetation. During our visit to Wonga-Wongué, Paul and I also found the tracks and droppings of forest buffalo on the beach, but no indication that they ever went into the sea.

The buffalo do not live in the true primary forest, but only around its edges and in the richer secondary forest. This choice of secondary forest habitat speaks also for the ebb and flow of the forest biome over time, creating the conditions under which this animal evolved. In modern times they have benefited from cultivation, which creates secondary conditions, and from exploitation of the forest, especially the resulting lush grass that grows along the timber extraction roads.

The isolation of the Wonga-Wongué grasslands, surrounded by dense primary forest, would seem to be a situation of long standing – yet, apart from the buffalo and western sitatunga, no other large grazing mammal is found. The western bushpig, appropriately also known as the red river hog (for its bright orange colour), uses the grasslands, as does the giant forest hog. However, they are essentially forest creatures and utilize the edges of the forest for feeding. The usual habitat of sitatunga is the dense, lush swamps and swamp edges. It was most unusual to find them out in such open country. When disturbed some of them crouched down quietly and, if not pressed, would not budge. When more seriously disturbed they made off in a bounding gait, much like a greater kudu, their tails curled up in alarm. The underside and edges of the tail are white but not as long-haired as that of kudu or reedbuck. The male western sitatunga is a dark chocolate-brown colour with distinct white stripes and spots and two striking white patches on either side of the bridge of the nose. The coat of the western sitatunga does not appear to be as long and shaggy as that of the southern or Selous' sitatunga.

Having grown accustomed to seeing the forest primates as dark objects bouncing high up in the trees, it came as quite a surprise to us one day to spot what looked like a troop of baboons foraging at the edge of a forest patch. A close approach revealed that they were a type of baboon, the exotically coloured mandrill. The adult male features a superb blend of colours – the sides of the muzzle are deeply grooved and a bright powder blue, the nose is signal red, the eyes bright chestnut, the moustache whitish and the beard a bright orange or dull yellow; all these colours are set against the grizzled grey background of his fur. Their buttocks are bright scarlet and shades of violet. Perhaps the bright facial colours of the adult males serve to identify them clearly in the gloom of the forest, and to advertise their status.

Claude Pradel and other hunters insist that there are two types of forest elephant. They call the one *cyclotis* or true forest elephant; the other they refer to as the assala or pygmy elephant. Although it seems unlikely that there could be another subspecies (*Loxodonta africana pumilio*) sharing the range of *cyclotis*, the issue is by no means settled. The debate seemed to have been decided when an animal taken to the United States and said to be *pumilio* just kept on growing to reach the eventual size of a *cyclotis*. An assala elephant is reputedly no more than two metres at the shoulder, whereas a big *cyclotis* bull can reach three metres. Though both

The rich red fruit of the oil palm (Elaeis guineensis) *is the source of commercial palm oil and is also eaten by birds and fruit bats.*

types occur in the same area, they are said never to mix. The hunting regulations of Gabon distinguish clearly between the pygmy and forest elephant. The licence fees for the large *cyclotis* are higher than those for the smaller animals. Most scientists, however, remain sceptical. If the debate is to be settled, and the existence of a pygmy elephant proved or disproved by field studies, the most likely place in which to do so is Gabon.

KAHUZI-
BIEGA
NATIONAL
PARK

ZAÏRE

(Above) *Largest of the forest antelopes, the bongo occurs throughout the lowland forest zone and in isolated montane forests.*
(Left) *Forest elephants seek out glades in the bamboo groves where a lush understorey of shrubs and herbs provides rich pickings, a feeding ground shared with the gorillas.*
(Tshibinda, Kahuzi-Biega National Park, Zaïre)

It was a damp, overcast day on the steep eastern slopes of Mount Kahuzi. In the distance the grey waters of Lake Kivu lay placid as it was early morning and the wind ruffled the lake only in the late afternoon, when the thunderheads had built up. The forest smelled musty, the greenery was shiny-wet, and the white flowers of the exotic lily *Lilium formosanum* had drops of moisture sparkling on their petals. Despite the dullness of the weather, a Natal robin sang a short, tuneful song and then fell silent. The small wizened Mbuti Pygmy tracker lopped a trailing vine with a much-used panga. In his left hand he carried a stout stick which he used as a support on steep slopes and to probe into the dense shrubbery, pushing aside the nettles (*Laportea* spp.) and wild celery (*Pencedanum* spp.) to check on the tell-tale signs that were clear to him. To those unfamiliar with this forest world there was not a trace of an animal's passing. He huddled with a companion; a cricket started some hopeful chirping and then stopped. The trackers turned to the guide and mumbled a few words, the guide turned to Conservateur Iyhemopo Bebu, who was escorting us through his park, and he turned to us with a wide, generous smile – 'Le gorille,' he whispered 'tout près'. The back of his hand hid his shining teeth, making his message conspiratorial.

A faint tapping, a gorilla beating its chest, was heard, but surely from far away. The trackers and guides were silent, expectant, staring into the dense darkness of the forest. We were all keyed up, tense, waiting for something to happen. A curtain of vines and branches suddenly shuddered and parted. A terrible high-pitched scream tore at the dark

61

Most secretive of birds, the Congo peacock of the lowland forest of Zaïre has never been seen in the wild by Western eyes.

glimpse of him, enough to appreciate his bulk fully, as he crossed our track. His shoulders were twice as wide as those of a grown man, the muscles rolling under the long, sleek black fur. He had a broad rump, like a brewery horse, solid, and a white saddle, the badge of status of the adult eastern gorillas, acquired only after 12 years of age. Maheshi then started to feed on some wild celery, plucking the leaf, then peeling the petiole in his teeth before biting off and chewing a piece. Some of his family were moving along behind him and feeding, dimly seen black shapes in the gloom. A youngster climbed a tree to get at some delicacy. The sun broke through the wispy grey cloud brightening the scene.

The trackers edged forwards, swishing away the soft-stemmed shrubbery of the secondary forest, slowly opening a path between us and the gorilla. Maheshi knew the routine. The Pygmies were careful not to make any sudden moves, as they did not want to surprise or offend him. The huge gorilla carried on feeding, allowing the Pygmies to nick away at all offending shrubbery with their razor sharp pangas and so give us a superb view of him. He sat feeding, unconcerned, peaceful, an animal whose gentle disposition had been so well hidden by his scream of anger when he charged. He had impressed us with his power and position. Now that we were suitably awed and humbled, and honour was satisfied, he could get on with the more important business of eating.

The gorillas of Kahuzi-Biega National Park look much like the mountain gorilla *Gorilla gorilla beringei* of the Virunga volcanoes which range over a small area of Zaïre, Rwan-

silence, followed by a cacophony of cries from the little trackers of 'Maheshi! Maheshi!', the name of the huge black, silver-backed gorilla that was rushing forward on his knuckles, his mouth open, the lips pulled back to expose his brown stained teeth, and to release the searing screams that poured out of him. The gorilla stopped his charge a scant two metres, virtually at arm's length, from the leading tracker, and reared up, not quite upright, but even so he towered over the man. The trackers scrambled backwards towards us, still calling Maheshi's name. The great ape stopped, then visibly relaxed, as he sank back into the tangle of vegetation. He stared at us, obliquely, not directly. He was so close that every wrinkle on his black face was plain, his eyes were a deep warm brown colour, deeply recessed in his craggy brows, his gaze was open and frank. As suddenly as he appeared, he disappeared, only the shaking of the shrubbery marking his passage.

The gorilla moved along slowly, circling behind us, always keeping between us and his group of 15, which included one infant born a week earlier. We caught another da and Uganda, some 100 kilometres to the north. Some authorities regard them as mountain gorillas; but others, who have studied their anatomy closely, consider them to be a distinct subspecies, the eastern lowland gorilla *G. g. graueri*. These two eastern forms are very different in appearance from the smaller, browner western lowland gorilla *G. g. gorilla* which is found far to the west, and on whose territory we had wandered in Gabon. The western gorilla males do not have the impressive white saddle of the eastern forms. Although the eastern gorillas are regarded as an endangered species, and their numbers in the Virungas have declined in the past two decades due to encroachment of farmland on their limited habitat and to poaching, the Kahuzi-Biega population is presently healthy, relatively stable and possibly even increasing.

The Kahuzi-Biega National Park, a hunting area in the past, was proclaimed a national park only in 1970. One of the men who knows it best is Adrian Deschryver, former warden of the park. He slowly, carefully, habituated two groups of gorillas to humans. The process took two years before he felt confident enough to take tourists into the forest and approach the gorillas closely. His pioneering work has reaped recognition for the park, for this is the only place in Zaïre where visitors can enjoy the thrill and the privilege of seeing these great apes at close quarters.

The Mbuti trackers, so fearless of the gorillas, were terrified of the forest elephants. They regarded them as extremely fierce, unpredictable and best avoided. As we moved through the forest, close to the bamboo zone, they cautiously pointed out fresh droppings and tracks to us. But they followed the elephant spoor with little enthusiasm. For us, seeing these elephants was one of our reasons for visiting Zaïre. So, with entreaties and cajolery, we kept our trackers to their task, on the strict understanding that if we found elephants we would not approach them closely.

The tracks of the small herd we followed indicated that they had moved from the bamboo forest during the night and fed in the secondary forest in a steep-sided valley just above the park gate at Tshibinda. In the early hours of the morning they had moved back up the mountain. By midday we were close to them in the zone where the mountain forest was replaced by tall feathery leaved bamboo. Our approach was painfully slow, cautious, silent. The little men were tense, and they did not make a sound – quite a contrast to their noisy approach to the gorillas, when they wanted to ensure that the gorillas knew we were approaching.

We started moving slowly down a slope, and then froze when one of the Pygmies stopped dead. In the gloom ahead of us he had heard a branch snap. We listened, straining every sense to locate the animals, until a low growl carried to us the contented communication rumble of a resting or feeding elephant. A slight breeze stirred the tall green stems of the bamboo, causing them to rattle and clack together gently. The elephants, we could not say for certain how many, stood in deep shadow, their backs visible, a patch of ear here, a gleaming amber tusk there, a swish of a tail further on, all dappled by the gentle light. A young elephant stepped out into a clearing, the bamboo towering above

The notice board at the entrance to Kahuzi-Biega proclaims the park's priority: it is a sanctuary for the gorilla.

Dappled by shadows and mottled by lichen the densely packed stems of tall mountain bamboo (Arundinaria alpina) *form a seemingly solid barrier in places.*

Rooting through the litter of the forest floor the bushpig or red river hog turns up the soil, creating ideal beds for the germination of seeds.

63

The fire-footed squirrel is common in eastern Zaïre. Various forms range throughout the Equatorial forest and into West Africa.

Chimpanzees occur across Africa in the forest zone and along its periphery. Though very agile in trees, they spend much of their time foraging and resting on the ground.

him, and gazed quizzically in our direction, his trunk raised as if scenting. The Pygmies were rooted in silence. The elephant dropped his trunk, picked up a leaf, idly put it into his mouth and casually sauntered back to the group.

The trackers, not wanting to test our luck further, edged backwards. We all moved away, down the mountain, breathing easier, wondering whether we had seen forest elephants or forest ghosts.

The park lies on the high eastern edge of the great Zaïre rain forest. The peaks of Mount Kahuzi and Mount Biega form the western wall of the Rift Valley. Unlike the peaks in the Virungas which are volcanic, these peaks are granite, the building blocks of Africa. The eastern section of the park contains a lot of secondary forest where land which was formerly cultivated is returning to a natural vegetation cover. *Hagenia abyssinica*, a silvery leafed, usually moss-covered, spreading, untidy tree is often found in these forests, as it is under similar conditions of rainfall and altitude on all the East African mountains.

Above the *Hagenia* zone there is tall, montane primary evergreen forest which has cedars among its canopy species. Further up the mountain this is replaced by bamboo forest. The mountain bamboo *Arundinaria alpina* is a member of the grass family, but grows to a height of 12 metres or more with hard woody, hollow stems having a diameter of about 10 centimetres. The bamboo plants flower only once and then die. The flowering is synchronized and occurs about every 15 years. Fortunately not all the bamboos in an area flower at the same time. The blooms appear in patches so there is always a good population left. Above the bamboo is a zone of subalpine vegetation, also very typically montane with *Erica* and other heather, which is found all the way down the east coast until it becomes the essence of the diverse Cape floral kingdom at the tip of the continent.

In the forest of Kahuzi-Biega the destinies of gorilla, elephant and man are somewhat intertwined. The best gorilla habitat is the secondary forest, where light penetration is good and where the low shrubbery at ground level can grow in profusion. Old cultivation sites, where the forest plants are recolonizing land cleared by the former human inhabitants of the area, are therefore prime gorilla habitat. These conditions also provide ideal feeding for elephants with an abundance of forage within easy reach. The elephants therefore, unless hunted and persecuted by man, also tend to favour the secondary or regenerating forest rather than the mature forest. To some extent they also help to maintain the secondary forest by occasionally felling trees, opening up the shrub layer, performing a function which may be the evolutionary predecessor of their impact on the savanna.

The forest elephants are also closely linked to the life cycle of many forest trees, especially those of the primary zone. The seeds of many species must pass through an elephant before they are able to germinate. The large size and strong smell of many forest fruits are possibly the result of a long period of co-evolution of the trees and the elephants. Size makes it easier for the elephants to handle the fruit, and in the dim light conditions, given the colour blindness and poor eyesight of the elephants, the strong smell of the fruits could act as an attractant for them.

In the mature forest there are fewer gorillas, the understorey is relatively open, and food sources close to the ground are somewhat limited. As the larger male gorillas cannot climb to get food they are limited to areas of denser understorey which is usually secondary forest. In the primary forest the arboreal monkeys and chimpanzees are abundant as there is plenty of food for them. The bamboo forest is a rich, but only seasonal, food source for the elephants and gorillas. They make the most use of this plant community from October to December when the new young bamboo shoots appear.

On the western side of Kahuzi a small stream, which becomes the Lua, rises and joins the Lualaba, the major tributary of the great Congo or Zaïre River. The Lua flows through untouched lowland evergreen forest, home to most of the animals also found on the eastern slopes of the mountain, but also guardian of one of the most enigmatic, beautiful and least known of Africa's birds, the 'paon de Congo' the Congo or Zaïre peacock. The western boundary of Kahuzi-Biega National Park passes close to the small village of Utu, where one of the great stories of African ornithology had its climax in 1949. Dr James Chapin, the ornithologist whose monumental work *Birds of the Belgian Congo* is still regarded as a classic field study, found a feather in the headdress of an African in 1913 at Avakubi in the Ituri forest. He could not identify the bird from which it had come and carried the feather around with him for 23 years – until 1936 when he was able to match it to the female of a pair of stuffed birds found in the Tervuren Museum, just outside Brussels. These birds were the first representatives known to science of a new genus and species, *Afropavo congensis*.

The male Congo peacock is a dark metallic green with brilliant blue wing patches and tail. Both sexes have a reddish neck patch, while the hen has greenish upperparts and russet below with black bars on the wings. The male bird has a wiry, regal, whitish peafowl-like crest. It was not until 1949 that the first live birds were examined by Westerners, bought from local people at the village of Utu. Chapin had previously only glimpsed one of the birds in 1937. The forest of Zaïre is so extensive, and the people so few, that the 'paon de Congo' may not be the only animal, scarcely known, or not known at all, to hide in its depths.

We had no realistic hope of seeing any Congo peacocks, but there was always the anticipation. It was thrilling to know that somewhere, perhaps close by, in the greenery which stretched westwards as though to infinity, there were new and strange creatures. The Congo peacocks, like the otter shrew, Bosman's potto and the aquatic civet, live their secret lives untouched by man.

On our way down the mountain we rested beneath an old, gnarled *Hagenia* tree. A touraco called, a harsh grating sound, and we saw the bird, emerald green with glossy maroon wings, as it clambered into a tree. This park, only 600 000 hectares in extent, preserves within it a sample of the complexity of natural life. Looking around me, I realized how small is our understanding of the vast and rapidly disappearing African forest.

The Western myth of the ferocious gorilla was only recently dispelled. The forest people of Africa, with whom this great ape has co-existed for millennia, have always known him to be a gentle vegetarian.

We do not understand how even the large organisms function or how the ecosystem works. We cannot yet fully comprehend the interaction of rain forest, elephant and gorilla, not to mention the mystery of the 'paon de Congo' and who knows how many other unknown forms of life there might be in this still, dark green world.

Our first view of elephants in Virunga was breathtaking. We had left Rwindi camp early in the morning with a guide and, after driving for about an hour on the southern Rwindi-Rutshuru plains, we came to a ridge of high ground. Much of the plains country had been recently burnt and was then green and verdant, but the grassland here was still fairly tall and a rich golden orange colour. Paul happened to glance back and spot four elephant bulls up to their knees in the golden waving grass. Beyond them, towering blue into a bluer sky, was the Massif du Kasali, a peninsula-like mountain range which extended on to the plains.

The elephants continued on their slow line of march, feeding, moving, feeding, flapping an ear, swishing a tail, heedless of our presence. Around us was silence, except for a lark of some kind, flying high and singing. I wondered why the elephants were in the relatively coarse, dry grass, and not on the short green newly flushed grasslands where the topi and kob thronged. We watched the elephants in peace, satisfied that they had chosen this spectacular setting for us, conscious of colour, form, balance and lighting, sufficient to delight the painter's eye.

Fire and ice, from the boiling lava of the Nyamlagira volcano to the Margarethe glacier, cold montane moorlands and baking plains, mist-shrouded forests and sombre savannas . . . Colours and contrasts, opposites and extremes on a grand scale make the Virunga National Park exciting and different. Not only is there a range of dramatically contrasting landscapes and climates, but the animal life is also rich and varied – there are rafts of hippo in Lake Edward, solitary okapi

VIRUNGA NATIONAL PARK

ZAÏRE

(Above) *The gentle okapi of the Ituri forest is related to the giraffe and was one of the last of the larger mammals to become known to science.*
(Right) *The Rwindi-Rutshuru plains are the last of the East African grasslands; from here the dense rain forest stretches westwards. Here, too, the eastern savanna elephant gives way to the forest elephant of the Zaïre basin.*
(Rwindi, Virunga National Park, Zaïre)

The candelabra euphorbia (Euphorbia candelabrum) *is a characteristic tree of the Rwindi-Rutshuru plains and of Queen Elizabeth National Park across the border in Uganda.*

Only rarely do man and elephant coexist in peace. At the fishing village of Vitshumbe, within the Virunga National Park, schoolchildren do their morning exercises oblivious of an elephant bull feeding nearby.

on the edge of the Ituri forest, elephants, mountain gorillas, buffalo and bongo. This is the premier national park of Zaïre and the first national park proclaimed on the continent.

In this park, men died for elephants. A rough stone and concrete memorial stands near the hot springs at May ya Moto which honours the memory of 23 park rangers who died resisting insurgents during the period of strife and civil war which followed upon independence. There are not many areas in Africa today where one would find such dedication to the ideal of maintaining the sanctity of a national park.

The Virunga National Park, proclaimed in 1925 as the Albert National Park in what was then still the Belgian Congo, covers about 8 000 km². The park lies in the western Rift Valley and its western wall, the Kabasha escarpment, is the park boundary, while to the east it stretches along the international boundary with Rwanda and Uganda. This region is the cradle of the Nile. From the Virunga volcanoes on the southern border of the park the rivers flow to the north following the trough of the Rift to Lake Edward. From the Zaïre side of the lake, the main tributary is the Rutshuru River which meanders across the flat, grass-covered Rwindi-Rutshuru plains. The Rwindi River picks up small streams on the west from the Kabasha escarpment, which is the watershed between the Nile drainage to the Mediterranean and the westward drainage of the Congo or Zaire River to the Atlantic.

Lake Edward also receives a major tributary from Lake George in Uganda via the Kazinga Channel, one of the most famous stretches of hippo habitat in Africa. The Semliki River starts from Lake Edward and flows past the Ruwenzori Mountains to Lake Mobutu (formerly Lake Albert). From there the White Nile flows northwards to meander through the sudd, a vast expanse of papyrus (*Cyperus papyrus*) swamp in southern Sudan and, a thousand kilometres on, it joins the Blue Nile at Khartoum.

North of Lake Edward rise the fabled Ruwenzoris, poetically named the 'Mountains of the Moon' by Ptolemy. The altitude at Vitshumbe on the southern shore of Lake Edward is 915 metres, and the highest point in the Ruwenzoris, Mount Stanley, reaches 5 119 metres. The peaks of the Ruwenzoris are usually lost in cloud; a silent, damp, cold world. Alpine plants, including huge cabbage-like groundsels (*Dendrosenecio* spp.,

Senecio spp.), giant lobelias (*Lobelia deckenii*), coarse tussock grasses and other plants adapted to withstand extremes of temperature are dominant. Tall heath and ericas, festooned by lichens and mosses, are the home of dassies and duiker, a few leopards and birds. It is generally an area where wildlife is seldom seen. From the foothills of the Ruwenzoris, the equatorial or lowland forest stretches westwards to the Atlantic.

The character of the plains vegetation has been dramatically changed by elephants and by fire. Photographs taken on the Rwindi-Rutshuru plains in 1934 show a vista of savanna and woodland dominated by flat-topped *Acacia* trees stretching into the distance. By 1959, only 25 years later, photographs taken at the same spot show vast open grasslands with hardly a tree in sight. In the Ugandan parks to the east of the Virunga National Park, the same phenomenon has been recorded. In the Murchison Falls National Park, the roles of elephants and fire were carefully documented in the work done by Dr Richard Laws and his colleagues. The elephant populations of the protected areas were augmented by others pushed in by the inexorable pressure of human population increase and development. These elephants crowded into wooded and even forested areas, destroying the trees. As the elephants opened up the vegetation, more grass could grow. When the annual dry-season fires swept through the area, seedlings and elephant-damaged trees were destroyed. In time the trees were eliminated, leaving only grassland.

To counteract this process, the first large-scale elephant culling operations in Africa were launched in Murchison Falls National

Park in 1965. The project was eventually abandoned but, as is so often the case in Africa, another more drastic form of elephant culling took over. The breakdown of law and order in Uganda during the presidency of Idi Amin resulted in large-scale elephant poaching. Between 1973 and 1976, the elephant population of the park was reduced from 14 300 to only 2 600 animals. Although fire still inhibits a rapid return to woodland, the almost complete cessation of elephant browsing has ensured that the trees stand a better chance. Various reports indicate that woodland regeneration is taking place and the elephant/woodland cycle has almost run its course.

Virunga lost many elephants during the turbulent years after independence and in the more recent plague of poaching. The situation in Uganda also affected the elephants of Virunga, as they could cross the border freely. They seldom returned.

The Rwindi-Rutshuru plains and their extension across the Ugandan border into the Queen Elizabeth National Park lie in a transition zone between the forest and forest woodland mosaic of West Africa and the great plains to the east. Yet they have an essentially East African character. Many West African forms reach as far as this general area, and no further. Most conspicuous of these is the kob, known here as the Uganda kob, which is very similar to the Buffon's or Senegal kob Paul and I first encountered in Comoé. There are conspicuous eastern absentees from Virunga, such as the zebra, impala and greater kudu. These species occur to the east and south. Greater kudu are also found in the north of the Nile basin, ranging as far west as the Cameroons.

White pelicans feed co-operatively, driving schools of fish before them or surrounding them and scooping up the catch in their large beak-pouches.

The silvery-white saddle of the male mountain gorilla appears when he reaches full maturity at about twelve years of age.

Before the recent depletion of wildlife by Amin's troops, the liberating Tanzanian forces and poachers, the Nile basin grasslands supported a higher biomass of large mammals than any other area in Africa. The explanation for this lies in the nutrient status of the rich volcanic soils, the high rainfall and the temperature – all of which make for an impressive rate of primary production. In this case, the growing season is longer. There is, therefore, not only greater potential for producing plant matter, but also more time. A further contributing factor to the high animal biomass was the composition of the fauna, which was dominated by large animals such as elephant, buffalo and hippo. The latter two species are grazers. While the elephant is generally a mixed feeder, it is dependent on grass on these now almost treeless plains. The other large mammals of the area, such as Uganda kob, topi, Defassa waterbuck and Bohor reedbuck, are also all grazers.

The Virunga National Park is representa-

tive of several major biomes – the plains with their complement of savanna animals, the forest, the lake and the montane plant and animal communities. Virunga is unique in that it has both forest elephants and buffalo in the Ituri Forest and Semliki Valley, and savanna elephants and buffalo on the Rwindi-Rutshuru plains. Nowhere else are both forms of elephant and buffalo found in one park. The elephants Paul and I studied and photographed in the Rwindi area were typically savanna animals. They had thick curved tusks and ears with pointed lappets (lobes), stood high at the shoulder, were massive in build, and moved around in large herds. We saw groups of up to eight bulls and breeding herds of 20 to 30 animals along the Rwindi River. The Semliki elephants, traditionally known as 'Congo rats' because of their small size, are similar to the smaller forest elephant, but may also include transitional forms.

Not only are there mountain gorillas in the

69

The marabou stork is largely a scavenger, equally at home in national parks and around villages and towns, where it readily takes to eating refuse.

In the slush and ooze of a crowded wallow a hippo bull – with mouth agape and gnashing of teeth – threatens the mud-encased carcass of another.

Virunga volcanoes in the south of the park, but also giant forest hogs and forest monkeys, such as the golden monkey. The okapi, known to Westerners only since the turn of the century, but hunted for millennia by the Mbuti pygmies, is found only in the Ituri forest of eastern Zaïre. Its range stretches into the upper part of the Virunga Park, where the forest crosses the Semliki valley to lap against the foothills of the Ruwenzoris.

The okapi is a fascinating, even-tempered, gentle creature. It weighs up to 250 kilograms, stands 1,7 metres at the shoulder, and is the closest living relative of the giraffe. It has a glossy coat, with a dark liver-brown, almost chestnut colouring typical of forest animals, and zebra-striped black and white buttocks, each individual having its own distinctive pattern. The first evidence of the okapi's existence examined by a scientist was a piece of buttock skin. As a result, and not surprisingly, the okapi was originally tentatively classified as a zebra of some kind. Only the males have short, skin-covered bony protrusions or 'horns' on the head. Okapi are browsers, have large funnel-shaped ears and, although they do not have the sloping forequarters so common among forest-adapted mammals, possess a short neck, more like an antelope than a giraffe.

The dominant animal in Virunga, in numbers and biomass, is the Nile hippopotamus, of which there are about 36 000. They are to be seen packed together in great herds all along the shores of Lake Edward and up the Rwindi and Rutshuru rivers. Every small pan or mudhole within reach of these areas is also home to as many hippo as can squeeze into them. We saw some muddy pools, so choked with hippos that it would have been easy to walk across on their backs without ever stepping into the water! Indeed, black crake, spurwinged plovers and blackwinged stilts were doing exactly that, chasing insects over the hippo islands. Among these densely packed schools, there were dead animals lying among the living.

One had its ears dried out and turned over – its nostrils were below the surface of the muddy ooze in which dominant male hippos defecated at will on their inferiors, a not very subtle (in human terms) means of showing superiority. Gas, presumably from the putrefying innards of the carcass, bubbled out of the nostrils and popped gently to the surface. A huge bull, demanding right of way, roared at the body, yawning widely to show off his magnificent and lethal canine teeth. There was no response. Even the potent threat of his restless gnashing and champing had no effect. Slightly puzzled, perhaps even intimidated by such a fearless adversary, he approached the carcass slowly, sliding through the ooze as though in slow motion. He sniffed cautiously at it, and then seemed to decide that it posed no threat, because he made himself comfortable, sinking slowly into the slush, at peace with his quiet, unresponsive neighbour.

The hippo have a marked affect on the grasslands, and virtually the whole area within five kilometres of the water had been grazed down to a short lawn by the veritable army of hippo which takes over the plains at night. There were also other signs of the over-abundance of this species. Most of them were in a poor condition and, in a sample of about 1 000 animals, we saw only one youngster, indicating very little reproduction. The hippo over-grazing was probably affecting the Defassa waterbuck, as well as the Bohor reedbuck, of which we saw very few adults and no young. Like the reedbuck, the waterbuck hide their youngsters in long grass during the first few weeks after birth. They return regularly to feed them, but are then free to forage over a wide area. The youngsters do not waste energy following their mothers, nor are they exposed to predators as they would be if they moved around. When they cannot hide anywhere, the calves are probably more vulnerable to predation by lion and spotted hyaena which are abundant on the plains.

The plant matter and nutrients from hippo dung provide food for a rich fish life which in turn attracts birds by the thousands but, surprisingly, no crocodiles. These reptiles were most likely killed off by noxious volcanic ash thousands of years ago, and have been unable to recolonize the area as they cannot move up the rapids in the Semliki River. Huge flocks of great white pelicans, pink-backed pelicans and cormorants hunt fish, squabble and roost around the lake. The white pelicans are particularly elegant as they swim in formation, like squadrons of sailing ships, dipping their yellow beaks under the water and scooping out the fish. Along the Rutshuru River, fish eagles are abundant, launching themselves from the dark green branches of tall *Euphorbia candelabrum* trees, their favourite perches whitened by their droppings. They scream defiance at neighbours and proudly patrol their waters, calling evocatively.

The abundant fish stocks support a thriving community of fishermen at Vitshumbe, inside the park boundaries. The daily catch is sold to buyers from outside the park. The fishermen, middlemen and transporters all pay a fee to the park authorities. There is, in a sense, a contradiction in that the harvesting of fish is accepted, but there is resistance to any suggestion of culling the abundant hippo. Many of the Virunga hippo could quite justifiably be culled to relieve pressure on the habitat.

It is a matter of opinion and philosophical outlook whether one regards the impact of

Spur-winged plovers and other waders pick their way among, around and over the countless hippos packed into wallows along the shores of Lake Edward.

the Virunga hippo population on the park environment as being detrimental or not. It is, however, apparent that by keeping the grass short, the hippo prevent fire from being a major factor in some areas and the woody plants, especially *Capparis tomentosa*, are forming fairly dense thickets close to the rivers. These thickets are fed on by elephants, and this may to some extent com-

pensate them for what they cannot get out of the hippo lawns. However, if taken too far, the over-grazed area could erode badly, as has happened across the border in Uganda. The abundant hippo are already in poor condition and if they are left alone they might literally eat themselves out of a food supply. Like the elephants of Tsavo, their population could then crash.

We saw the Serengeti and Mara plains at the beginning of the long rains in May. The vegetation was lush, with flowering red oat grass, *Themeda triandra*, giving a rich, warm orange tinge to the green landscape. It was the fiery colour of life, not the dull colour of the dry season. Cloud masses moved across the plains as though following appointed paths, and in the distance, across a river, the sky was dark and grey. In the foreground the scene was brightly lit by the slanting light of late afternoon; buffalo stood chewing the cud, with yellow-billed oxpeckers busily searching through their sparse coats, taking ticks, scabs and perhaps also flies. The mustardy colours of the kongoni and eland were bright against the green, heavy-headed grass, and a small heard of elephants trudged past, outlined in darkest black.

The Serengeti is widely regarded as an example of Africa's pristine past and it is not difficult to understand why. From the summit of a rocky kopje, or better still, taking a bateleur's view from a low-flying aircraft, the vastness, the grandeur, the great sweep of the grasslands under the wide blue sky, all impart a sense of timelessness. This feeling is enhanced when one drives through herds of 2 000 buffalo or 10 000 wildebeest, so stretched out that one cannot see one end of the herd from the other, or when one sees these animals from the air, like ants spread out endlessly below. Yet Serengeti is not representative of Africa. Its rich soils, derived from volcanic ash, and favourable climate ensure a level of biological productivity not readily matched elsewhere on the continent. What we see now is also very different from the Serengeti of only thirty-five years ago, when there were some 250 000 wilde-

MAASAI MARA NATIONAL RESERVE

KENYA

SERENGETI NATIONAL PARK

TANZANIA

(Above) *White-bearded wildebeest form the bulk of the animal biomass of the Serengeti-Mara Plains and probably represent the biggest concentration of large wild ungulates on earth.*
(Right) *Elephants pale into insignificance against the vast landscapes of the East African plains.*
(Governors Camp, Maasai Mara National Reserve, Kenya)

The kori bustard, the heaviest flying bird, stalks the grasslands of Africa from the Cape to Ethiopia.

beest, a mere sixth of the number there today.

The Serengeti-Mara ecosystem covers about 40 000 km² of upland country between Lake Victoria and the eastern arm of the Rift Valley. This system contains the largest wild ungulate population on earth. The wildebeest that migrate annually from one end of the system to the other now number well over a million animals. Their movements are a stunning spectacle with herds containing thousands of individuals converging like rivers and flowing across the landscape.

Although the Kenya/Tanzania border bisects Serengeti-Mara unequally from west to east, both countries have taken steps to conserve as much of the ecosystem as possible; on the Kenyan side is the Maasai Mara National Reserve of some 3 780 km², and contiguous to it, stretching away 200 kilometres to the south, is the great 18 400 km² Serengeti National Park and adjoining controlled areas. Over half of the ecosystem is therefore currently under legislation that makes wildlife conservation the primary land use and debars agriculture, pastoralism and human residence. The remaining parts of the ecosystem are, west of the Serengeti, used increasingly by cultivators and, east of the reserve and park, by Maasai pastoralists.

During the middle of the last century, the Maasai and their cattle were widespread in the Serengeti ecosystem and not restricted to only a part of it. Alongside them were numerous game animals. Grazing ungulates such as white-bearded wildebeest, zebra, kongoni, Thomson's gazelle and buffalo were widespread. In addition there were the browsers – eland, Grant's gazelle, impala, giraffe, black rhino and elephants. We will never know quite how many there were of each, although we can assume that the overall weight of wild ungulates was limited to some degree by the numbers of Maasai domestic stock. Conditions are presumed to have favoured grazers rather than browsers because the Maasai and their stock used the whole area and this, in turn, implies that grassland predominated.

In the 1880s a series of catastrophes followed one another to bring about massive changes. Early in that decade an epidemic of bovine pleuropneumonia ravaged the Maasai herds. No sooner had this run its course than the great rinderpest epidemic swept the region. Maasai cattle were reduced by perhaps as much as 95 per cent. The tribesmen themselves were then stricken by a series of smallpox epidemics. Thus, by the mid-1890s, the Maasai people were not only much reduced in number, but had drawn back upon the heartlands in the Kenyan and Tanzanian highlands. Cattle were not the only animals affected by rinderpest; many game species also succumbed, particularly wildebeest and buffalo, and the Serengeti system lost a large proportion of its grazers. The departure of the Maasai probably resulted in a steep decline in seasonal fires, as they had burnt the grassland frequently to remove dry grass and suppress tree and shrub regeneration in order to improve grazing.

The loss of grazers and a decrease in fires led to the rapid development of bush and woodland wherever rainfall and soil conditions allowed. And this is what happened throughout what is now the Mara and the

Migrating wildebeest move across the plains, like endless columns of ants, plodding on steadily to pastures new.

whole of the northern half of the Serengeti. Only the southern Serengeti and its contiguous areas remained open grassland – a condition dictated by low rainfall and particular soil circumstances.

These new developments favoured browsers and, in particular, elephants. However, the expansion of the elephant population is likely to have been delayed by a rise in the demand for ivory. There are records from the area of considerable elephant hunting, much of it inspired by Maasai who were trying to recoup their cattle losses and who sought ivory to exchange for stock. Thus, when the first white men got to know the Serengeti ecosystem they found it moderately to heavily wooded over much of its northern half. Indeed, thicket density had risen to such a degree that tsetse had become established widely and a very large area was now denied to domestic stock.

There was still a seasonal migration of wildebeest, as the dry southern, short-grass plains were an ideal habitat for them while there was water in the seasonal pans and pools. When this dried up, however, they had to move elsewhere, predominantly westwards towards Lake Victoria, where there was higher rainfall and permanent water. As scientists and conservationists got to know the region, it was apparent that rinderpest had become a regular feature of the ecosystem. It appeared in a mild form known as 'yearling disease' and killed off a substantial proportion of every year's wildebeest calf crop. The survivors, however, acquired a lifelong immunity to the sickness.

Rinderpest also occurred with distressing regularity among Maasai cattle all along the eastern Serengeti ecosystem. Naturally, the

wildebeest and other game were blamed as being the source of infection. However, the reverse turned out to be true. When an effective rinderpest vaccine was developed by Dr Walter Plowright some 30 years ago, all the Maasai cattle were rapidly immunized. No sooner had this been done than yearling disease disappeared from the wildebeest. It would therefore seem that the cattle had been the disease reservoir for the game. Quite what the detailed relationship was is now only of historical value. Of great importance to the ecosystem, however, was the removal of a major source of mortality. The population started to increase rapidly.

When the rinderpest disappeared from the Serengeti, several other influences were making themselves apparent. To the west of the national park, human cultivation was encroaching into the wildebeest dry-season areas. This had the effect of both inhibiting egress from the park and somewhat deflecting the seasonal movement northwards. To the east, a growing Maasai population with its stock was competing more for such dry-weather resources as there were and it is highly likely that the incidence of seasonal burning was increasing. It was also first reported during this period that elephants were seriously thinning woodlands in the Mara. In the 1960s this trend continued over the border into the northern Serengeti woodlands.

The thinning of the woodlands produced more food for wildebeest and other grazers, fueling their rates of increase. It also produced more grass for fire, allowing flames deeper into the thickets. Tsetse habitats were thus destroyed, allowing stock to graze these areas and open them up even further

The zebra occurs in large numbers on the Serengeti plains and, like the wildebeest, epitomizes the abundant animal life of an age that has all but passed.

through trampling. A series of influences were thus set in motion that rapidly directed the landscape back towards what it must have been like in the middle of the last century. However, in the park and reserve, where cattle are not allowed today, the wild grazers take advantage of the situation. The million and more wildebeest now add their weight – quite literally – to the process of maintaining grassland, for their hooves trample and cut down a huge proportion of the tree seedlings that show their heads above ground. Those that do break through may not escape fire, and the small proportion that get to this stage increasingly fall prey to elephants before they attain any size. For the moment, openness prevails and once again grazing animals dominate the scene.

The famous black-maned lions of the Mara and the other large predators – leopard, spotted hyaena, wild dog and the sleek,

Wildebeest know that there is safety in numbers and when in flight the herd members keep close together.

The yellow-spotted dassie lives in colonies on outcrops of rock throughout the Serengeti plains. This animal is a distant relative of the elephant, with whom it shares several anatomical features.

Topi bulls are often seen guarding females or standing on termite mounds to advertise themselves more effectively to rivals.

lithe cheetah – as well as a host of smaller animals, scarcely make a dent in the ungulate populations. The Serengeti system, therefore, provides the most convincing evidence of the futility of the once widely held view that African predators in a natural system control their prey populations. Far more wildebeest die of disease than from predation.

The typical animals of the plains, such as the wildebeest that live in large herds in open country, have precocial young – calves that can run and keep up with their mothers within a few minutes of birth. In their preferred open habitat, where predators can watch from afar, this is apparently an essential adaptation. Another survival feature of the wildebeest, also seen in the predominantly grazing species of East Africa and the southern savannas, is the synchronization of breeding activity.

Most wildebeest confine calving to a period of about three to four weeks on calving grounds where they gather from over vast areas. The choreography is so precise that a grassy plain empty of animals one month can be crawling with grunting mothers and bleating, spindly-legged, wide-eyed calves the next. The calves usually arrive when the first flush of green grass has appeared and when water is plentiful. For the nursing mothers these are the best dietary conditions of the year and will ensure a sufficient supply of quality milk to give the calf the best start in life. The flood of young, vulnerable animals creates a temporary overabundance of potential food on which the local carnivores cannot make much impact. The territorial systems of the predators excludes their gathering to make better use of the short-lived glut. The resident lions or hyaenas must ensure that their territories can sustain them through lean as well as good times, and they brook no influx of strangers.

Elephants were absent from the central Serengeti area for most of this century, and they became numerous only in the 1960s. The cause of their move southwards has been much debated. A not unreasonable suggestion links it to the increase in human and cattle populations in areas traditionally occupied by the elephants, such as Loliondo. Increased hunting and disturbance resulted in the beginnings of the compression syndrome seen so often in Africa. The Serengeti, although not ideal for elephant habitat because of its lack of shade and browse, was passable, and disturbance was minimal. The more heavily wooded Mara area, on the other hand, has always had some elephants. That elephants, the most adaptable of all large African mammals with the possible exception of the leopard, have been able to establish themselves in the Serengeti region is shown by their steady increase in numbers. In the northern Serengeti, where poaching is rife, the elephants have tended to form larger herds than would normally be the case, and this presumably aggravates the 'elephant problem'.

There are only about 1 000 elephants on the Mara Plains, and 3 000 on the Serengeti, and their numbers are declining. As these reserves together cover more than 22 000 km², the elephants are at a fairly moderate density compared with that of many savanna regions. However, density, as normally calculated, takes into account only the area and the number of animals. In the case of elephants, it would be more useful to derive an index of elephants to trees. Even though there are so few elephants in the Serengeti, their impact on trees is regarded as a significant problem. It has been argued, for example, that the destruction of fever trees (*Acacia xanthophloea*) in the Seronera area by elephant bulls is undesirable for several reasons: the elephants are competing with giraffe for food; they are destroying cover and resting places for leopards and they are changing the character of the landscape. A perfectly logical management decision to control their numbers was made, and since then elephant bulls have been shot regularly in the area.

The salient lesson from the Serengeti is how change is perhaps the most prominent long-term feature of African ecosystems. Woodlands are replaced by grasslands for a while but eventually regain their position. The continent's ecology is one of tides in a pattern of largely unsynchronized ebb and flow. Many of the causes are far beyond man's understanding, let alone control. Of the complex set of facets that have determined Serengeti's development in recent times, one has been ten years of higher than average rainfall. If this now drops back to normal or to a lower than average sequence, we can expect sudden changes such as those that happened in the last century. The Serengeti/Mara wildebeest today contain few individuals, if any, that have been naturally immunized against rinderpest. The last animal to have survived an infection of yearling disease is gone, and virtually the whole one-and-a-half million population is as vulnerable now as it was a century ago.

Though lions may kill thousands of wildebeest every year on the plains, they make hardly a dent in the population.

Recently, rinderpest reappeared in Tanzania. Even if it does not devastate the wildebeest, the odds are that in due course something will do so and thereby demonstrate yet again the continuous nature of change in African ecosystems.

Tsavo is elephant country. The arid nyika – scrub and *Commiphora* bushland – which covers a huge swathe of eastern Kenya, is inhospitable to cattle and cultivation. And so this wilderness of thorn thicket, rocky inselbergs such as the legendary Dakadima, sand rivers and sparse grazing, was left to the wild animals that could use it most productively, and to the Wata. These people, attuned to their harsh environment, lived off the land, hunted for meat, gathered the fruits of the wilderness and for several thousand years made the elephant and ivory their special quarry. First among the elephant hunting tribes of Africa, the Wata (or Waliangulu) raised the killing of these great beasts to an exact science, and a fine art.

Their weapon was a bow, more powerful than the English longbow of Agincourt and Crecy. With draw weights of 54 to 77 kilograms, these were the most powerful handmade bows ever known. They cast arrows with speed and precision, but the secret of the kill was arrow poison. Like the Bushmen (San) and various other hunting tribes, the Wata had a thorough knowledge of plant poisons. The most common source of the poison was *Acokanthera schimperi,* a common plant containing a cardiac glycoside capable of stopping the most powerful

TSAVO NATIONAL PARK

KENYA

(Above) *Gerenuk can stand up on their hind legs, enabling them to reach the tender leaves at the very tops of the small trees and shrubs on which they feed.*
(Right) *Elephants have brought about profound changes to the vegetation of Tsavo, creating open savanna, which is ideal for grazers such as buffalo.*
(Aruba, Tsavo East National Park, Kenya)

Vultures, congregating in trees or spiralling down to the ground, are the ubiquitous proclaimers of death on the African veld.

The dik-dik's enlarged nose, which assists in cooling the blood, is one of the adaptations that enable it to cope with high temperatures.

heart. The Wata placed their arrows in the most vulnerable part of the elephant, the left lower abdomen, where absorption of the poison was fastest. An elephant hit in the right place by a Wata arrow would be dead within minutes – faster than an elephant culled today using a drug-filled dart fired from a helicopter.

The Wata hunters fitted easily into the natural system. They lived in small clans, were nomadic, and made few demands on the environment. Their hunting traditions, upon which their culture and society depended, were passed on from father to son. Their best hunters, the aces, specialized in elephant and black rhino, while lesser hunters took other game for meat and hides. They used the ivory and rhino horn to barter with neighbouring tribes for sheep, goats, cloth, brass bracelets and iron for arrowheads.

With the wilderness as their classroom, the Wata children were taught the lore of their people. They had to be finely attuned to the signs and sounds of the bush, and because there was always the potential reward of ivory, they would learn how to tell from spoor whether hyaenas were feeding on an elephant carcass, whether vultures were at an elephant, and how to find the carcass. The boys would learn to stalk and hunt, and were taught the traditional names of different classes of elephants. Thus a young bull of about eight years with small tusks was a *dudurucha*, a *boro* was a bull with tusks of about 15 kilograms each, a *tofa* had tusks between 30 and 45 kilograms apiece; a *dadnaba* was a large cow. But the stuff of dreams was an *usho*, a bull elephant with each tusk weighing 45 kilograms or more.

The heartland of the Wata hunting grounds, which became the 20 000 km² Tsavo National Park in 1947, was bisected at the turn of the century by the Mombasa-Nairobi railway. At that time Tsavo first became known to the outside world, not for its elephants or its Wata hunters, but for its man-eating lions, which held up construction of the railway until the famous Colonel Patterson eliminated them. The regions to the east and the west of the railway (later administered as two separate parks, Tsavo East and Tsavo West) are quite different in character, yet with many similarities imposed by the overriding nyika system.

Tsavo East generally has lower rainfall than the western section. It is flat country, its major topographic feature being the long, flat-topped Yatta plateau. Isolated hills break the monotony of the even, dull, green to grey bushveld landscape. In the north, Tsavo East gives way to more arid country in which small *Acacia* predominate.

Tsavo West, with a higher rainfall, generally has larger trees and an appearance of lushness in contrast to the east. The topography is also far more variable, with great ridges of bare granitic rock, such as Kichwa Tembo (meaning 'The Head of the Elephant'), rising high above the plain. New lava flows still lie dark and barren across the green land, and black cinder cones from volcanic eruptions are bare, with only an occasional struggling green plant. The older cones are already green, having been subjected to weathering processes long enough to produce a shallow soil cover in which pioneer vegetation has taken root. To the south-west lies Lake Jipe, a broad stretch of open water fringed with reed beds and a haven for bird life. To the west, dominating every scene in Tsavo West, lies the distant, brooding snow-covered dome of Kibo, the main peak of Kilimanjaro, the highest mountain in Africa.

Only two permanent rivers flow in Tsavo. One is the Athi, which bisects the park from west to east. The other is the Tsavo, which rises in a series of springs just off the north-eastern slopes of Kilimanjaro. However, the Tsavo's main volume of water derives from a set of crystal-clear pools at the mouth of Mzima, a vast subterranean spring fed by the high rainfall of the nearby Chyulu hills. This young volcanic range is composed of so porous a soil that water percolates down into it with virtually no run-off. Reaching impervious rocks deeper down, the water then flows underground until it gains access to the surface at Mzima. The large translucent pools are inhabited by hippo, Nile crocodiles, turtles and fish, all of which can be seen quite clearly from the bank. The Mzima water flows out of the pools and into the Tsavo. Lined with doum palms (*Hyphaene coriacea*), which are as typical of lowland East Africa as ilala palms are of Southern Africa, the river wends its way to join the Athi in the middle of the National Parks. From the Tsavo-Athi confluence to the Indian Ocean, the combined flow is known as either the Sabaki or the Galana. Rain in the nyika thornveld falls in two seasons with dry periods between, the rains beginning soon after the equinox in April and November. But the total rainfall is low, ranging from as little as 250 mm to 500 mm. For annual plants the growing seasons are short and are soon cut off by the dry periods. Succulence, deciduousness and underground storage organs are some of the strategies adopted by plants to survive under these conditions. Because of the nature of the vegetation, the large mammals that occupied the nyika thornveld were predominantly browsers, with the elephant population overwhelming the other species in terms of biomass. The vegetation, a generally dense tangle of dry, thorny scrub and thicket dominated by *Commiphora*, was also an ideal habitat for the black rhino, and there were at least 5 000 or more of them in the Tsavo area. Other browsers were common, such as the lesser kudu – a smaller, more colourful version of the greater kudu of the southern savannas – and the gerenuk, a long-necked gazelle that resorts to

Their ochre-red skins resembling the baked earth of Tsavo, elephants emerge from the thinned woodlands to drink at Voi.

rearing up on its hind legs to reach the tops of the low *Acacia* bushes on which it feeds. Giraffe and Kirk's dik-dik were also found in Tsavo. Grazers such as buffalo and zebra were few, and wildebeest, so abundant on the grassland to the east, were absent except for a few south of the Chyulus in an area known as 'Little Serengeti'.

The Tsavo elephants, with their red and terracotta colours picked up from dusting with or wallowing in the red-tinged soil of the area, played an important role in opening up the thicket and making it more accessible to other species, including man. The

elephant population was large, but because of the dense bush few early observers gained an accurate impression of their numbers. However, Ian Parker estimates the annual Wata offtake of elephants at 600-750 animals. At a likely reproductive rate of about five per cent a year, this harvest alone, without considering deaths during bad droughts, would have kept a population of 12 000 - 15 000 elephants at a stable level.

In the nyika there are a number of species of large mammals that also occur in the arid zone of Southern Africa and which, like many birds, have no representation in the in-

The vulturine guinea fowl – a ground dweller – is confined to the Horn of Africa and the adjoining arid savanna.

tervening areas. The dik-dik, steenbok, aardwolf and fringe-eared oryx are such mammals with discontinuous distribution. There are also many animals that link Tsavo to Arabia and India. The striped hyaena occurs throughout this zone, and in the south-west arid zone is replaced by the congeneric brown hyaena, with the spotted hyaena occurring in both areas and in between. The striped hyaena has many habits in common with the brown, and is almost purely a scavenger – also taking beetles and other insects.

In earlier times fire was not an important factor in the ecology of the nyika thornveld because fire requires grass for fuel. In the nyika system, where all the advantages in utilizing the sparse rainfall lay with the woody plants, there was little grass available. The Tsavo bushlands were characterized by tall, spreading, scraggly baobab (*Adansonia digitata*) trees. These trees, some as much as 1 000 years old, are still found throughout

the drier regions of Africa as far south as the Kruger National Park, and in West Africa they reach down to the Atlantic in Togo – in the arid Dahomey Gap – and across to Senegal. Baobabs are centres of life for many creatures. Being tall, they provide nesting sites for the larger eagles and also accommodate the untidy stick nests of the red-billed buffalo weaver, which is also common in the southern savanna. The similarities of the avifauna of the nyika thornveld and the arid regions of the southern savanna are striking.

Many birds are found in these two areas, yet are absent for long distances in between. One of these is the smallest African bird of prey, the pygmy falcon. This tiny bird, weighing only 60 grams, feeds mainly on insects, but it also kills small birds, lizards and other reptiles. In Southern Africa, the pygmy falcon commonly occupies a nest chamber in the huge, haystack-like structures built by the sociable weaver. In East Africa the pygmy falcon uses the nests of buffalo weavers, but according to Leslie Brown, usually moves in only after the somewhat untidy constructions of the weavers have been modified and re-lined with soft grasses by starlings.

Although most animals are in keen competition for food and other resources, there are some situations in this harsh environment where species cooperate to their mutual benefit. A recently described example concerns the dwarf mongoose, a small sociable predator that lives in colonies of up to 20 animals – usually in termite mounds. These mongooses have a close relationship with yellow-billed hornbills and von der Decken's hornbills. The mongooses and hornbills forage together during the day, the mongooses flushing out insects for the hornbills

to catch, and in return the hornbills warn the mongooses of the approach of predators.

When the Tsavo National Park was proclaimed in 1947 the Wata were not taken into consideration, and their hunters became, by this short-sighted decree, poachers and criminals on their ancestral hunting grounds. This exclusion without compensation or consideration for people who had lived for generations in an area taken over for conservation was an example of the kind of blunder perpetrated by many colonial governments. The newly-appointed wardens of Tsavo set about stamping out the 'menace' of the Wata. In this they were supported by Western morality and the greatest of the Wata hunters of modern times (men such as Galogalo Kafonde, Boru Debassa and Abakuna Gumundi) were portrayed in the media as criminals. That they were superb hunters and fine men was ignored. Eventually even the white wardens who imprisoned them admired the Wata for their skill, courage, honesty and decency. The wardens were caught in a clash of different cultures and were equally honest, doing their duty as they saw it. The social consequences for the Wata were calamitous, and even though an attempt was later made to right some of the wrongs, it merely compounded the tragedy.

A major check on the growth of the elephants was removed, and numbers increased rapidly. In addition, other elephants, displaced by settlement, also crowded into Tsavo. The elephants devastated the bush, breaking down, tearing apart and uprooting trees; even mighty baobabs were demolished, creating ideal conditions for grass. With the grass and the more open environment came fires, which were particularly fierce after years of good rainfall and damaged the remaining woody plants and seedlings. The vegetation changed, was opened up, conditions for other animals and birds were altered, and new opportunities were presented for grazers. A growing 'elephant problem' was diagnosed. Culling was recommended by some and vigorously opposed by others. While the arguments raged, the rains failed. During the drought of 1970-72, at least 6 000 elephants and many black rhino starved to death. With well over 10 000 tusks lying around, there was an unprecedented influx of 'poachers' to harvest the ivory. At about the same time, the demand for ivory and rhino horn soared, as did the prices. Hunting the remaining elephants, thought to number at least 36 000 after the die-off, was a much easier proposition in the relatively open country of the new Tsavo. The hunters too were new, mostly Somalis driven south by drought and armed with AK47 automatic rifles. In the space of a decade about 6 000 elephants had starved; an estimated further 20 000 had been killed by poachers. About 5 000 black rhino had died, so wiping out the largest population of modern times.

Tsavo is now recovering and the woodlands will eventually return if they can escape the fires. Indeed, there is even some evidence to show that what happened was simply part of a long-term cycle. The elephants, their population structure sadly ravaged by the deaths, will probably decline further because the prime breeding cows were hardest hit by the drought. The black rhino now number less than 100. Plains game has increased, as could be expected, and the life of the park goes on. The Wata, a people with a sentience for their environment which modern man can never hope to equal, have virtually disappeared.

The Tsavo story might have taken another course. Had the elephants been culled, as is done in some other parks, the vegetation changes that resulted from the impact of elephants could have been avoided. Nevertheless, Tsavo demonstrates the alternative to culling in a large African park. The system recovers, albeit with a different balance between plant and animal communities.

Where elephants are culled, the diversity of the vegetation and animal systems are largely maintained in a fairly stable state, as in Kruger. This is regarded as a desirable management objective. The larger the system, the more resilient and the better able it is to absorb fluctuations in animal or plant communities with little if any loss of diversity. But in parks smaller than about 10 000 km², like the majority in Africa, there is little room for manoeuvre. If diversity is to be maintained in these small units there is no alternative to controlling elephant numbers.

There can be no quarrel with non-interference in a national park if it is large enough for natural processes to operate unimpeded by man. But in small parks, control and utilization are inevitable. The consequences of a

Found north of Tsavo, the reticulated giraffe has striking colouration. Sharp eyes and acute hearing make it one of the most difficult animals to stalk.

particular course of action must, however, be weighed against the alternatives. In Africa there will ultimately be only one. The elephant problem will have only a marginal influence on the future of national parks. What will carry far more weight is the problem of providing food and living space for people.

AMBOSELI NATIONAL PARK

KENYA

(Above) *Amboseli elephants have the typically soft, white East African ivory that commands higher prices in the trade than the harder ivory from West Africa.*
(Left) *The eternal image of Africa – a herd of elephants pacing across the bleached bed of Amboseli's dead lake, while the snow-covered peak of Kilimanjaro rides above the clouds.*
(Loginye, Amboseli National Park, Kenya)

Kilimanjaro is Africa's highest mountain, its domed, icy peak, Kibo, reaching 5 894 metres. It soars out of the vast East African plain into the path of the rain-bearing winds that blow from the Indian Ocean, far to the east. Milking the air of its moisture, the windward eastern and southern slopes have a high rainfall, producing luxuriant vegetation. Above 3 000 metres, the flora is uniquely alpine, consisting mainly of open tussocky grasslands and bogs, scattered with giant groundsels (*Senecio* spp.) and lobelias (*Lobelia* spp.). Below the alpine zone are bands of forest, each typical of the altitude in which it occurs, ranging from *Podocarpus* in the higher zones, to mahoganies (*Entandrophragma* sp. and *Khaya* sp.) on the lowest slopes.

In keeping with its massive size, Kilimanjaro produces a large rain-shadow that lies across its north-western slopes and extends far out into the lands beyond. In the centre of the rain-shadow at the north-western foot of the mountain is the bed of an extinct alkaline lake, Amboseli. In wetter times it once held water all the year round, as did Etosha Pan, more than 3 000 kilometres to the south-west, but both now hold water only after exceptional rains. Today, like Etosha, it has a dusty white surface alive with whirling dust devils in the heat of the day, where saline-adapted plants (such as *Sporobolus spicatus* and *Sueda* sp.) grow sparsely, and where the elephants are grey from the fine, powdery dust. So dry are the north-western slopes of Kilimanjaro that no streams flow off them to support life below. However, there are a number of springs that give rise to short watercourses that end in a series of swamps named Ol Tukai, Enkongo Narok

The waterbuck bull, an impressively large animal, has a quiet and placid disposition.

Impala are hardy antelopes and are still common in national parks, wilderness areas and on cattle ranches.

and Loginye by the Maasai. They form oases of lush greenery in an otherwise arid landscape, a little to the east of the former lake bed.

Zoologically, Amboseli lies at something of a crossroad. It is near enough to the Somali region to exhibit mammals particularly associated with that area and with the arid nyika of eastern, hinterland Kenya, such as Kirk's dik-dik, fringe-eared oryx, gerenuk and lesser kudu. At the same time it has numerous representatives of the ecosystems of the East African highland plains, for example wildebeest, zebra, and Thomson's and Grant's gazelles. High above on the slopes of Kilimanjaro, the fauna and flora indicate distant connections with the West African forests. The most striking of these are Abbot's duiker and the spectacularly attired Kilimanjaro colobus monkey. Abbot's duiker is a large, dark, forest antelope closely related to the yellow-backed duiker of the western forests. It is an animal that few white men have ever seen in the wild and the species is virtually unknown to science.

Kilimanjaro is one of the most spectacular backdrops for photography in all Africa. It is so vast and majestic that it is difficult to conceive that it was once nearly twice its present height. At some stage several million years ago the mountain erupted in an enormous explosion, showering the surrounding area with volcanic ash that is now seen as the powdery soil of the Amboseli area. Kibo is not the original peak of the volcano, but a parasitic cone that was formed when a new vent opened in the side of the original volcano. To the east of Kibo lies Kilimanjaro's second peak, Mawenzi. One is the antithesis of the other. Where Kibo is rounded and se-

rene, Mawenzi is saw-toothed and jagged; where Kibo is white and glistening, Mawenzi is dark and forbidding. Mawenzi is a relict plug of solidified magma, which cooled and hardened in the throat of the volcano that preceded Kibo, and from which the soft mantle of volcanic ash has long ago eroded. It is inconceivable that a feature so majestic as the Kilimanjaro massif should be without elephants. And, of course, it has them.

It is somehow fitting that the largest tusks on record from an African elephant are said to come from Kilimanjaro. They were reputedly obtained from an elephant shot by an Arab hunter employed by Hamed bin Muhammed, a Zanzibari potentate otherwise known as Tippu Tib – a nickname that may have been an onomatopoeic rendering of the sound of the musketry with which his slaving ventures were widely associated. These enormous tusks weighed 103 and 97 kilograms respectively, and were 311 and 317 centimetres long. At the lip line they were 62 and 60 centimetres in circumference. They are so large that it is difficult to envisage them as part of a living animal. Today they lie in one of the British Museum's dusty storerooms, somewhat yellowed, but unsurpassed in magnificence.

On the mountain, elephants are ever more restricted by human increase, which results in the removal of their habitat and its replacement by crops. The southern and eastern slopes are among the most densely populated areas of Tanzania. They are the tribal lands of the Chagga, who are renowned for their industry and success as coffee producers. The clash between them and elephants is, of course, nothing new. It is widely thought that elephant ditches placed between cultivators and wildlife areas are products of modern conservation. However, the Chagga were digging them far back in the last century and have always regarded them as an obvious and sensible barrier to keep elephants out of cultivated areas. Elephants also frequent the Amboseli swamps, far below the mountain slopes. Their range is small for they concentrate on the three swamps and can almost always be found at one or the other. Their accessibility, small range and exposure to a large number of tourists have made them tame. Of all the elephants that I have come across, those of Amboseli are the easiest to observe and are ideal subjects for behavioural studies.

Cynthia Moss has been watching them for more than a decade and knows almost every individual in the 500-strong population. She and the students working with her have compiled careful records of births, deaths, rates of growth, social events and general behaviour, making this population the best documented in Africa. The only comparable records are from Addo Elephant National Park in South Africa where I worked for eight years, and Manyara, Tanzania where Iain and Oria Douglas-Hamilton worked in the 1960s.

The only alternative to long-term studies such as these is the infinitely less attractive option of shooting large samples. Important details such as calving intervals, age, growth, and onset of sexual maturity can be derived in this way and can be used, with discretion, to help us to understand elephant problems and populations elsewhere.

One particularly worthwhile finding from Amboseli concerned the response of a population's reproduction to drought. A long dry

A leopard at ease is beguiling; but the casually draped and relaxed paws can instantly be transformed into murderous hooks to catch unwary prey.

spell of several years led to very low survival among the young. This was followed by a bad drought and for two years no calves were born. When the rains came most cows conceived and produced a bumper crop of calves 22 months later. Such a cohort of animals, all much the same age, moving through a population easily explains the cycles in recruitment that were first described by Dr Richard Laws. If the cows that produced the large calf crop stayed in rough synchrony with one another, and it would be odd if they did not, they would all have conceived again at approximately the same

time about one year after the post-drought 'baby boom', to give rise to another batch of calves about five years after the drought.

Yet another important finding comes from Amboseli. In many African national parks elephants have destroyed woodland and much of the associated life. In Amboseli it was noted that many of the fever trees (*Acacia xanthophloea*) in the swamps were dying and, superficially, it seemed that elephants were once again responsible. It would have been all too easy to have been guided by the results from elsewhere when searching for a solution to the problem, and to have culled the elephants. However, culling would have been wrong, for the death of the Amboseli trees was caused by the rising level of salinity in the soil in which they stood. Nothing could have made the case more strongly for examining each situation on its own merits.

The yellow baboon, which occurs in Amboseli, has been even more intensively studied than the Amboseli elephants. Teams of scientists have been recording every detail of the lives of two troops for more than a decade. The value of these studies lies in their contribution to ecological and behavioural theory. These ideas help to explain many basic responses and processes, which might also be at work in man, a distant relative of the baboon.

The Amboseli swamps lie in the traditional lands of the Maasai, a nomadic, cattle-keeping people. For at least several centuries, the Maasai have used these oases as dry-season refuges for their stock. Much wildlife has followed similar routines. Annually, a population of wildebeest, zebra, gazelle and other grazers, as well as elephants, have ranged away from the swamps in the wet seasons when everything is green and the pools are temporarily full, and drifted back to the swamps with the return of the dry weather. The ecosystem covered by these seasonal movements is some 3 000 km², of

Wildebeest are only rarely found in areas where water is not readily available.

88

which the national park comprises less than ten per cent. The Maasai have always been generally tolerant of wildlife, and when white men first arrived in East Africa they were impressed by the co-existence that prevailed.

This earlier apparent stability is changing. Throughout this century the Maasai and their stock have been increasing, and with this rise in numbers and densities their earlier tolerance has worn ever thinner. Many now see wild animals as competitors for grazing and, to a substantial degree, this is true. The conservation systems of the white man in Africa, particularly national parks, demanded the absence of humans. In view of the spectacular concentrations of wild animals in Maasailand, it was inevitable that there would be moves to set aside some of the land for wildlife. Such moves exacerbated the existing ill will among the Maasai over land loss, for in Kenya they had surrendered a large proportion of their territory for occupation by British settler farmers.

This initial conflict had several negative consequences for the wildlife of Amboseli. No species suffered more than the rhino. The Amboseli black rhinos gained pictorial distinction, not only from the superb backdrop against which they were usually photographed, but because one family had very unusual horns. Instead of growing upwards off the snout in the conventional fashion, Gertie and her daughter Gladys had horns that were not only very long but also thin, slightly undulating and pointed forwards.

Another striking feature of the Amboseli rhinos was the frequency of specimens that were born without ears. This odd congenital defect is known in seven other black rhino

populations, ranging from Hluhluwe in the south to Kenya's Samburu in the north. The affected animals have only one external ear or sometimes none at all. The animals seem to suffer no particular disadvantage under natural conditions, though I found that a one-eared rhino introduced into Addo from Hluhluwe was always easier to approach than animals with normal hearing. Black rhino hearing is usually acute and this, combined with a fine sense of smell, compensates for its poor eyesight. Perhaps the earless Amboseli rhino were easier to approach than others. Whether this was true or not is debatable, but Maasai spearmen reduced Amboseli's rhino from around 150 in 1950 to about 30 in 1973 and only 8 in 1977.

Why did the Maasai selectively spear Amboseli's rhino? Traditionally, rhino are animals of bad omen to the Maasai, and should one cross ahead of a herd of cattle, special cleansing rituals have to be performed to avert catastrophe. There was thus a cultural base for perceiving rhino as unwanted elements. While this may not have been an incentive to go out and kill them, it would have created a general attitude in which this action would not be condemned. This mildly hostile outlook was greatly exacerbated by endeavours to dispossess the Maasai of the Amboseli swamps, particularly when the tribesmen could see that white men were enthusiastic about preserving rhino. Spearing these objects of particular conservation concern was an effective way of cocking a snook at authority. It was also in keeping with the Maasai belief that spearing a large, dangerous animal demonstrated bravery. An ultimate exhibition of manhood was for a 'moran' (warrior) to spear a lion. Only one act could improve upon this: it was for a man to dart forward, when the lion was at bay surrounded by spear-wielding moran, and grab the great cat by its tail. While lion killers were placed at the top of the tribe's hierarchy of valour, rhino spearers were not far behind.

To these factors – tribal superstition, political antagonism towards alienation of land for wild animals, and a society that approved of any young man who could spear a large dangerous animal – was added the soaring price of rhino horn during the 1970s. This virtually guaranteed the demise of the Amboseli rhino. Since then the situation has improved; a high birth rate and the reintroduction of two rhino from elsewhere in Kenya increased the population to 17 in 1984, but only time will tell whether the species will survive in Amboseli. This story clearly demonstrates that tribal lore, political feelings and the need to show bravery may be important factors to take into account in many other conflict situations involving 'poaching'.

The key to Amboseli continuing as a sanctuary lies in winning Maasai approval of this goal. No one has been more aware of this, or done more to work for it, than Dr David Western. Now well into his second decade studying the Amboseli ecosystem, he believes that, through careful research and planning, it may be possible to meet the conflicting demands of both the Maasai and the area's fauna. In part his argument stresses the

The repetitive call of the yellow-billed hornbill is characteristic of the drier savanna regions of eastern and southern Africa.

revenues that the Maasai can derive from Amboseli's wildlife through tourism. The local district council and landowners, who obtain substantial sums annually from this, now constitute a strong lobby of Maasai who are no longer eager to do away with the park. The developments in Amboseli, largely stimulated by David Western are, like Operation Windfall (Wildlife Industry for All) in the Sebungwe region of Zimbabwe, landmarks in the evolution of Africa's conservation policies.

If African parks are to survive they will have to be accepted by the people most directly affected by them. At Amboseli great steps have been taken towards ensuring that the park is acceptable to the Maasai as well as to the Kenyan government. Only when such a state exists can the Amboseli elephant be considered safe. There will then be some hope that the calves that wade through the Longinye swamp today will one day lead their own young through its lush greenery.

In the miombo woodlands of Malaŵi I had my first encounters with the African elephant. While living in the Kasungu National Park I studied these grey giants and gained a smattering of an understanding of their ways. It was also in Kasungu that I first faced the charge of an angry elephant, and there I first killed an elephant. Nurtured on Hemingway and Ruark, my first elephant kill was a holy grail, as no doubt it would be to many young men born and bred in Africa. The aftermath of the kill was, however, somewhat different. Adrenalin makes it quick and unreal. Then the dark blood oozing out of an elephant's head, the last pathetic scuffle of a wrinkled foot in the dirt, the last involuntary passing of faeces, the later stink of death, the buzz of flies, the seeming obscenity of vultures squabbling to tear out its eyes, bring one to face reality. For me there was no glory in this game. I have shot other elephants since, in other parts of Africa, but never again with anything other than cold detachment, only as a necessary task of management, or to perform the merciful act of killing a desperately crippled or injured animal.

Kasungu is one of the two largest of Malaŵi's national parks and covers 2 316 km², hugging the border with Zambia. It is a fine example of a miombo woodland landscape incorporating most of the major habitats typical of the miombo system throughout its extensive range.

The miombo woodlands cover the heartland of Africa – a vast plateau formed from the weathering of the most ancient rocks on earth, the basement complex rocks of the Central African Plateau. It is a seemingly endless expanse of trees, canopy touching cano-

KASUNGU NATIONAL PARK

MALAŴI

(Above) *The bateleur eagle appears short and squat when perched, but unfolds to become a graceful aerial acrobat.*
(Right) *Isolated granite inselbergs – the oldest rocks on earth – tower above the miombo woodlands, which shelter the largest elephant population in Malaŵi.*
(Wangombe Rume, Kasungu National Park, Malaŵi)

Paul Bosman ©

The inselbergs, or island mountains, of Central Africa provide relief in an otherwise featureless landscape.

To get to the shortest grasses and to dig out rhizomes, the warthog spends much of his feeding time on his 'knees'.

Malaŵian hunters relied on home-made guns (upper) or antique trade muskets (lower) to sow devastation among the Kasungu elephants.

With head raised and ears spread wide, an elephant is at its most impressive when it faces and intimidates a more humble foe.

py, dissected by grassy drainage lines known as dambos. The miombo is one of the largest vegetation zones on earth, extending about 1 500 kilometres from Zaïre and central Tanzania to the Limpopo and about 2 500 kilometres from east to west, from the Atlantic to the Indian oceans. It is a woodland or tree savanna in which several species of *Brachystegia, Julbernardia* and *Isoberlinia* reign supreme. This woodland covers most of Angola, Zambia, southern Zaïre and Tanzania, Malaŵi, Moçambique and Zimbabwe, and some of its elements cross into Kenya and Botswana. To the north it is bounded by the rain forest and the East African savanna. The miombo effectively forms a barrier between the East African savanna and the great southern savanna. This habitat barrier divides many savanna species into two distinct populations, e.g. black-backed jackal, giraffe and steenbok.

The elephant is the most important wildlife species, in terms of biomass and impact on the vegetation, in this system which is characterized by low density wildlife populations. This is because of the inherently low nutrient status of the sandy soils derived from the weathering of rocks of the acid basement complex, or original rock surface of the African continent. Over vast spans of time this soil has been leached of most of its nutrients by the action of water, which easily penetrates the sand, and then seeps into the dambos taking the nutrients away. These sandy soils are covered by a typically closed canopy miombo woodland, which forms the characteristic landscape of the Central African Plateau. In places the plateau surface is penetrated by different rock types, richer in minerals, which produce pockets of more

The wattled crane is one of Africa's endangered wetland birds and is distinguished by the conspicuous wattles at the base of the bill.

fertile soils and a somewhat different vegetation, generally savanna with taller grassland dominated by *Hyparrhenia*. The trees are spaced further apart, and savanna species like *Albizzia versicolor, Pericopsis angolensis, Combretum* spp. and *Terminalia sericea* are common. Such more fertile soils are also found in Kasungu along the lower margins of the major dambos where the process of soil formation from the underlying rock is still actively taking place. As leaching has not yet occurred to the same extent as elsewhere in the park, the soils are richer in minerals and nutrients; these are known as 'sweet' dambos.

The Kasungu elephants appreciate these differences of soil type, which are reflected not only in the vegetation but also in the quality of water yielded. The research of Dr Richard Bell in Kasungu, has gone a long way towards unravelling the intricate relationships between soils, vegetation, animal distribution and utilization of the Kasungu miombo. The highest densities of elephants have always been found on the better soil types. The elephants' preference for certain sources of water is, not surprisingly, also influenced by taste. So, in the dry season, the elephants prefer to drink in the dambos on leached soils, where the water contains more minerals. As these sandy soils have a higher infiltration rate, the rainwater passes into the soil to seep out slowly on the dambo margins, forming pools of cloudy, grey water. These waterholes have been enlarged, over time, by the action of the elephants. Every time they come to drink, shower or wallow, they remove mud on their feet and bodies and so, over many years, the waterholes have become deeper and wider. In the sweet dambos, however, the soils are less permeable. The slower infiltration rate results in more run-off rainwater which is almost pure, containing few minerals. This water is clearer and cleaner looking but is not favoured by the fastidious elephants.

The feeding habits of the Kasungu elephants are equally attuned to the quality of the environment. Therefore, they concentrate for feeding in the woodlands on more fertile soils. Through this selection they have converted the woodland over large parts of the park into a dense, shrubby, coppice growth. This structure is maintained by heavy browsing pressure.

Many of the plants growing on the infertile sandy soils have, over time, developed what is thought to be a mechanism to prevent their being browsed excessively. Thus they contain indigestible chemical compounds which render the plant unpalatable to herbivores like elephants. Presumably this mechanism has evolved because of the inability of these plants to replace leaves quickly due to the poor soil fertility.

The effect of these unpalatable plants, which appear so lush, green and rich to the human eye, but which are anything but attractive to animals, can be seen in the composition of the large mammal fauna of Kasungu and the other miombo areas. There are thus few browsers such as kudu, black rhino and impala, and giraffe are absent entirely from this zone. On the other hand sable antelope are largely confined to the miombo and occur only marginally in other habitat types to the north, east and south of the miombo. Lichtenstein's hartebeest is the only exclusively miombo antelope, and is rarely found elsewhere. Others such as the roan, reedbuck and oribi are common in the miombo and other similar habitats. These antelopes are all highly specialized grazers, particularly dependent on the dambo grasslands.

In Kasungu, bornhardt inselbergs – grey, streaked and speckled – loom up out of the otherwise featureless mosaic of woodland and dambos. The highest in the park reaches 230 metres above the surrounding woodlands. It is a long, narrow, hump-backed mass of rock which towers above several smaller inselbergs and carries the lyrical name of 'Wangombe Rume', which means 'The Big Bull' in Tumbuka. The name is apt as it refers to the hump of a bull, so typical of the Zebu-type cattle of Africa, rising above the backs of the lesser cattle in the forms of the other rocks round about. These island mountains are usually surrounded by an apron of denser woodland on the slightly deeper soil around their base. The rock face, crevices, gulleys, cracks and flat weathering surfaces also support a flora highly adapted to such specialized habitats, and include lichens, mosses, aloes, tussock grasses and

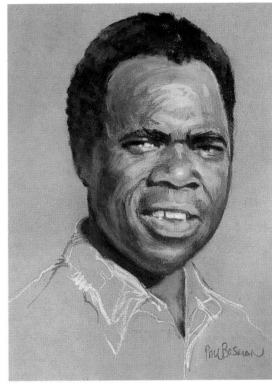

Matthew Matemba, the dedicated warden who led the skilful law-enforcement campaign that stopped elephant poaching in the Kasungu National Park.

the aptly named resurrection plant (*Myrothamnus flabellifolius*). This plant shrivels up and dries, and appears dead, but within 24 hours of rain falling, it comes alive and is green and verdant. The rock masses are also home to many specialized birds such as the freckled nightjar, reptiles such as the dragon-like rock leguaan which can be up to 1,5 metres long, and mammals such as the klipspringer which seldom venture far from their rocky sanctuaries. Klipspringers are superbly adapted for their life on the rocks. Their blunt, yet pliable hooves enable them to get a firm foothold on bare rock and bound up a rock face with ease. Their col-

Greater kudu bulls live in bachelor groups and only consort with cows during the rut.

ouring is a grizzled mustardy brown which blends in superbly with the background colour of the rocks and lichen.

The freckled nightjar is perfectly adapted to nest on even the slightest nook or cranny on the face of the rock domes. Using nothing more than gravel and lichen, it builds an inconspicuous nest on which it sits out in the open, blending almost invisibly into the background of lichen-covered rock. This bird knows that its giveaway is the bright jewel of its eye and so when an intruder approaches it on the nest, it closes the eye nearest to him. If one walks around the bird, it slowly closes the other eye and opens the one of the safe side. The trust these birds have in the security of their camouflage is further demonstrated by their tenaciousness at the nest – they do not fly away unless one gets closer than about two metres.

As a biologist working in Kasungu at the end of the 1960s I set out to count the park's elephants and to map their distribution. Years later Richard Bell repeated the surveys and found marked changes in distribution of elephants, but no distinct changes in the distribution of other large mammals. This is almost entirely due to the effects of an epidemic of elephant poaching which hit

Kasungu from 1975. By 1981 the elephant population had been severely reduced and was concentrated in a relatively protected triangle of tourist roads close to the game lodge and administrative headquarters. On a return visit in 1981, I was amazed to find that almost 80 per cent of the park had been completely depopulated of elephants. With poaching beginning in the 'Lifupa Triangle', it seemed as if the disastrous elimination of elephants from the war-ravaged parks of Uganda was about to be repeated in peaceful Malaŵi.

Fortunately the crisis brought out the best in Matthew Matemba, the first Malaŵian warden of Kasungu, who was appointed at the beginning of 1982. Matemba had been trained in wildlife management in the United States, and he brought to his new post an enthusiasm and dedication which was vital if poaching was to be controlled. He planned what must rate as the most successful, short-term anti-poaching operation that I know of in Africa. Matemba's rangers, assisted by Richard Bell and his research staff, set about gathering information on the poachers, the middlemen, the traders and possible informants in a methodical and strategic manner, with no fanfare and fuss, just guts and brains. They were fortunate to get the full backing of the government and the Party – this is essential in any sphere of activity in Africa, especially one where alien norms are being propagated. Informants were richly rewarded for their information, clandestine deals with traders were set up and several 'Mr Big' operators were netted. Virtually all the Malaŵian poachers involved were caught and jailed. Significantly, very few arrests of ivory poachers were made in the park – most of

them were arrested at home. Informants had been used to devastating effect. Within a few months the problem was solved. Significantly no handouts had been solicited or received from the international conservation money generally thrown at such problems to no avail. The Malaŵians did not depend on radios, aircraft, new boots and expensive vehicles to get their men; they simply relied on their own ingenuity and hard work. What a lesson it could be for the rest of Africa, and how sad that the Malaŵian example has not yet been emulated elsewhere.

The Kasungu elephant poachers took meat as well as ivory and that placed them somewhat above poachers who take only ivory. It was not easy to overlook the many parallels between them and the Wata hunters of Tsavo. Most of their families had lived in the Kasungu National Park area before it was cleared of people to combat sleeping sickness outbreaks in 1920. They were professionals. Some of them, such as Langton Chinseu, had a lifetime of hunting to their credit, or discredit. Chinseu was a well-known rhino hunter when I first moved to Kasungu in 1969 and had many brushes with ranger patrols in those days. He was a man of the bush and knew his environment and quarry. His technique was to stalk close to a black rhino, climb a tree and then call the animal to him by imitating another rhino. When the curious, or offended, animal had approached close enough, he would shoot it in the heart or lungs with a muzzle loader, firing ball bearings or pieces of reinforcing steel rod. Sometimes he would fire a lead slug from a borrowed 12-bore shotgun. The wounded rhino would dash away, only to be tracked down by Chinseu later on. In about

1975 his trusted Tower muzzle loader of nineteenth century vintage burst and blew off the thumb of his left hand. As a result of this accident, he became known far and wide as Nineteen (for his 19 fingers and toes). Another gun burst some time later, severely injuring his hand. The wound became gangrenous and eventually the proud hunter ended up in a government hospital where his left hand was amputated. He nevertheless pursued his career, one-handed, but as deadly as ever. His status was enhanced by a bracelet of woven elephant tail hairs worn on his right wrist. Attached to the bracelet were several small sticks taken from the temporal glands of bull elephants he had shot. These sticks, which are probably pushed into the opening of the gland by the elephant, perhaps to ease an irritation, are worn as a powerful talisman. Chinseu was eventually caught making a delivery of poached ivory and sent off to prison.

Elephant poaching, which is rampant in other African parks, is now virtually limited in Kasungu to the activities of Zambians crossing the international border into the park. Because follow-up operations by Malaŵian game rangers into Zambia are not possible this poaching will be much harder to crack.

The elephants of Malaŵi have had to give way to agricultural development and a thriving human population of more than six million people at a density of more than 100 per square kilometre – for the vast spaces of Africa, a very dense human population indeed. Malaŵi, unlike many other African nations, can however produce sufficient food for its needs and even exports agricultural produce. Because Malaŵi has no mineral resources, its development and progress has been closely tied to the extent to which it has been able to develop an agricultural base for the nation. Malaŵian agriculture is, therefore, efficient and intensive – there is no room for elephants outside the national parks, game reserves or forest reserves. There are few unsettled buffer zones surrounding conserved areas, and in many places cultivation continues right up to the park or reserve boundary.

Despite these constraints, the Malaŵian government has managed to set aside a representative range of national parks and has maintained them in the face of various political and population pressures. Malaŵi is an example for Africa. If this nation can keep its elephants then there are grounds for optimism, but if Malaŵi should fail, if the park boundaries should be pushed back by the tide of people, then the writing will be on the wall, not only for the elephants in Malaŵi, but ultimately also for all the elephants of Africa.

The agile klipspringer, sure-footed on its rubbery hooves, bounds with spectacular speed and ease up steep rock faces and curving granite domes.

In the Luangwa Valley one is seldom far from elephants or signs of them: a shattered tree; a broken branch; some leaves dropped to the ground by a feeding cow; an idle, twisting scribble in the dust of a dirt road, marking the course where a bull trailed the relaxed tip of his trunk on the sand, the great platters of their footprints, a heap of fresh yellowish-green dung, its smell reminiscent of a stable, steaming in the chilly dawn; the pungent earth where an elephant has urinated; Luangwa is a place for elephants.

The Luangwa trough, a branch of the Rift Valley system, intersects the main eastern and western branches just north of Lake Malaŵi. From there it slices through the Central African Plateau to connect with the Zambezi. The Luangwa Valley is about 700 kilometres long and on its floor lies a river, the course of which is erratic. It changes with the floods, cutting off loops which may remain isolated from the main course of the river for centuries, forming quiet lagoons fringed by ebony *Diospyros mespiliformis* and sausage trees *Kigelia africana*. When the river bursts its banks in a new flood, the lagoon joins the main course once again, and new oxbows are cut off elsewhere. The Luangwa River has high banks and a wide flood plain of rich alluvial soil, which is highly productive and supports enormous concentrations of animals dominated by elephant, hippo and buffalo. The flood plains are also the home of specialist grazers, such as waterbuck and puku, the Central African equivalent of the kob found in the Nile basin and in West Africa. The clay soils support *Colophospermum mopane* woodlands which line the valley and then give way to *Brachystegia* woodland on the escarpments on either side.

SOUTH LUANGWA NATIONAL PARK

ZAMBIA

(Above) *A bird of regal bearing, the crowned crane is esteemed in some parts of Africa as the bird that brings rain.*
(Right) *Through the drowsy heat of the midday hours elephants stand quietly in the shade, conserving energy, keeping cool and giving the small calves time to rest.*
(Nsefu, South Luangwa National Park, Zambia)

The yellow-billed stork or wood ibis migrates with the seasons in southern Africa, but is permanently resident in Zambia, where it breeds in large communal nesting sites.

The southern savanna with all its characteristic components of plants, birds and game animals is separated from the East African savanna, with which it shares so many features, by the huge block of the miombo or *Brachystegia* woodlands. The savanna does, however, intrude into the miombo in the generally low-lying river valleys of the Central African region. Thus the Zambezi and the Shire Valley, which runs up to Lake Malaŵi, penetrate deep into the miombo. The Luang-

The puku of Central Africa is the ecological equivalent of the West African kob, being a grazer on flood plains and along drainage lines.

wa Valley penetrates further, carrying its characteristic life forms far north of the Zambezi to within 200 kilometres of the Ruaha trough in Tanzania. This is the most likely connection, during previous dry periods, between the arid zones in the south-west and north-east, whereby the oryx, dik-dik, aardwolf and other animals now isolated in these zones might have had a continuous distribution. Even today, giraffe and impala are found in the Luangwa and Ruaha, but not in the miombo on either side or between them.

At Mfuwe, in South Luangwa, one of four national parks in the valley, we watched an elephant bull feeding in a lagoon. These oxbows are known as *Luangwa wafwa* or 'dead Luangwa' in the Chewa tongue. The lagoon was covered by a bright green layer of Nile cabbage, a floating lettuce-like plant, *Pistia stratiotes*. Growing up among them, rooted in the deep rich mud, was wild rice (*Oryza sativa*). The elephant bull kept to the shallows, sloshing and splashing his way forward as his trunk twined around the grasses and pulled them out. He was fastidious, beating the muddy grass against his knees before raising it to his mouth. An elephant feeding so industriously is a picture of single-minded devotion to an occupation unequalled by the other large mammals. The elephant does not stand guard, constantly testing the breeze or scanning the horizon for danger, the whiff of a predator, an ear flicking here, a tail curled up there. The elephant feeds in peace, at least where he is not hunted by man.

Being intelligent creatures, the Luangwa elephants know where they are safe, and where not. In the late afternoon, when the setting sun is golden on their dusty grey flanks, herds drift towards the river and

coalesce into larger groups. They wade through the darkening shallows, to drink and then to feed through the night on the east bank in the settled zones. By daybreak they are sure to be back in the safety of the South Luangwa National Park on the west bank.

The marula trees *Sclerocarya caffra* had dropped their sweet-scented, yellow, plum-like fruits when we visited the valley. Fruiting trees were skirted by a patch of bare ground, cleared and beaten by elephants. They investigated every tree heavy with fruit. They slowly reached up with eager trunks, laying them along the stems, pressing with the bases of their trunks, and then shaking the trees vigorously. Fruits rained down. If the shaker was alone, he could shuffle and snuffle around collecting his meal at leisure. If he had a companion who was also picking up fruit, there was fierce competition for the booty, and as much time and energy was required to keep the rival away from the fruit as to collect it.

Impressions of the Luangwa Valley, as of other places, are often shaped by the people one meets there. Paul and I had the good fortune of getting to know Norman Carr at Mfuwe. Formerly a game warden, he started his career as an elephant hunter for the government before the Second World War when a rampaging elephant created a vacant post by trampling his predecessor. Norman took us to the Nsefu sector of the park, on the east bank of the Luangwa, and showed us scenes from an Africa which has almost gone.

The landscape of Nsefu has two major features, the Luangwa River and, some distance away, the Mutanda Plains. When we drove across the plains at midmorning, it was already hot and in the distance zebra and Cookson's wildebeest danced in the heat haze. The zebra, like their East African cousins, have only black and white stripes, without the brown shadow stripes of the animals to the south. The wildebeest of Luangwa have been isolated for a long time, and are recognized as a distinct subspecies. Their nearest conspecifics are found in southern Tanzania and northern Moçambique. They are superficially much like other wildebeest, with long scraggly beards and long tails with the dense bunches of coarse tail hairs that are always in vogue as fly wisks.

We saw Cookson's wildebeest moving across the plains in large herds, and always scattered along the edges were territorial bulls, snorting, swishing their long tails, galloping in circles to proclaim their fitness. When the herds of cows and young had moved off, the bulls remained, snorting defiance, stamping their feet, and seeking the company of zebra, impala and other creatures which chose to associate with them. Norman took us to a salt pan on the edge of the plains where a hundreds-strong herd of buffalo, the humped and black wild cattle of Africa, had gathered for the tangy salt and nearby water which was pouring and bubbling out of an artesian borehole. The buffalo, curious as always, started moving towards us, spread out in a phalanx in the traditional bull's-head manoeuvre of the Zulu impi (regiment), with a solid mass of animals forming the head, and its ranks growing thinner to the sides as the horns.

The buffalo advanced, noses lifted, wet and shining. Their long ears, tassled and torn, flicked constantly to discourage the persistent tsetse flies. A low bellow came

Norman Carr, elder-statesman of the Luangwa Valley, readily shares a lifetime of wildlife and conservation experience with visitors.

from an old bull, two youngsters scuffled, the advance petered out and stopped, leaving only silence and expectation. The dust from their hooves slowly drifted away and settled. The clashing of horns, stamping of feet, a snort, the distant eerie call of a flock of crowned cranes, a sound heard on earth for at least 60 million years, a distant bateleur, banking, swooping, wheeling. Heat, dust, flies, Africa.

Norman Carr turned to us from his seat behind the wheel of his Toyota safari car, a host welcoming guests for a feast. His arms swept up and outwards, forming an arc to encompass so much of his life and his ex-

perience. An old buffalo cow saw the movement, tossed her head, curled up her tail and spun around. Her action started a ripple of movement in the middle of the herd which quickly spread to the outermost animals. The herd bubbled, boiled and then seemed to coalesce into a galloping mass of animals which chose a course west to Luangwa, and surged away. We were left, with the dust, silence and warm smell of cow dung.

We drove slowly down the valley in the wake of the buffalo herd towards a large flock of crowned cranes. They strutted along, heads high, their honking calls still sounding occasionally and echoing across the dull, iron grey of the dead mopane trees and the dry yellow grass. Their golden crowns in the bright sunlight were like the halos of early Christian icons, their velvety black foreheads, white eye patches and red wattles flashed as they bobbed and turned, wings outstretched, curtsied and danced. The elegance of these birds was breathtaking. Paul and I wanted to take photographs to try to capture their spirit. Norman smiled indulgently, knowing that the birds would decamp as soon as we left the vehicle. And so they did, the flock of cranes, their pale grey bodies suddenly flashing white as they spread their wings, ran for speed and then floated away, higher and effortlessly faster, over the plains to where the buffalo had been reduced to black dots, white dust and a stunning memory.

Norman was pensive as he drove us towards the Luangwa, this river which is the lifeline, the reference point, the fulcrum of all the swarming life of the valley. Perhaps his thoughts went back to his first safari to this area, some 40 years before. He took us to

The enormous gape of the hippo, and the enlarged canines and incisors, are adaptations for defence and ritualized fighting.

Until recently Luangwa had one of the largest populations of black rhino in Africa, but poaching for horn has decimated their numbers.

The isolated population of Cookson's wildebeest is found only in the Luangwa Valley.

Contentedly feeding in the muddy shallows of a lagoon, a Luangwa elephant bull shows ivory of a size that is now rare in Central Africa.

what he had known as a grove of great winterthorn or ana trees *Acacia albida*, in which a colony of yellow-billed storks had nested. Only a few trees were left. The rest, debarked by elephants, had died, and collapsed into heaps of rotting logs. A small herd of elephants moved through the dead grove, feeding on the short green grass. A calf played with his trunk, twisting and twirling it, thumping it on the ground like a garden hose, then flapped his ears and lay down in the shadow of his mother to rest, to sleep, perhaps to dream.

Norman Carr knows the Nsefu area, on the east bank of the Luangwa, as though he had lived there all his life. For almost half a century, he has patrolled it, walked it, driven through it and seen it develop from a tribal hunting ground into a game reserve set aside by Chief Nsefu, in whose domain it lay. Later, Nsefu proclaimed it a game reserve. Over the decades Carr's knowledge of Nsefu, and indeed the entire Luangwa Valley, has been nurtured, grown and blossomed. That he loves this piece of Africa is abundantly clear from his books and from simply chatting to him. He knew this area when the only 'elephant problem' anyone mentioned was the occasional raid on a garden or cropland. He saw the follies of the original Luangwa elephant cropping scheme, but realized that it was a good idea that foundered.

Norman Carr is wizened and grey haired, but his sparkling eyes, firm step and consuming passion for the valley keep him younger than his years. His camp is at Chinzombo, where he intends to retire one day when he gives up leading tours and imparting a lifetime of experience and knowledge to all fortunate enough to go out with him. Chinzom-

bo is built on the east bank of the Luangwa, amid groves of mopane trees, overlooking the river. In a way, it is a centre of wildlife art, for Norman's daughter, Pamela, and her husband, Vic Guhrs, are renowned painters. Norman's assistant, Patrick Ansell, is also a talented artist. His father, W. F. H. Ansell, the mammal taxonomist after whom the local subspecies of sable antelope is named, also lived in Zambia for many years and was one of Norman's colleagues in the Game Department.

Fifteen years ago there were more elephants in the Luangwa Valley than in any other single area in Africa. Estimates, based on extensive aerial surveys, put the number at about 100 000 animals in one major population which occupied the series of national parks, game reserves and controlled hunting areas which are spread down the valley. Within the space of a few years, however, a plague of ivory and rhino horn poaching had descended on this, one of the many, spectacular wildlife areas on the continent. By 1982, as many as 20 elephants a day were being poached, and scores of black rhino were being shot each year. The thinly stretched personnel of the national parks could no longer cope with the situation. A voluntary body, the Save the Rhino Trust, raised sufficient funds to put Phil Berry into the field with the cream of Zambian rangers, as an anti-poaching force. They were soon rewarded by a steadily increasing number of arrests and, although they have not stamped out poaching, these law-enforcement teams have at least put a damper on it.

The story is a familiar one in Africa, but in the case of Luangwa, as of Tsavo, there is an ecological sting in the tail. Both these areas carried elephant populations far in excess of what they could support without serious change being wrought on the vegetation. In Luangwa, the elephants increased rapidly, and the expanding human population probably also caused a compression effect. Large areas of the mopane woodland were devastated and baobabs destroyed, so that huge tracts of the wildlife reserves looked like scenes from First World War battlefields, with little more than smashed skeletons of trees left standing. Virtually all the damage was concentrated on the west bank of the Luangwa River, the national park side. On the east bank, where elephants were harried and hunted, there was hardly any evidence of an elephant problem and large areas of the woodlands were in almost pristine condition.

A short-lived attempt at elephant population control was made in the 1960s, when an abattoir was built. However, there were many staff, logistic and policy problems, and the scheme folded. The elephant population continued to increase, and its impact on the vegetation was studied and described by a new generation of expatriate wildlife experts. The cropping scheme was not revived, however, and the vegetation damage described as serious in the 1960s still continues today. Heavy poaching has caused a decline

Elephants regularly cross the Luangwa River to reach the feeding grounds of their choice outside the Park, but promptly return when danger threatens.

in elephant numbers, but also an undesirable further compression of animals into relatively safe areas, thus compounding the problem. One of the dilemmas is that poachers cull for their own benefit and are, in effect, making private use of a resource which belongs to the nation. Their methods are wasteful, and at best a gang of poachers is a poor substitute for an efficient culling and utilization team.

With the hungry human population growing steadily in Zambia, it is inevitable that so great a natural resource as the country's wildlife stocks will one day be required to provide food and other benefits for the people. Far better for this potential to be tapped by the authorities, than by poachers. If the park managers cull with discretion, it will be possible to maintain the Luangwa as one of the world's greatest wildlife areas, and derive a benefit from it which can enrich and improve the lives of its neighbours.

Paul Bosman ©

LIWONDE
NATIONAL
PARK

MALAŴI

(Above) *Late in the dry season the leafless, grey stems of the impala lily* (Adenium multiflorum) *are covered with pink and white blooms, which splash colour on the bleached savanna undergrowth.*
(Left) *An elephant bull feeding on the Shire flood plains attracts cattle egrets and other birds, which feast on the insects flushed by his passage.*
(Likwenu, Liwonde National Park, Malaŵi)

Standing on Chiunguni Hill one can survey the entire Upper Shire Valley and the Liwonde National Park which lies in it. Stretching from north to south is the deep Shire River. Close to the foot of the hill are the Shire Swamps, a mosaic of grey-green *Phragmites mauritianus* reed beds with darker columns of papyrus (*Cyperus papyrus*) marching alongside the channels. Rising above the reeds are occasional termite mounds, clothed darkly with dense thicket. On the edge of the swamp, the grass is cropped short, its even greenness broken by the tussocks of longer grasses and sedges, pools thronged by egrets and ducks, channels which lead back to a sparkling lagoon, and tall groves of *Hyphaene* palms. Some of these trees with their tops gone are reminders that not so long ago people cut and tapped them for sweet and heady palm wine.

Fingers of higher ground reach into the swamp and carry tall mopane (*Colophospermum mopane*) woodland, with occasional dark blue-green candelabra trees, *Euphorbia ingens*. Beyond the Shire, the blue hills of the Kirk Range, named for Livingstone's companion, only just stand out above the haze. To the south looms the dark massif of Zomba Mountain which rises a sheer 2 000 metres above the valley floor. To the east, the Mangoche Hills, which form the wall of the Rift Valley, are far away, and where they emerge from the valley floor, the vegetation changes abruptly from mopane to the darker miombo woodlands. The flatness of the valley is broken by isolated dark hills of volcanic origin which rise above the green mopane-covered plain, like whales breaching in a calm sea. To the north the waters of Lake Malombe glitter in the distance. Up the river, 103

Awesome in the defence of her herd, the elephant matriarch is far more likely to charge at an intruder than is the more placid bull.

whose course can be seen outlined in dark green, the distant, wide, golden flood plains are dotted about by groups and columns of dark animals moving out towards the greener grass along the river – these are the elephants of Liwonde.

The great Rift Valley enters Africa in the Danakil Depression, a God-forsaken desert wasteland in Ethiopia, and then slices for 3 000 kilometres through this vast continent until it loses itself in the Indian Ocean off the coast of Moçambique. Threaded along its course are the great lakes of Africa. The largest lake, Victoria, fills a shallow basin between two branches of the Rift, but her deepest lakes, Tanganyika and Malaŵi, fill the cracks in the earth's crust made by these rift valleys to a depth of over 1 000 metres, deeper than any lake in the world after Russia's Lake Baikal. Malaŵi is a beautiful lake, some 585 kilometres long and up to 90 kilometres wide. The country of Malaŵi lies along the western catchment of this lake and the catchment areas in the Shire Valley; the eastern catchment of the lake is covered by Tanzania and Moçambique. The Shire River, the outlet at the southern end of the lake, takes water down the course of the Rift Valley to join the Zambezi. Soon after leaving Lake Malaŵi, this river widens into Lake Malombe, a second, much smaller lake. At Lake Malombe, the Rift Valley swings south-westerly, and is lined by the mountain walls of the Kirk Range and the Mangoche Hills. The Shire River winds along the floor of the Rift, plunging down a long series of rapids into the Lower Shire Valley and then to the Zambezi.

As recently as 1973, the land from the Shire River almost as far as the eastern wall of the Rift Valley and from Lake Malombe to the town of Liwonde was set aside as Liwonde National Park. This is a paradise of 580 km² of river, marshes, savanna, woodland and hills, containing a wide variety of wildlife. Liwonde is one of several national parks proclaimed in Africa since independence, and not based on an equivalent area set aside previously by a colonial power. Liwonde is the product of an African government which, led by President H. Kamuzu Banda, has proved to be farsighted, not only in conservation but in many other respects as well.

Although the heavy clay soils of Liwonde are fertile, they are not of great agricultural value as they are difficult to work and the area is infested by tsetse flies. There were thus very few people resident in the area when I visited it in 1969 on my first assignment as a wildlife biologist. My brief was to investigate the potential for national park development of the Liwonde area. For days I criss-crossed this wilderness with two Malaŵian hunters who knew it well. We found signs of elephants – tracks, droppings, well-used paths, broken branches – but did not actually see any. One of the hunters, Richard Shaba, carelessly walked into a buffalo bean (*Mucuna pruriens*) and paid the agonizing price, and in the process taught me a useful lesson. This plant is an innocuous-looking creeper, which produces scimitar-shaped pods covered by fine, shiny, golden hairs. When the plant is touched, the hairs detach and on contact with human skin they cause a fiery, maddening itch which is many times worse than a nettle. I went down with malaria, but not before I had concluded that Liwonde was a pearl of great price. My report was accepted by the government and in due course the Liwonde area was proclaimed a reserve and later achieved full national park status.

The most impressive features of Liwonde were, to me, in those far-off days, the untouched mopane woodlands, the elephant herds and the magnificent sable antelope which, even though the area was heavily hunted, were still holding their own. The Liwonde elephants are typical of the East African form, and therefore very different from their fellows in the Kasungu National Park which lies to the north, and west of the Rift. Like the elephants of Moçambique and the Kruger National Park further south, they have somewhat larger ears and bodies than the Central African form. Their ivory is typically heavier than that of the elephants of the miombo woodlands of central Malaŵi and Zambia. The sable bulls are as impressive as they are anywhere, with their inky, glossy hides against which the brilliant white of their bellies and facial stripes is starkly contrasted. However, the cows are more choco-

An iridescent emerald-green neck patch distinguishes the male pygmy goose from his less brightly coloured mate.

late-brown than those of the western parts of the central plateau such as in Zambia or Angola.

The Liwonde elephants have a long history of disturbance. They are known to have migrated regularly from the Upper Shire Valley to the Mangoche Forest on the eastern wall of the Rift, and across the watershed into Moçambique. This movement took them through settled areas where they raided crops and gardens. Control shooting resulted, and over the years, many elephants died while moving from the Shire to the hills. Once in the Mangoche Hills, which is a forest reserve, they enjoyed some protection. To eliminate this friction between the Liwonde elephants and man, the government added to the park a narrow, but essential, corridor of land linking the heartland of Liwonde to Mangoche. This allows the elephants to move freely from the Rift Valley to the mountains without being shot. However, the many years of persecution have probably left their mark, and the Liwonde elephants are among the most aggressive in Africa. They often charge vehicles on sight, much to the surprise and

terror of visitors. Only a gradual campaign of standing up to them at the slight risk of damaging a few vehicles will teach them not to be aggressive. Every time a terrified driver takes fright and roars off, the elephant's dominance over vehicles is reinforced and the problem grows.

Because of the years of control shooting most of the Liwonde bulls are relatively young. It is extremely rare, therefore, to find bulls with heavy ivory. This situation exactly parallels that found in the Addo area in the 1940s, when there were only two adult bulls to 10 adult cows, the other bulls having been shot while marauding in farmlands.

The Liwonde elephants are slowly learning that they are protected in the park and they seem less inclined to move away during the wet season now than in the past. Their traditional movements take them eastwards to higher ground after the summer rains have turned the valley floor into a vast bog with swamps along the banks of the Shire. As the area dries out and water supplies in the highlands become attenuated, they move back towards the valley floor, where water is abundant. A further attraction is that, as the floodwaters retreat, the grassland on the flood plains dries out and becomes available to animals. Later in the season when the grassland along the edge of the woodlands is yellow and dry, it is still green and nutritious closer to the river. By following the retreating green grass the elephants are ensured of a high quality diet for most of the dry season.

The sable antelope and other game species follow the same pattern of annual movements as the elephants. During the rains they move eastwards to higher and drier ground; during the dry season they move back on to

On the shore of Lake Malombe an ambitious strangler fig (Ficus sp.) has grown around an ancient baobab tree (Adansonia digitata), enclosing it and slowly killing it.

When the male greater kudu has reached his prime at the age of eight years, his magnificent horns complete two full spirals and begin a third.

Waterbuck bulls guard the females on their territories, and are quick to see off rival males.

the flood plains to take advantage of the better feeding conditions there.

The other wildlife species which survived in the Liwonde area are also making a spectacular recovery. Greater kudu, oribi, impala, waterbuck, bushbuck, warthog, lion and hippo are all common. However, the hunting pressure of the past did succeed in eliminating black rhino, zebra and buffalo. Striking absentees from these mopane woodlands are the giraffe, black-backed jackal and steenbok which are found in all the other mopane areas south of the Zambezi. Giraffe are also found up the Luangwa Valley in Zambia.

The Shire River is a lifeline for birds. White-breasted cormorants are common around the Mvuu camp. Here the Shire drowned a grove of trees along its banks when a barrage was built downstream to control the flow of the river for the Nkula Falls hydroelectric scheme. These dead trees provide ideal roosts for the cormorants which gather by the thousand. There is a constant pulsing of sound around the roosts as the birds come and go, fight, feed their young, croak and cackle. The trees are whitened by guano and the grass under them stands dense and lush, fertilized by the birds' droppings.

Further along the banks of the Shire, many other large trees, which had probably stood for years above the flood levels before they were inundated, now provide sought-after perches for the numerous fish eagles which stake out their territories and vigilantly guard them against incursions. The call of the fish eagle – that thrilling, rending sound – is made by the bird as it throws back its head in a wild series of screams, which carry far across the water and the dull green-grey of the bush, to announce occupancy. Like the whoop of the spotted hyaena, it is the voice of Africa, as poignant as the trumpet of an elephant or the distant booming roar of a lion.

The Liwonde lions, like the elephants and other game, were also reputed to undertake seasonal movements from the Shire as far to the east as Moçambique. When the game left the area during the rains, some of the lions followed – those that remained behind courted starvation, or turned to the terrifying habit of killing people. For years, man-eating lions plagued the Liwonde, Namweras and Kasupe districts. The Game Department employed hunters to track and shoot several lions each year. They were usually quite thin, but were not the injured lions or cripples of legend. These lions were also aided in their man-eating careers by the habits of the local people. As the Shire Valley was unbearably hot and humid, people were tempted to cool off by sleeping out of doors and thus became easy prey for lions. As game populations in the park have built up, the incidence of man-eating by the Liwonde lions has declined.

The mopane woodlands of Liwonde are still in a nearly perfect climax state. Their seasonal use by a relatively small elephant popu-lation has resulted in little or no significant damage. However, with the stabilizing of the elephant population in the park and their permanent residence, the situation is slowly and ominously beginning to change. Even now, while the elephant population is still in an early phase of growth, there are areas which show signs of heavy elephant usage. The first areas to be affected are those on the mineral-rich raised beaches near the camp. Here the mopane woodland is replaced by a richer savanna with *Acacia* spp. and *Combretum* spp., baobabs (*Adansonia digitata*) and *Albizia harveyi*. Even now, trees with their bark pulled off and branches broken, and even trees that have been pushed over by elephants, are a common sight. Liwonde is a small park, and among its greatest assets are its untouched woodlands. Somewhere a balance between elephants and woodlands will have to be established, as has been necessary in every other park in Africa where elephant protection has been successful. If the Liwonde wardens do not adhere to a limit of this kind, the park could follow the Luangwa Valley, and end up with its woodlands destroyed and impoverished. However, the Department of National Parks and Wildlife is aware of this problem and in its management plan for the area has specified limits to the woodland change that will be permitted.

In the northern parts of the park, the mopane woodlands break up into large grassy glades, the habitat of a healthy population of the small grassland antelope, the oribi. Close to Lake Malombe, a sizeable patch of dry forest and thicket on deep sandy soils offers a home to bushbuck and crested guinea fowl. These forests are so similar to those of the Shire Valley below the Nkulu Falls that one wonders why nyala, the most common large antelope there, did not reach the Liwonde area – they are presumably very sensitive to small differences in the habitat.

In the southern parts of the park where Chiunguni Hill rises above the flood plains, the slopes are covered in tall mixed woodlands with *Albizia tanganyicensis* and *Brachystegia* spp., and with taller grasses than are found out on the plains, or among the mopane.

Along the Shire one finds the water dikkop. This bird's call is uttered at night and is an eerie, piping sound. There are many African traditions associated with night sounds, one of the most interesting being the belief that the ghostly call of the buff-spotted flufftail is the voice of a singing chameleon. A striking avian feature of Liwonde is the countless untidy grass nests of the white-browed sparrow weaver.

On a hot morning, sitting in the shade on a termite mound and looking over the flood plains to the hills on the far western side of the valley, one would feel as much at home in Liwonde as in any area of the vast southern savanna. The birds, the sounds and the animals are the same. This is the last of the southern savanna; north of it, except for the

Sable antelope, which congregate seasonally into herds of 100 animals or more, are one of the wildlife attractions of Liwonde.

slender finger of the Luangwa Valley, lies the miombo woodland of the Central African Plateau, an area with many similarities to the southern savanna, but where different plants and birds make for an unmistakably different biome. Liwonde is a unique park. It is the only area in Malawî where the southern savanna is so completely represented. In the richness and diversity of its wildlife and habitats lies the potential for Liwonde to become, in a very short space of time, not only a superb elephant sanctuary, but also one of the most exciting wildlife viewing areas of Africa.

We travelled to Mana Pools by the most exciting route, flying low along the Zambezi River from Kariba. Our journey started at Tashinga in the Matusadona National Park. From there we flew along the southern shore of Lake Kariba and over the dam wall in Kariba Gorge. The Zambezi breaks out of the confines of the gorge at Nyamuomba. As the escarpments retreat to the north and south, a wide, flat valley stretches away on either side of the river. The vegetation changes abruptly – the alluvial plains are covered by park-like open savanna, with an occasional, enormous baobab tree (*Adansonia digitata*) dominating the scene. Along the river bank spreading Natal mahogany trees (*Trichilia emetica*) cast shade so deep that few plants grow under them. There are also tall *Kigelia africana* trees whose large sausage-like fruits, up to a metre long and weighing up to 10 kilograms, hang like grey-brown and green lanterns.

The Zambezi River ran clean and clear, with long, white sandbanks and shoals breaking the crystalline blue. Crocodiles were abundant, and seemingly always sunning themselves on sandbanks from where they could slip quickly into deeper water. Hippo crowded together in herds of 30 or more, heads ducking under the water as we passed, and then bobbing up behind us, pinkish ears flipping away silver droplets of water. In one of the herds we saw an animal which lacked the dark pigmentation of his fellows. The unfortunate creature was a brilliant sunburnt pink and was covered with sores and scabs, most likely keratoses or a form of skin cancer. I instinctively felt a stab of sympathy for the animal, for I too suffer from a sensitive skin and must forever go

MANA POOLS NATIONAL PARK

ZIMBABWE

(Above) *Inquisitive and intelligent, the spotted hyaena is a highly efficient and social hunter – not the skulking, loathsome scavenger of legend.*
(Right) *Wildlife knows no political boundaries: an elephant bull easily crosses the Zambezi River from Zimbabwe to the wilderness on the Zambian bank.*
(Chivure Mouth, Mana Pools National Park, Zimbabwe)

The gentlemen's club – old buffalo bulls retired from the busy life of the breeding herd, yet still seeking company and protection, live peacefully together.

through the bush fully-clothed, with hat, mask, dark glasses, gloves and layers of barrier cream. The Nile hippo is more exposed to the sun than any of the other African mammals. It is said to have subcutaneous glands on the neck and back which secrete an oily substance regarded by some as a healing agent; others believe it serves to block ultra-violet light. The hippo, it seems, was coping with sunburn long before man.

Water birds were not particularly varied – pied kingfishers fled to the banks; Egyptian geese clattered into the sky, white wing patches flashing as they frantically flapped away; cattle egrets were abundant, and occasionally a heron took to the air as the plane passed low overhead. We could clearly see large shoals of fish darting hither and thither. The great river constantly changed mood and colour as we skimmed over the water. The deep channels were marked by darker blue-green water and the pale stripes of underwater hippo paths; where sandbanks lay just below the surface the shallow water sparkled. The water was calm in places, elsewhere rippled, wrinkled and dappled by the breeze. Sandbanks were fringed by silver-topped reed beds of *Phragmites mauritianus*, and some even had a green covering of star grass (*Cynodon* sp.) cropped to the texture of a country lawn by the broad mouths and rubbery lips of the hippo.

The river banks rose steep and high above the dry-season water level. Hippo paths snaked up the steep banks, twin tracks distinguishing them from elephant paths. When an elephant walks, its footprints overlap, hind on fore, left close to right, forming one broad smoothly beaten path when a route is regularly used. Hippos have their feet relatively further apart and when they walk, they make two distinct narrow parallel tracks. The scouring effect of recent floods had left many trees clinging precariously to the bank, while most of their roots hung out over the water.

Some fallen trees had lost their last foothold and tumbled into the water where they lay half submerged, a tenuous connection of a few roots keeping some branches green, yet most of the tree bare and dead, a perch for cormorants and kingfishers. The remains of other trees, swept down the river, scoured by the sand, baked and bleached by the sun, lay like corpses half-buried on the sandbanks. White trimmings of guano showed where some of the dead trees served as roosting sites for herons and darters. On some sandbanks, the ashes of a watch fire showed where a small party of fishermen had spent a cold night. Occasionally we flew over dugout canoes holding two or three of them. They flashed beneath our wings, a momentary glance of an upturned smiling face, a wave of greeting and they were left far behind.

There was a marked change in the vegetation when we passed the mouth of the Rukomechi River, the boundary of the Mana Pools National Park. The low-lying land stretched away from the river to the distant and receding escarpment to the south, and the scrubby mopane (*Colophospermum mopane*) vegetation gave way to open winter thorn (*Acacia albida*) woodland, with tall spreading trees and yellowing grass. It was soon apparent that in this open country game was more abundant. A small herd of timid eland trotted away, the dewlaps of the bulls swinging to and fro under their throats, their long ox-like tails swishing in time. Buffalo bulls stood in the shade of an immense winterthorn, chewing the cud, scarcely bothering to look up at us as we passed. Warthogs ran for cover, youngsters crowding against their elders, tails aloft like cavalry pennants.

Mana Pools National Park occupies only 2 196 km² and lies like a narrow slice from the Zambezi across the wide flood plain or river terraces reaching into the hilly escarpment country. But, although it is small, it is sandwiched between safari areas, and is, therefore, the heartland of more than 10 000 km² of wildlife estate. The whole area supports more than 12 000 elephants, 16 000 buffalo and despite heavy poaching, still has numbers of black rhinoceros.

The flat country, rich alluvial soil and perennial pools are all a legacy of the Zambezi River. Over immense spans of time the river has been migrating northwards and leaving the Mana terraces behind on the south bank. As the river moved, the remains of its older channels, cut off from the main body of water became long, still, perennial pools. When the river is in flood, these pools are recharged and flushed out. During the dry season the pools and flood plain become a magnet for the animals which move down from the *Brachystegia* woodland of the southern escarpment hills, through the tall open mopane, the dense swathes of 'jesse' thicket, a deciduous close-growing tangle of

vegetation, to the open park-like *Acacia albida* woodlands formed on the flat river terraces and flood plains.

The open park-like country close to the river showed its seasonally changing character in the dark clay soils, cracked and dry in August, but in which we saw the deep imprints of elephant, hippo, rhino and buffalo tracks embedded, evidence of how wet and waterlogged the area becomes during the rains. Groves of *Trichilia* trees, *Lonchocarpus* and *Acacia* stood on raised terraces, while the low-lying areas were covered by *Paspalum scrobiculatum* and other grasses. Elsewhere, there were extensive stands of *Vetiveria nigritana*, into which a rhino disappeared, his passage shown only by a waving and rippling of these tall grasses. On termite mounds the deeply coloured soils were covered by tangles of creepers, such as the climbing *Combretum paniculatum* whose fiery red blooms form dense mats known as the 'flame of the forest'. All around the tall stands of *Panicum maximum* that had been lush and dark green during the rains were now collapsed, yellowed and sparse looking, but still nutritious.

The lower branches of most *Acacia albida* trees were neatly trimmed up to a height of about six metres, clearly an elephant browsing line. These trees produce an abundant harvest of 'apple ring' pods, reddish, curved and curling, rich and much sought after by elephants, baboons, kudu, impala and rhino. These trees, the subject of an intensive investigation by Kevin Dunham, the park's biologist, make a substantial contribution to the region's food supply. Baboons and impala are constant companions in these woodlands, the impala gathering to pick up the

A remnant of war, Fort Mana is now used to house game scouts, who face an equally dangerous fight against the ubiquitous rhino poacher.

A sleeping bag, a folding stretcher and a nearby rifle provide warmth, comfort and security when one sleeps out in the open.

*Like an enormous snake, the tendrils of the python vine (*Fockea multiflora*) twine around the stem and branches of a mopane tree.*

111

The foxy charaxes (Charaxes jasius saturnus), a powerful, high-flying butterfly, is widely distributed in the lower-lying areas of the southern savanna.

pods dropped by the baboons, feeding or frolicking way above their heads. For the impala this is a fairly productive source of food as the baboons usually pop only the seeds into their mouths, discarding the pods.

Elephant bulls shake trees, pushing with the base of their trunks against them, first leaning forwards, then rocking backwards to get the tree to sway and whiplash, raining pods to the ground. These are then avidly picked up by dextrous trunks and shoved into cavernous mouths. Baboons and impala also gather near feeding elephants to share their harvest. Elephant bulls reach high above their heads, stretching their trunks almost vertically upwards, to pull down the tender green branches of the winterthorns. One huge bull reared up on his hind legs, his forefeet off the ground, as he stretched a little further to pull down succulent branches and to devour them, leaves, twigs, bark, wood and all.

There were two much younger askari bulls with him, and they stood around nervously, eager to share in the feast, but too afraid of the big bull to make a direct grab. One reversed up to him in a submissive female posture, hind legs well apart, until he stood next to him and, as the branches and twigs dropped out of the mouth of the feeding bull, the youngster eagerly picked them up and chewed them with relish. After feasting for some time, the big bull waded off slowly, but steadily, into the Zambezi, moving north to Zambia. Two cattle egrets, snow white with bright yellow legs, flew up from the grass where they had been hunting insects disturbed by the elephants and followed the bull, landing on his back. They sat there, contented passengers, as the animal steadily crossed the wide, shallow river.

The elephants of Mana, like those of Liwonde in Malaŵi which also utilize a floodplain system, have daily and seasonal patterns of movement. As the dry season progresses, the elephants tend to move closer to the flood plains where water is abundant and food still plentiful. Late in the dry season, there is the added attraction of the significant crop of *Acacia albida* fruits which are rich in protein and carbohydrates. At this time of year, the breeding herds move on to the flood plain during the day and back to the denser, protective mopane woodland and jesse thicket at night. Bulls are more inclined to stay on the flood plain continuously. When it rains, and Mana receives 802 millimetres in an average year, the flood plains quickly become waterlogged and the elephants move to higher and drier ground.

The Mana elephants move around in the fairly large breeding herds typical of savanna elephants, and we saw groups of 20 or more. They are reputed to have a high proportion of tuskless cows, some estimates going as high as 10 per cent. Although tuskless cows are found in all savanna elephant populations, they are generally uncommon. Only in the Addo elephant population in South Africa is tusklessness the usual condition of cows, and tusked cows are the exception. Many writers have referred to tuskless bulls, known in Tanzania as 'boodies' but there is to my knowledge no recorded case of a congenitally tuskless male elephant. They may break their tusks, but all males start off with them.

We slept in the open, with only a canvas tarpaulin as a roof. The African night is alive with the sounds of many animals, and at Mana Pools we experienced some of the most interesting nights of all our travels. There were lions about, so I borrowed a rifle from Kevin and propped it up on a folding camp chair where I could grab it in an emergency. Because I have a fear of a hyaena walking off with my face during the night, I slept with my hat over my face, a habit cultivated over many years.

It was a cold night and our sleep was fitful, the moon full and they dry-season sky clear. The stars glittered brightly. We could hear animals, unseen, moving around in the grass. Hippos grunted and bellowed, the resonance of their deep voices echoing under the trees. Lions roared way across the Zambezi in the wilderness on the Zambian bank. The eerie call of water dikkops, large-eyed nocturnal birds, rose and fell.

A shuffling in the grass announced the arrival of a buffalo bull who came quite close, stared at us contemplatively and then ambled off to lie down, ruminating, near the still glowing embers of our fire. I wondered whether he was keeping close to us as a protection against lions. Elephant bulls moved past, stopping a while to feed off the trees around our fragile camp and then padding away, huge in the moonlight, silent as ghosts, floating dreamlike now in the silver moonlight, now wafting into deep shadow and then disappearing without a trace of their passing save the wrinkled tracks which we would inspect in the morning.

Occasionally a turtle dove called, a few liquid notes, hesitant, uncertain, as though the bird had woken, cooed fitfully and then nodded off to sleep. A fish eagle called – the first time I had ever heard that evocative sound at night. Just past midnight I woke to see a solitary spotted hyaena lying close to us, his head resting on his paws and his bright eyes watching us intently. I sat up and he stood up lazily and moved off. The following night it was Paul who woke to find a large hyaena sniffling and snuffling around our camp site, watching us and coming closer to our makeshift beds. Paul moved, the hyaena took fright and loped off. We wondered what the hyaenas would have done, had we not disturbed them. There are many records of their attacking people sleeping out in the open, but I suppose there are many more occasions when they have come and gone without the sleepers knowing they were there.

The spotted hyaena is traditionally linked to witchcraft in Africa, and it is reputed to be the nocturnal steed of witches and wizards. Early European observers took the legends to heart, and regarded the hyaena as the loathsome incarnation of evil, shuffling hunchbacked through the night, moaning and giggling like a creature possessed. The stigma was attached, I suppose, to its scavenging habits, the role with which it was most often associated, and it was assumed to rob kills from the noble lion. The reality, however, is quite different. The hyaena is an intelligent, highly social carnivore that may forage singly or hunt in deadly efficient packs, bringing down animals as large as wildebeest and sometimes even tackling buffalo and hippo. They have an effective clan structure, maintaining territories which they mark with secretions from their anal glands, leaving chemical messages which are easily interpreted by others of their clan, or strangers. Their behaviour is fascinating, and it is only within the last two decades that the complexity of their lives, and the order and logic of their behaviour, has been unravelled.

It was chilly just before dawn. The moon had sunk low in the west, and the stars faded as the light strengthened. The turtle doves started to call, one bird here, another there, without enthusiasm at first, and then slowly

Tuskless cows occur in most elephant populations. They seem little inconvenienced by this condition, and are usually even more aggressive than their tusked sisters.

they seemed to warm up and start calling in earnest. Other birds too were greeting the dawn. A warbler called, and far away the booming notes of a ground hornbill duet floated over the bush – *le hu, le hu, le hu tu tu*. 'I'm going back, I'm going back to my family,' says the unhappy female. 'You can go, you can go, you can go back to your family,' replies the strutting male.

Matusadona is a place of sunsets, fish eagles and elephants. The setting sun is in our faces as our boat moves slowly down the Ume River, late on a wintry afternoon. Far across Lake Kariba it sinks into the distant grey haze of Zambia, setting alight and uniting water and sky with a flaming orange glow. As the orb drops lower, the colours change to red, to carmine, to softest pink. The pink transmutes to pastel grey, the sky and water pale, the flat-topped Bumi Hills becomes the darkest grey and the gaunt drowned trees stand black against the light, their reflections zigzagging across the water. A fish eagle is still perched on the skeleton of what was once a shady tree, the bird is indistinct, more suggestion than reality.

As the boat draws closer to the shore, we cut the engines and drift. All is still, save for the gentle lapping of the waves. The eagle stares at us, turns away, ruffles his feathers in annoyance, then launches himself aloft, his great dark wings seeming almost to meet above and below him, the long primary feathers raked out like fingers clawing at the air to lift him up high. He soars, the wing beats relax, the head is thrown back and the liquid scream comes pouring out, echoing across the leaden water, eerie, defiant. Two elephants, wading in the shallows, pause, half turning towards us; are they listening to the bird, or have they picked up our scent wafting across the water?

Paul and I had been gong out every day with Russell Taylor, the biologist at Matusadona National Park. He guided us through the park, and explained the intricate ecological process which developed with the formation of the lake, as fish, birds, mammals and vegetation adapted to changed circum-

MATUSADONA NATIONAL PARK

ZIMBABWE

(Above) *Sensitive, sometimes aggressive and quick to charge, the black rhino, because of the demand for its horn, is one of the most threatened large mammals in Africa.*
(Right) *A dry-season sunset on Lake Kariba – with elephants in the shallows and a watchful fish eagle – presents a spectacle of rare beauty.*
(Ume Estuary, Matusadona National Park, Zimbabwe)

114

Various forms of the vervet monkey, which lives in small troops, are found almost throughout the savanna and woodland regions of Africa.

stances. He spoke with calm authority, showing a profound understanding of natural processes and man's role in the system.

The easiest way to see elephants in Matusadona is to take a boat and explore the multitude of bays along the lakeshore. In places the shallows are marked by stark forests of drowned trees, still standing, more than 20 years after the dam was closed. Along the shore, a green fringe of *Panicum repens* grassland has developed into a highly productive and sought-after habitat for elephant, buffalo, hippo and waterbuck. The elephants spend a great deal of time feeding in this zone and also in the plant-choked shallows of quiet bays where Goliath herons stalk tilapias.

Skimming over the pale surface of the lake towards the Sanyati River, we spotted the familiar dark silhouettes of elephants along the hazy shore. Russel piloted the boat skillfully through the snags and dead trees until we reached a sandbank. We waded through the water, among the gloomy, drowned trees, to get a closer look at the elephants. Because crocodiles are abundant in the lake, Russel carried a rifle, a distinct comfort. The elephants fed peacefully and, when it grew hotter, moved to the water's edge where some showered and splashed mud on themselves, while others stood dreaming in the heat. Around us stood the trees, dead and decaying, yet they were the focus of a whole new dimension of life systems. Insects, geckos and lizards lived on the trees, fish took shelter among them aquatic weeds grew around them, and they served as perches for fish-eating birds.

The elephants did not react to the boat, and we once drifted quite close to a party of bulls which ignored us. We stayed further away from breeding herds, but they too seemed unconcerned and small calves splashed in the shallows while the adults drank and showered. These elephants had, in the past, used the mopane (*Colophospermum mopane*) woodlands on the floor of the wide Zambezi valley as a dry season concentration area. During the wet season, they moved away into the gently undulating foothills, the more rugged escarpment country covered by miombo or *Brachystegia* woodlands and the highlands beyond.

Matusadona, like all the wildlife areas strung out along the Zambezi valley, carries a healthy population of black rhino. Like the elephant, this species is incompatible with man and it is only in national parks that they will ultimately survive. The trade in rhino horn has encouraged poaching of black rhino in most parks throughout Africa, and numbers have declined dramatically over the past decade. In Zimbabwe, as in the other Southern African countries, poaching is still under control, and the black rhino is still secure. While driving out towards the southern boundary of the park one afternoon, we saw a black rhino bull close to the road. Russell stopped the vehicle as the alarmed animal lifted his head and stared myopically in our direction. His supple nostrils flared and closed as he tried to scent us, but we were safely downwind. Four oxpeckers flew off, chirring noisily, but the rhino did not dash away in reaction to the bird's warning. He stood his ground defiantly.

The bull had several long cuts and scratches on his face, and metallic green flies crawled over the dry and darkening blood. Perhaps he had been in a fight. Julie, Russell

and Lynne's two-year-old daughter, was sitting on her mother's lap, apparently as fascinated by the rhino as we were. She gently called him with soft baby talk. The large cupped ears flicked and turned, and the animal moved closer. We stared in awe, wondering what it would do next. Julie continued her conversation and the animal approached to a few metres, then perhaps recognizing the vehicle as something strange, snorted loudly, turned around and moved off, grumpily puffing at us over his shoulder as he disappeared into the bush.

One usually knows animal species by their signs, tracks, droppings and other indications of their presence, or from pictures. But the first sighting of the creature is always memorable, for only then does its scale, texture, form and movement assume reality. Matusadona provided me with one of these unforgettable experiences. The Taylors, Paul and I were all sitting around the camp fire on the edge of the Maronga River talking about the park and the problems facing it. We heard a clicking sound from the river which I took to be two buffalo clashing horns. As I got up to have a look with a flashlight, I realized the sound was that of stones in the river bed being rolled around. I still thought of a buffalo, carelessly crossing the river, and was unprepared for the sight of five Cape clawless otters gambolling down the river bed, busily rolling rocks over looking for food. Two of the otters were larger than the others, and we assumed that they were a pair of adults with their young. They scampered over the rocks with a graceful flowing motion, dived into pools and porpoised out the other side. They moved in such a compact group that they seemed to twine over and

around one another as they ran. Their sleek wet fur shone in the weak beam of the flashlight, their eyes like dark jewels.

On December 3, 1958, Lake Kariba was born. Two sluice gates in the newly completed dam wall at Kariba Gorge were closed, forming the first dam on the Zambezi River. Behind the wall, the largest man-made lake on earth at that time started to take shape. The birth of the lake marked the beginning of great, and rapid, ecological changes. Arid mopane woodlands, dark green riverine forest, glades, gulleys, animals and villages, all would disappear in time under the clear blue waters of the Zambezi, and a whole new ecosystem would take their place.

The microscopic aquatic life, plants, fish and birds of the Zambezi system, as well as several introduced forms, have settled into new, sometimes still changing relationships with one another. A South American water fern, *Salvinia molesta* (present in the Zambezi before the dam was built), spread rapidly under the new conditions. It colonized large areas and various efforts were made to control it, including the introduction of *Paulinia acuminata*, a South American semi-aquatic grasshopper which eats *Salvinia*. However, a balance was soon reached between the conditions suitable for the fern, known by then as 'Kariba weed' and the insect. The weed provides shelter for fish, and *Paulinia* is eaten by many birds. The indigenous fish of the Zambezi and its tributaries reacted to the new conditions in the lake with increases in the numbers of those able to utilise deeper water, and a decline in those preferring a riverine habitat. There has also been a successful introduction of freshwater sardines, or kapenta, from Lake Tanganyika.

117

Elephant herds bunch together when moving onto the exposed short grasslands along the shores of Lake Kariba, even though there is little risk of danger.

Towing a boat through a drowned mopane forest in the shallows of Lake Kariba is a somewhat unusual way of stalking elephants.

These small fish live in the open, deep water and now support a profitable fishery, as well as influencing the habits of predators like tigerfish and pied kingfishers which move far out of their normal haunts to feed on them.

As the waters of the Zambezi rose to form the lake, every little hillock or ridge became an island. Each had its complement of animals, great and small, that had retreated before the rising water to higher ground, only to end up trapped. Thousands of animals perished, either from starvation on islands after eating every scrap of green plant material, or from drowning. But the renowned rescue campaign known as Operation Noah, mounted by what was then Southern Rhodesia and led by the legendary Rupert Fothergill saved at least 6 000 animals. The authorities on the north bank, now Zambia, rescued 4 000 animals. Although Operation Noah took care of mostly large animals, even bush squirrels, galagos, snakes and birds were captured and moved to the mainland. The marooned animals were studied by Graham Child, later Zimbabwe's Director of National Parks, and much new information on how populations of large mammals respond to such traumatic events was gathered. On a less important, but no less interesting level, the swimming abilities of many large mammals were recorded. Elephants moved ahead of the water, or swam when necessary. Adults could swim for miles, but small calves had to be helped by their mothers, and many drowned. One of the saddest incidents occurred when three elephant cows with two small calves were trapped on an island. The rescuers tried to chase them off into the water, but to no avail. Perhaps the cows knew that their little ones would not be able to last the long swim to safety. The calves were then caught and taken to the shore, in the hope that the cows would leave, but they stubbornly stayed on the island. The rescuers later returned the calves as they were too small to fend for themselves. A week later the cows were gone and the bodies of the two calves, badly battered and bruised, were found. They had been killed by their mothers.

To provide a permanent home for the thousands of animals displaced by the rising waters, the Matusadona Game Reserve, later upgraded to a national park, was proclaimed in 1963. Covering some 1 370 km², it is a park with an unsettling past, yet a hopeful future. The dramatic decrease in the valley floor habitats after inundation, and the concentration of the animal populations into the remaining area, put severe pressure on the ecosystem. Yet the impact of the lake is not the only cause of ecological stress. Of far greater consequence has been the insidious pressure on the park originating from human development to the south, throughout that part of Zimbabwe known as the Sebungwe. The story has been carefully documented and Matusadona provides a classic case of the genesis of an elephant problem in a national park. Unlike the policy of most other park authorities, the problem has been tackled on a broad front in Matusadona, as it is clearly recognized that the elephant problem is a consequence of land use patterns in a much larger area.

The entire Sebungwe region covers some 40 000 km² and contains two national parks, Matusadona and Chizarira, two safari areas, four forest areas and ten blocks of tribal or communal lands. Most of the area is of marginal value for agriculture, yet subsistence agriculture is essential to provide for a human population which has increased tenfold over the past 80 years. The tsetse fly, which originally limited the extent of the settlement, has been pushed back to the northern areas of the Sebungwe, and southward movement of game animals, the hosts of the fly, is prevented by a control fence. The fence is accompanied by a road along which people have moved and settled. Their crops are invariably raided by elephants, animals are poached to the north of the fence, anti-poaching measures are intensified and conflict grows.

As the human population has increased, the available elephant range has decreased from about 30 000 km² in 1955 to its current area of 10 000 km², while the elephants have increased from about 5 000 to 8 300 – despite over 5 000 having been culled during this time. The compression of the elephants into the conserved areas has raised their density fourfold, with a resultant opening up of woodland habitats through tree destruction, increasing the vulnerability of the habitat to fire, which the expanding human population readily provides. Under such pressures, the habitat is being changed to the detriment of other species, such as sable and some small mammals. Even raptors are losing nesting sites as the large trees are toppled. To think of letting nature take its course under such circumstances is unrealistic – the problem is man-induced; it is not a natural occurrence.

The first step would be to regulate the numbers of elephant, and other over-abundant animals such as buffalo, within the national park, but that is recognized in this instance as only a partial short-term solution. A long-term solution, which takes into account the needs of the 300 000 people of the area, and which must give some hope for the maintenance of the parks, is now being actively sought. Russell Taylor and Rowan Martin, his colleague in the Zimbabwe Department of National Parks and Wildlife Management, drew up an ambitious plan for resolving the conflict between human and wildlife interests on a regional basis. They suggested buffer zones in which a gradation of wildlife and human use could be established. These range from wildlife priority areas, such as the national parks, through multiple-use zones (for wildlife, subsistence crops, harvesting of natural resources, and beekeeping) to intensive human use zones where no wildlife would survive. These areas would also encompass the range of the tsetse fly within parks to areas free of the fly where cattle could be kept.

Operation Windfall (Wildlife Industry for All) is an example of such a system working. Where elephants had to be culled to protect habitat in a safari area, the products, including meat and skins, were sold to the local population at minimal cost. Since its inception nine years ago the scheme has been expanded as the response has been positive – the shortage of meat has been alleviated in some areas, the need to poach has declined, and the recognition of wildlife as a resource

The serval is a long-legged hunter of rodents and birds, catching them with its outsize paws.

belonging to the community has been encouraged. The buffer zone concept requires clear definition, because it must benefit not only the settled areas but also the parks. This will happen only if the buffer zones absorb the increase from animal populations inside the park. The objective, in other words, is to create a zone in which the compression of elephants can be reversed.

If Operation Windfall succeeds, we may see the development of a stable land-use system which provides for the needs of the wildlife and eliminates or dampens the desperate scrabble for land by the park's neighbours. If the buffer zone alternative to a fence line marking a park boundary succeeds, there need be less fear for the future of elephants in Matusadona.

Botswana lies at the heart of Southern Africa. A vast, arid, flat, sparsely populated land, most of it blanketed by the desert sands of the Kalahari. In the north of the country there is an almost pristine tract of wilderness which includes the Linyanti Swamp, the Chobe National Park covering 11 700 km², forestry reserves where stately teak (*Baikiaea plurijuga*) woodlands stretch to the horizon, the Okavango Delta and seemingly endless safari hunting areas. One travels for miles on narrow winding sandy tracks through virgin country teeming with herds of game, among which are 50 000 elephants, the largest concentration in Southern Africa.

Although it is dry country, it is an area where, paradoxically, water has influenced much of the vegetation and the fauna. Rivers, swamps and lakes are vital keys in the functioning of the ecosystem.

The water comes from Angola. The Kwando River rises in the moist highlands of Angola and then flows southwards to spread out across the land as the Linyanti Swamp which straddles the frontier between the Caprivi area of Namibia and Botswana. The Linyanti then feeds most of its outflow along an extended swamp, marsh and lake system to the Chobe River. The Chobe has a wide flood plain which is one of the richest and most important wildlife habitats in northern Botswana and which has been a magnet for elephant hunters since 1870. Although the elephants have been protected for many years the Chobe flood plains are still a killing ground. Now the elephants are hunted illegally, by poachers. When Paul and I visited Chobe in 1983 we counted 11 fresh elephant carcasses along a 20 km-long strip of flood plain. The bitter irony of Chobe, however, is

CHOBE NATIONAL PARK

BOTSWANA

(Above) *A fish eagle, the evocative avian voice of Africa, keeps watch over its territory from a perch near the water's edge.*
(Right) *His skin wet, glistening and comfortably cool, an elephant bull emerges from a bathe in deep water.*
(Serondela, Chobe National Park, Botswana)

Elephant bulls can reach as high as six metres with their dextrous trunks to pick leaves and fruit.

that if it is to survive with its plant communities intact, many more elephants will have to die.

The Chobe River is the watering place for thousands of elephants during the dry season as there is no natural water within 60 kilometres of the river. One can sit on any high point overlooking the flood plains and watch a daily procession of tens and hundreds of dark, thirsty elephants streaming down to the water's edge. They drink from the bank, dipping their trunks into the clear swamp-filtered water, or wade eagerly into the shallows. Drinking is often followed by showering and bathing, particularly if it is a hot day when the elephants spread out to feed along the flood plains or simply to stand, resting contemplatively, in the shade of some tall riverine tree.

However, this concentration of elephants, which has been building up steadily over the years, is increasingly disastrous for the riverine vegetation. The gallery-type forest which lined the banks of the Chobe was opened up and broken down. What Selous described as dense, almost impenetrable jungle has long since changed, and the signs of heavy use by elephants – the broken, coppiced, dead and dying trees – stretch many kilometres back into the hinterland of the Chobe National Park. The number of elephants has risen not only through natural increase, but also from their being gradually compressed into the sanctuary by increasing human populations in Botswana and neighbouring Caprivi and Zimbabwe.

The only short-term solution which will allow the riverine zone to recover is to cull the elephants. This is a course of action which the Botswana authorities have not been inclined to take, in keeping with their policy of minimum interference in the system. The most likely outcome of their no-culling policy is that the elephants will continue to increase until the food resource is depleted to such an extent that the population is vulnerable during severe drought. Under such circumstances, it is likely that thousands of elephants will die and the vegetation will then be accorded a respite. This is a probable scenario for the future, and in the light of what is known of elephant population dynamics, the same cycle probably occurred in the past as well. For the moment the Chobe/Linyanti area is still a paradise, but to the trained eye it is a looming elephant tragedy.

The Linyanti Swamp is a sea of reed beds, papyrus (*Cyperus papyrus*) groves, islands, crystal-clear open lagoons dotted with lily pads and aquatic meadows of hippo grass (*Vossia cuspidata*). Narrow winding channels cut through the papyrus beds and carry the water to flood plains where elephants graze unconcerned and thousands of red lechwe splash like dancers through the shallows. The islands vary in size, but most are small, fringed by dense riparian forest and tall makololo palms (*Hyphaene petersiana*) whose fronds are chewed to fibre by elephants, and then spat out. The centres of the islands are usually open short grassland, sometimes with large, whitish termite mounds which are the favoured resting place of the secretive shaggy-haired sitatunga.

This almost aquatic antelope, a small relative of the kudu, has elongated, splayed hooves, enabling it to move across reed beds and mud flats where its dryland cousins would quickly be bogged down. It can also swim, but in deep water its greatest enemy, the Nile crocodile, lies in wait.

Sometimes huge clumps of papyrus move with the flood, lifted by the rising water, and float downstream forming a mass dense enough to block the channels. During dry years the papyrus blockages may dry out, and are sometimes burnt, to open the channels once more. Elephants, hippopotamus and buffalo tramp and open paths through the papyrus and reeds to keep open narrow channels which are then in turn used by the swamp people, the baYei, poling skilfully in their dugout canoes or mekoros.

Many species of birds occupy the varied habitats in the swamps and along the river. Fish-eaters are plentiful, and the distinctive ringing call of the African fish eagle is a constant feature of the Chobe River. Deeper in

The red lechwe of the Okavango, Linyanti and Chobe flood plains is one of four lechwe types found in Africa.

the swamps, where small islands form patches of forest dominated by the motsodi tree (*Garcinia livingstonei*), lives one of the rarest and strangest of Africa's birds, the elusive Pel's fishing owl. This large bird is active at night, swooping down to the water and grabbing fish from near the surface with its talons. Its lifestyle is, therefore, similar to that of the fish eagle, but it is hidden under the

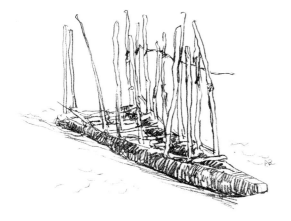

At Kachikau, an ox-drawn sledge, fashioned from a forked tree, provides an easily maintained form of transport.

cloak of darkness when the eagles roost. Generally fishing owls are confined to the quiet backwaters rather than the open lagoons and river. At night, and in the still hours before dawn, the hooting duets of fishing owl pairs float across the swamps, eerie and mysterious. In the classic field guide *Roberts Birds of South Africa*, the call is described somewhat poetically, but accurately as '. . . a weird screechy howl, which rises in a nerve-shattering crescendo, to peter out like a cry of a lost soul falling into a bottomless pit'.

As the Chobe draws away from the swamp country of Linyanti and Lake Liambezi, it becomes a classical river. Wide flood plains are characteristic of the northern (Caprivi) bank, while in places there are steep banks on the south, alternating with narrower flood plains. The puku antelope is at home on the grassy flood plains, sharing this habitat with its close relatives, the red lechwe and waterbuck. Buffalo, impala, zebra and thousands of elephants also concentrate on the flood

Comfort and luxury in the wilderness: the Chobe Game Lodge provides visitors with every facility for a memorable stay.

plain grasslands during the dry season. Egyptian geese clatter along the flood plains and waterways, and jacana diligently inspect lily pads and water weeds in quiet creeks. On the Pookoo Flats, so named by the hunter-naturalist Selous, who described the Chobe River as an earthly paradise when he visited it in 1874, are gently sloping banks and hummocks where enormous colonies of brilliant carmine bee-eaters excavate their nest holes. When the birds are breeding, from September to October, the colonies are a flutter and buzz of activity. Birds are constantly hovering and twittering, bringing food for the young and then flashing away – carmine and turquoise jewels, long-tailed, elegant.

The abundant water ensures a dense growth of shrubbery and tall trees along the raised southern banks of the river. This narrow strip of riverine forest is the home of the chestnut Chobe bushbuck which is gaily marked with striking white spots and stripes. In the past this riverine strip was also occupied by the beautiful green and red Narina trogon. This typical bird of the evergreen forest was named by the gallant French naturalist Francois le Vaillant for the enchanting Khoi-Khoi maiden, Nerina. But the trogon has almost disappeared from this forest strip and the bushbuck too has declined because of the intense and unremitting seasonal utilization of this habitat by the Chobe elephants.

The wildlife authorities in Botswana have encouraged research into the elephant problems of Chobe and much useful data has already been accumulated. It has been found that the park supports two distinct elephant populations, one centred on the Chobe River in the north of the park and one on the

123

The design of the dugout canoe, carved from a single log, is much the same throughout Africa.

Linyanti area to the south-west, the two being separated by the settlements in the Kachikau enclave between Ngoma and Linyanti where the park boundary sweeps well away from the river. The elephants show a distinctive pattern of seasonal movements, with dry-season concentrations along the Chobe and Linyanti, and when there is water, also at the Savuti Marsh and Ngwezumba River to the south. When the rains come and small pans are filled in the hinterland, the elephants rapidly disperse away from the rivers. In October 1983, there were 900 elephants grazing within a kilometre of the Chobe Game Lodge, a luxurious hospice in the wild, but after one night of heavy rain the elephants were gone. This ensures a fairly rotational usage of plant communities. As in other elephant ranges there are also clearly defined breeding herd areas, and bull ranges, such as those around the park headquarters at Kasane.

Elephants marked with coloured neckbands have yielded some interesting data on the distances over which they move. Breeding herds from Chobe move about 70 kilometres towards Mababe and herds from the Linyanti population travel up to 50 kilometres south across the Savuti Channel towards the Khwai River. Marked bulls from Chobe have moved as much as 150 kilometres to the south, and 90 kilometres west deep into Caprivi. These long-distance movements of bulls ensure genetic exchange within and between populations and so prevent inbreeding. In addition to the elephants which migrate away from the Chobe River, there is a small resident population which does not move more than 20 kilometres.

The vegetation of the northern half of the Chobe National Park dominated by teak woodlands appears far more lush than the scant 500 millimetres of annual rainfall would suggest. The teak grows on loose, deep Kalahari sand on slightly undulating country, with shallow drainage lines. The Chobe area also supports *Brachystegia boehmii*, a tree confirming that this is a southern extension of the vast miombo woodlands of Central Africa. It brings roan and sable antelope and other typical miombo animals to almost within range of desert animals, such as gemsbok and springbok.

Even though the Chobe River flows through one of the most remote stretches of country in Southern Africa, it has not escaped the scourge of alien plants which are invading and displacing indigenous vegetation everywhere. The South American water fern *Salvinia molesta* is spreading up the Chobe from the Zambezi, creating dense mats of vegetation on the surface of the water. In one recent tragic incident a herd of buffalo feeding on the north bank of the Chobe was startled by rifle fire from Caprivian hunters. The animals fled for the safety of the park, galloping across the short green grass of the flood plain. The herd plunged into the river in a section which was choked by *Salvinia*. The leading animals broke through the weed mat, floundering helplessly, unable to move on top of the choking layer of weeds, unable to swim, unable to turn back. From behind, the rest of the herd kept pressing forward, trampling those ahead, struggling across the backs of the tightly packed drowning animals. Bellowing and splashing, the herd surged and pressed forward. Most of the buffalo got across, but more than 80 drowned.

The Chobe game reserve was proclaimed only in 1961; before that the area had been sporadically settled by pastoralists and used as a major cattle grazing area on the traditional stock route north to Zambia. For a time, also, the teak woodlands were exploited and even supported a sawmill where the Serondela camping ground is located today. Cattle could use the area only in the absence of the tsetse fly, and the boundary between fly country and cattle country seems to have moved backwards and forwards over the past century. The historical record indicates much of the Chobe area was open grassland when Livingstone passed through it. The cattle grazers moved in and, with the combined impact of their over-grazing and early burning, they caused vegetation changes over large areas. As the grass was wiped out, woody scrub encroached. Its dominant species, the Kalahari Christmas tree (*Dichrostachys cinerea*) which has colourful purple and yellow flowering spikes, was ideal habitat for the tsetse fly. Nagana and human sleeping sickness, two dreaded diseases spread by this insect, then caused the people and their cattle to move, and as they degraded new areas, the tsetse followed. There have also, however, been natural declines in the tsetse fly zones, brought about perhaps by fluctuations in the numbers of game animals upon which the flies depend for food. The great rinderpest epidemic, which swept through Africa between 1894 and 1896, killing most of the game, also contributed to the decline of the tsetse.

This ebb and flow of animal populations, plant communities and tsetse flies has been going on for millennia. However, cattle and people have been a part of the equation for only little more than 200 years. Before then the fluctuations and permutations of the system would have been due entirely to natural processes like drought, flood, fire and animal populations.

The Chobe National Park is, unlike most other conservation areas in Southern Africa, still relatively undisturbed by the actions of wildlife managers, although the effects of settlements and early burning by foresters are evident everywhere. However, this situation is unlikely to last very much longer. One of the suggested strategies for relaxing the intensive dry-season pressure on the riverine areas is to put down a series of boreholes and drinking troughs a few kilometres away from the river. This might keep a portion of the elephant population away from the Chobe,

The southern white rhino was hunted nearly to extinction. From the survivors in the Umfolozi Game Reserve of Natal, animals were reintroduced to Chobe.

but ultimately these animals will also hammer the eastern woodlands into oblivion, causing even greater disturbance to the system. It might, therefore, be just as well to leave the park alone, if culling is not an option to be considered, because the elephant population will then crash more quickly and a new state of affairs, less damaging to the rest of the park and its wildlife, will assert itself. The loss of thousands of Chobe elephants will be sad, but no sadder than the loss of trees and trogons.

125

Elephants by tens and scores . . . herd upon herd of dusty grey elephant cows, youngsters and calves, solitary bulls and groups of bulls, all plodding through an endless dusty wilderness of mopane (*Colophospermum mopane*) woodlands. Elephants and space are the abiding images of northern Botswana and bull elephants are the undisputed lords of Savuti.

Cutting into the south-western quadrant of the Chobe National Park is a meandering, narrow channel which starts at the Linyanti Swamp, on the border of the Caprivi. It winds away in a south-easterly direction, twisting, turning, doubling back as though uncertain of its course until it reaches the isolated rock piles of the Gubatsa Hills. Then it becomes a confident channel, striking south to lose itself in the Mababe Depression, the bed of a long dead lake.

The Savuti Channel knew times of feast when it served as the watering place for thousands of animals, and times of famine when it dried up, save for a few small pools or seeps where thirsty animals fought for water. When David Livingstone crossed it in 1849, the Savuti was flowing strongly, but 30 years later, when the great hunter Selous reached the area in search of ivory the channel was dry. It remained so until 1957. After heavy rain and floods on the Linyanti, the channel carried water again, bringing life and death in its wake – life for the game populations which soon built up as the Savuti became a perennial water source, and death for the tall camelthorn (*Acacia erioloba*) trees which had grown up in the channel during the long years without water. Some of these giants had a girth of as much as 260 centimetres, but unable to live in water, they died, and

SAVUTI

BOTSWANA

(Above) *Wild dogs are highly social; they live and hunt in closely co-ordinated packs and are seldom found alone.*
(Right) *Dramas are constantly played out at waterholes during the dry season, as life for many species revolves around diminishing sources of moisture.*
(Gubatsa Seep, Savuti, Chobe National Park, Botswana)

Old buffalo bulls sometimes break the tips of their horns, which are then gradually worn smooth.

their gaunt skeletons stand today as mute and stark testimony of the ever-changing nature of a natural system.

In recent years the Savuti flowed all year long to Mababe and created a rich wetland known as the Savuti Marsh. During the 1982-83 drought, when the channel dried up again, the marsh slowly disappeared, its water evaporated, and tsessebe kicked up dust where soft-plumaged red-billed teal had once risen in flocks from the sparkling water. This drought ravaged the southern hemisphere. In Peru the perfidious wind of El Nino was blamed, but in the summer rainfall regions of Southern Africa the drought fitted a clearly predictable cyclic variation in rainfall.

At the end of the 1983 dry season Paul and I teamed up with our friend Clive Walker on a safari to northern Botswana. We stayed with Lloyd Wilmot, who has a bush camp on the channel near the Gubatsa Hills. We had all visited Savuti before, on many occasions. Where we had known water we now saw dry, white sand. Elephants dug deep holes in the sandy bed of the channel in search of water. But even these bulldozers of the wild could not provide for the many other animals which had concentrated in the area, and then either died or moved on.

Scattered along the channel were a few small seeps where a little precious water still oozed from under the deep sand. These seeps were the centres of life and activity for the remaining wildlife of the Gubatsa area. At one seep near our camp a slow flow of water barely succeeded in keeping the mud moist. All day, every day, thirsty elephant bulls crowded into the mudhole, sucking up the surface layer of water as it formed. Around the seep, where the ground had been trampled flat and hard by thousands of feet, the elephants dug drinking holes. From these they could extract water, slowly and carefully. They inserted thirsty trunks into the holes, waited for the slow seepage to fill these reservoirs, and then sucked it up, perhaps no more than a litre at a time, squirting the precious liquid down their throats. These drinking holes were large enough for only one animal at a time. So, as elephant society dictates, the dominant bulls had their fill while subordinates, the younger, smaller and weaker bulls, patiently waited their turn, or waded into the mud.

Cowering in the mud, usually close up against a bank, was a sub-adult hippo. Grateful to have a wallow where he could at least stay partly wet, he lay still, moving only when an elephant was about to step on him, or threatened him. The hippo's predicament was a sad one, yet he was far better off than the herd of 26 hippo further up the channel to the west of Gubatsa. There, a pool had been reduced to a tiny saucer-shaped depression, no more than three metres across and about 50 centimetres deep. When chased out by thirsty elephants, the hippos stood, dejected, packed together in the sparse shade of tall, leafless marula (*Sclerocarya caffra*) trees, waiting for dusk to bring relief from the burning sun.

Day after day we returned to the seep. Lloyd's bush-green Land Rover did not dis-

128

turb the elephants at all. We parked only a few yards from the elephants, revelling in being so close to such magnificent creatures. We stayed through the days and well into the cool moonlit nights, and the Savuti elephant bulls were always there. As one or two left, their places would be eagerly taken by others who had trekked many miles to this tiny, ungenerous oasis. Moving through the parched woodlands with the flowing grace of elephants, dusty ears flapping and heads bobbing rhythmically, they came pacing across the hot sand.

For those denied a drinking hole there was the consolation of a moist and cooling muddy shower. Usually the elephant bulls observed the hierarchical system, but not always, especially when strangers, drawn to this, the only source of moisture for many miles, came hurrying down the sloping banks of the channel. They would sum up the bulls at the water points as they drew near, either stopping cautiously, or sailing straight into the attack with a deep bellowing roar. Huge heads lunged forward in a frenzy of thirst to stab at an opponent with superb fighting teeth. Trunks entwined momentarily, rough, mud- and dust-covered skin rasping audibly. Heavy bodies met with a solid thud, feet scuffed the ground, raising white and grey dust in billowing clouds as the bulls pushed against each other. Occasionally the tip of a tusk snapped off on impact with a rifle-sharp crack and arched through the air like a white-hot tracer shell. Every few days we found pieces of ivory lying near the waterholes, sometimes with ominous splashes of darkening red blood as proof of the desperate fights.

The breeding herds did not linger at these unprofitable places. They set off westwards to the water of the Linyanti Swamp, or south to the Khwai River and Moremi on the fringes of the Okavango. The upper reaches of the Savuti Channel, west of the park boundary, also held water which lasted throughout the drought. The herds were attracted not only by the crystal clear water, but also by the belt of lush vegetation lining the channel. This riverine strip was in sharp contrast with the grey, dry country surrounding it. Grass grew green along the banks and on the narrow flood plains where the channel twisted and turned. Water birds were abundant and elegant saddlebill storks marched sedately through the shallows. Even red lechwe, which are swamp and flood plain animals, were found along the upper Savuti. Hippo rafted lazily in the cool water, unaware of the fate of others of their kind further down the channel.

At the Gubatsa seep a resident pride of 19 lions, buffalo killers, had to wait for only a few hours for their next meal. Hard times for herbivores are times of plenty for flesh-eaters. The buffalo, weakened by the shortage of grazing and water, were easier prey than usual. Driven by thirst they would advance into the mud hole *en masse* while the lions lay in full view, no more than a few paces away. On one occasion a young male of the pride stalked across the open ground. But the buffalo knew that there was safety in numbers and that their scythe-like horns could disembowel a lion, so two of them charged defensively at the lion, which jumped up and bounded away, proof that if the buffalo kept together they would be safe. Alone, they stood little chance against the lions.

Though they forage on the ground most of the day, baboons retire to the tallest trees at sunset.

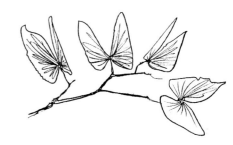

Shaped like an exotic butterfly, the double leaves of the mopane tree (Colophospermum mopane) are emerald green in the early summer.

Tsessebe, the southern representative of the topi, tiang and korrigum group, are the fleetest of antelopes. 129

The graceful impala is the most abundant antelope of the southern savanna, and the staple food of the larger carnivores.

The elephant bulls at the seep were intolerant of other animals when they were thirsty, charging even at lions and hyaenas. The chase, with ears spread and trunk flailing, usually ended with a roar to speed the fleeing carnivore on its way, unharmed. Only occasionally do elephants kill other animals when competition for water is desperate. Only when the lordly elephants had quenched their thirst, or driven by the pangs of hunger, had left the seep to feed, did the other animals venture down to the water. At dawn and at sunset the seeps were a magnet for birds. Turtle doves flocked there by the hundreds, landing, strutting, cooing, drinking, and then winging away in an hour-long stream of grey and white bodies.

The Savuti area, like most of Botswana, lies on Kalahari sand which ensures that there is virtually no surface run-off rainwater – it sinks away almost immediately. Pools or pans are formed only where there is clay and firmer soil or rock. The vegetation consists of mostly open tree savanna with camelthorn, leadwood (*Combretum imberbe*), silverleaf (*Terminalia sericea*) and the ubiquitous mopane dominating the scene. On sand ridges, the remnants of old dune systems, there is a sparser grass cover than in the valleys between. North of the channel there is generally more stunted mopane, with taller trees around the bare patches where pans are formed. The woodland grasses are generally wiry and tough, like *Aristida uniplumis, Schmidtia bulbosa* and *Eragrostis rigidior.* They are able to withstand the desiccating droughts of this arid area where rainfall seldom exceeds 500 millimetres per annum.

The bed of the Mababe Depression, when dry, is covered by a rich growth of grassland dominated by *Cenchrus ciliaris* and *Chloris gayana*, both excellent feed. The lowerlying heavier soils where water accumulates during the rains support tall *Sorghum* and *Cymbopogon* grasses. When the Savuti flows, or when the Ngwezumba River from the north-east floods, the grassland is transformed into a large sheet of shallow water which fosters an abundant growth of water plants and reeds. Around the edges of the marsh, above the flood levels, are scattered flat-topped, crooked-stemmed *Acacia tortilis* trees, and grey termite mounds – the quintessential image of the great plains of Africa.

Fire, ever a feature of the African savanna, regularly sweeps across large parts of Botswana, providing that the grass has built up sufficient material to provide fuel. When dry-season fires are followed by rain, the grass sprouts and grows again with vigour, sustained by nutrient reserves stored in its roots.

This flush forms a bright green sward for a few weeks which in the Savuti area attracts zebra, wildebeest, tsessebe and other grazers by the thousand.

In this arid country the rains determine whether there is an abundance of food, or a shortage. The major grazers like zebras, buffalo and wildebeest are, therefore, migratory. They concentrate at the dwindling water as the dry season advances. When the spring rains break, usually in the second half of October, they migrate in herds of hundreds to the north-east to feed on the new green pastures for a few short months where rain-filled pans provide abundant water. When the pans dry out, becoming mud and then dust, the animals retreat once again, westwards to Savuti and the Linyanti, or south to the Khwai and Okavango.

Those animals, like the giraffe and kudu, which seem to live without water if they must, make the best of the dry times and hope to survive until it rains again. Crocodiles generally retreat with the water, but three crept into small caves at Gubatsa when the channel dried up, lying immobile and torpid in the shadowy depths, as though hibernating, waiting for the water to rouse them from their state of almost permanent sleep.

The thunderclouds which build up every October afternoon lend an oppressive air to the scene. But, when the rains break, the hardships are forgotten. After the first rains, when every pan and depression contains water, the seeps are abandoned overnight; the trampled bare ground is left to rest, and be covered once again by grass, until it is exposed again during the next dry season. The relief of the first rain is almost tangible. The somnolent lions become frisky and energetic, though wet and bedraggled. The herds of zebra start moving off within a day. From deep below the ground, winged termites or flying ants come pouring to the surface to leave the colony and fly off to be eaten, to die, or to found new colonies. So abundant are the termites that many birds including red-billed hornbills, drongos, buffalo weavers, white storks and tawny eagles perch on the ground near the colonies, eating them as fast as they emerge. Even the African fish eagles, whose savage talons can so effortlessly pluck a rising fish from the surface of the Linyanti, move out to feast on termites.

Whereas the Savuti Marsh comes alive only when the channel flows, the Okavango is permanent and has an annual flood. The water is brought down the Okavango River from the highlands of Angola. The flood enters the delta and slowly moves through a complex web of swamps, lagoons, papyrus and reed beds until it reaches the Thamalakane and Khwai rivers. The Khwai takes water eastwards to Moremi, where elephants and thousands of other animals from the Savuti and Mababe areas concentrate during the dry season.

The future of this system, which is so important for Savuti, depends on people and

Never at ease in each other's company, elephants readily chase lions, especially if there are young calves nearby.

the tsetse fly. While the country between the Savuti and Okavango is empty of people, as it is at present because of the tsetse, the game can migrate freely. But if the tsetse is cleared from along the Khwai – and aerial spraying of endosulfan, an insecticide, indicates that this is now likely – then people and cattle could be settled there and throughout the Okavango. The game migrations will almost certainly then be disrupted. A new Savuti system will have to develop, and something of the glory of Savuti as we have known it for the past two decades may then belong to history.

Paul Bosman

ETOSHA
NATIONAL
PARK

NAMIBIA

(Above) *Adapted to desert life, gemsbok usually derive sufficient moisture from their food, but in Etosha they drink regularly at fountains and waterholes.*
(Left) *Elephants drink and shower at the small perennial fountains that are scattered around the edge of the vast Etosha Pan.*
(Okondeka, Etosha National Park, Namibia)

The Etosha National Park is one of the largest in Africa, covering 22 270 km². It lies in the pre-Namib, the slightly more hospitable country to the east of the barren Namib desert. It is an arid land. The rainfall, of between 250 and 500 millimetres, is erratic, but it usually arrives in the late summer, turning the land green. But to appreciate it fully, one must see Etosha during the dry season. The light is hard in the dry atmosphere, and the glare from the vast saline Etosha Pan, makes the eyes ache. When the wind blows across the baking surface of the pan, huge dust clouds are raised, blotting out the sun and hanging a grey pall in the sky.

An artist must experience the ambience of Etosha before painting it. It is only by silently watching the daily events around a waterhole, touching the hot, white surface of the pan, eyes screwed up against the glare, or listening to the distant rolling thunder of a lion's roar that one can sense the essence of Etosha.

And so Paul and I spent our time watching and waiting at waterholes like Ombika and Okondeka, becoming attuned to the rhythm of this great game reserve. At Ombika an artesian fountain delivers a constant flow of water into a small pool at the edge of a large limestone outcrop. Whitened rocks and rubble lie scattered around in a clearing up to 100 metres across and the thirsty animals carefully pick their way across the glaring calcrete to the water's edge. The dusty grey elephants of this parched land gather in the heat of the day to drink and shower, and here we passed many hours with them.

Small herds of elephants trooping through the sere bush regularly appeared on the edge of the clearing. The closeness of the water

133

Ungainly looking on the ground, the greater flamingo is a picture of grace in the air, its long neck and legs outstretched and its sedately beating wings flashing crimson and black.

The communal nest mass of the sociable weaver is added to and renovated all year round, so that nest chambers are available whenever conditions are suitable for breeding.

would set off a hurried, roaring, bunched stampede. Not for elephants the cautious, tail-flicking, sense-straining approach of the black-faced impala or greater kudu. No lion lies in wait for them. The elephants arrive and take command. Other animals are wary of them and stand aside, or approach carefully, but confidently, as they know that the elephants would quickly detect any lions and the matriarchs would see them off.

There is much jostling and bustling among the elephants at the edge of the water and, if the pool is large enough, they simply wade in, drinking as they go. Shallow pools offer a shower and a roll in the wetness, but it is in deep pools, such as the beautiful fountain at Goas, that elephants can bathe, play and splash like contented whales. Large-bodied animals, such as elephants need to keep cool, hence their love of shady places. If they cannot cool off by immersing themselves in water, they rely on the cooling mechanism built into their enormous ears, which have tissue-thin skin and large blood vessels. They create a cooling effect by flapping their ears. When the ears are wet from a shower or bathe, the cooling is enhanced by evaporation which dissipates heat from the surface of the ear, thus cooling the underlying blood. The greater the need to lose heat, the faster the ears are moved.

The scenes at the waterholes of Etosha are a constant kaleidoscope of colour and action. Young elephants playfully chase giraffe or gemsbok away. There are constant swarms of red-billed quelea, coming, going, settling and moving amoeba-like from the water to low bushes nearby – these small finches gather in flocks of thousands, which at times float across the veld like swarms of locusts. The high-stepping graceful gompou or Kori bustard struts around and a pair of blacksmith plovers fret and scold as animals approach too closely to the nest. As the sun sets in a murky sky – a brilliant orb through the haze – flights of double-banded sandgrouse come winging in to drink and collect water on their breast feathers which is then transported over many dusty miles to their patiently waiting chicks.

At a time beyond mankind's knowing the rainfall of northern Namibia was higher than it is today. The rivers of the Ovamboland plain poured a constant stream of water into a large, shallow lake. The vegetation of the area most probably resembled that of the Okavango delta of Botswana today. Papyrus and reed beds fringed the shallows, *Hyphaene* palms and scattered clumps of thicket studded the grasslands. Further away tall mopane woodland blanketed the plains on the clay soils to the south of the lake, to the west and east the deep sandy soils were dotted by patches of dry forest set in *Combretum* woodlands. The plains around the lake were the home of a wide array of game – and lord of all was the elephant.

Then the climate changed – as it has over the entire continent at different times – and the rainfall declined. The rivers carried less water, and then only during the short wet season. Slowly the lake shrank, and the plant communities were replaced by those adapted to drier conditions. When evaporation from the lake's surface exceeded the input of water from the rivers, the lake died. The salts, leached out of the soil over the ages and collected in the lake, were concentrated as the water evaporated, leaving a salty bed of silt on which virtually no plant life could grow. It became a vast, wind-blown dusty salt pan, a desert covering nearly 6 000 km², later known as Etosha – 'the place of dry water' – to the San hunters who wandered there.

Today, the absolutely flat, barren surface of the pan sometimes has a sparse cover of *Sporobolus tenellus* grass following good rains. The low country surrounding the pan, which is the major habitat of the wildebeest, is covered by short, coarse grasses. Scattered small shrubs are browsed by springbok, and low thorn thickets are sought after by lions for the shade they provide and cover from which to hunt. Most of the park is covered by woodland and savanna about four metres high in which the mopane tree (*Colophospermum mopane*) is most common. Other trees like *Combretum, Commiphora* and *Acacia* also occur in patches and as scattered individuals. The wispy perennial grasses, whitened in the dry season, are emerald-green and lush in the summer with the occasional brilliance of a flame lily (*Gloriosa superba*) to give a splash of blood-red colour.

In the extreme west of the park, around Otjovasandu, the flat dreary plains are broken by weathered granite outcrops, reminiscent of Kaokoland. The watercourses are distinct channels with sandy washed beds, lined by ana or winterthorn trees (*Acacia albida*) and giant leadwoods (*Combretum imberbe*). To the north-east, near the historic German fort of Namutoni where a stirring battle was fought in 1904, the broken and stony ground supports a dense tall thicket of tambotie (*Spirostachys africana*). This tree is poisonous to humans, and its smoke can contaminate food cooked over it. The dense shrub layer of these thickets, interspersed with open glades, is home of the Damara dik-dik. This tiny antelope has a large nose with an inflatable proboscis which is extended when it calls in high-pitched quavering notes. The dik-dik live in pairs on a territory which they mark by secretions from their prominent facial glands, warning other dik-diks that their patch of thicket is occupied.

On the edge of the plains large camelthorns (*Acacia erioloba*) betray the links of this country with the Kalahari desert, true home of this tree. The camelthorns are the preferred nesting site of sociable weavers.

The bat-eared fox forages with head lowered and ears cocked forward to listen for sounds made by termites and other insects upon which it feeds.

These small seed-eating birds build colossal communal nests to which they return year after year, renovating them, adding to them, and raising their chicks in the relative safety of numbers. These nests can spread over as much as nine square metres and occupy most of a large tree. Some have been occupied regularly for 50 years or more and many last as long as the tree can carry the weight. In time the tree completes its life and dies. The branches dry out quickly in the heat and break, destroying the nest. The colony moves elsewhere and builds again, labouring with bee-like persistence, each generation leaving a home for the next.

As the rainfall declined and the plains dried

135

Moving cautiously in the moonlight, a black rhino arrives at Ombika waterhole. After drinking, it will leave as silently as it came, along the same well-used path, and melt into the night.

out, an arid corridor was formed which extended from the south-west edge of the continent right across to the Horn of Africa on the shores of the Red Sea. The increasing aridity slowly changed the spectrum of mammals and birds, and only those which adapted to arid conditions occupied the expanding sub-desert. Species such as gemsbok, dik-dik, aardwolf and springbok took over the land from sitatunga, lechwe and waterbuck. When the climate changed again and rainfall increased, though not to its former levels, the arid belt across the continent was breached in Central Africa, but the extremities, Namibia and Somalia, remained as semi-desert and arid shrubland with the closely related arid zone fauna which they have today.

Through all the changes, through the wet periods of thousands of years and through the equally long periods of drought and desiccation, the elephant remained, adapting its feeding habits to the changing world around it, swinging from a species which fed, belly-deep in the lush green swamplands to one which trooped for dusty miles through the parched yellow grasslands taking its fill from the leaf and bark of stunted mopane trees, the bright yellow flowers of the *Acacia*, the sere sun-bleached grasses and succulent roots dug up from beneath the soil.

The Etosha elephants entered the twentieth century with an enormous range. During the dry season they concentrated near the fountains and waterholes that are scattered around the pan. When the rains broke over the dusty veld, the elephants moved further afield, making use of the rejuvenated veld as it burst into bloom and new leaf. This pattern of movement took animals from the western parts of Etosha to the edge of the Kaokoveld and from the east to the heart of Kavango.

Other species, such as wildebeest and zebra, followed by nomadic prides of lions, also migrated in their thousands with the changing seasons. From Andoni in the north-east the wildebeest herds would move along the southern edge of the pan as far as Okaukuejo and even further to the west. The green of summer would find them on the Grootvlakte, near the spectacular 'sprokieswoud' or fantasy forest of *Moringa ovalifolia* trees all twisted, bloated and gnarled like miniature baobabs. The dry season would move them back to the east, to the better-watered areas.

When good rains fall, the ancient lake is reconstituted, fleetingly and only as a poor reflection of what it once was. The flood water comes from Angola. Rushing southwards down the course of the Kuvelai River it fills Lake Oponono and then moves down the ancient, long dry river channels, such as the Ekuma and Oshigambo to Etosha. With the water comes life. Fish and tiny creatures are swept along to repopulate the pan. In the briny, warm waters, the blue-green algae multiply, sufficient to sustain gatherings of up to a million greater flamingoes. The fish also attract white pelicans by the thousands. But the short-lived lake is not as bountiful as its predecessors. As it dries up at the end of the rains, the pelicans must undertake a return journey of 200 kilometres every second day to feed in the higher reaches of the Ekuma River and in Lake Oponono and then wing back to the breeding colonies to feed their voracious chicks. The flamingoes build their strange mound-like nests of mud and lay their eggs on top of them. As the waters dry up the chicks are gathered together in large nurseries and start to walk across the dried and cracked surface of the pan, travelling about 80 kilometres to the north-west like some croaking, chattering organism with a life of its own. The parents also fly great distances to feed in the shallows of the receding waters and then back to the nursery to pick out their chick from among thousands of others, all looking exactly alike, fluffy grey brown bundles of down standing on long dark legs. No parent makes a mistake and probably finds its chick by recognizing its voice.

Modern man – the modifier and destroyer of Africa's age-old rhythms – has also touched this system. The Ovambo cultivators pressed down from the north and white colonists established cattle ranches to the south. Boreholes cut through the calcrete, and water for livestock was pumped to the surface. This was water which elephants could also use, and so the conflict began.

The elephants were left with only a small part of their original range, the area demarcated as a game reserve by the German colonial government in 1907, part of which was the Etosha National Park. Other animals, such as wildebeest competed with livestock for food and water and could transmit diseases to the growing cattle population. Thus came the game fences. But elephants broke through these fences at will. Peter Stark and other Etosha rangers earned their spurs chasing elephants back into the park on horseback – a hazardous, exciting and ultimately futile occupation. Eventually the most critical areas of the fence were reinforced and made elephant-proof.

The elephant population, which had ranged over wide areas, was more or less confined to the park. Boreholes and windmills made the park habitable in the dry season for the elephants. The population increased and by 1979 there were nearly 2 000 resident elephants. The vegetation, adapted over the ages to low-intensity utilization was now subject to year-round feeding. Branches broken off a tree by an elephant are no cause for concern if the tree has time to repair the damage, but when the elephants are eating up the trees faster than they can grow, then some biologists and park managers perceive a problem.

It is not inherently wrong that elephants destroy trees – they do this all the time to

some extent. But when they change the structure of the vegetation and affect the habitability of the area for other species, the park system is altered from one state of being to another. When woodland is converted to scrubland, and scrubland becomes open grassland, then the character and atmosphere of a park can be dramatically changed. When the changes become unacceptable there is usually only one solution, cull the herds. For park managers this is a difficult decision, based on vaguely defined aesthetic values, no more perhaps than a picture of what we want a park to look like. But that decision has now been reached in Etosha and the population will be closely controlled in the future.

Fortunately, there is a balance. Elephants can be maintained in some harmony with other species, such as black rhino, which are vulnerable to the habitat change wrought by the elephants. If the guardians of Etosha maintain this balance, we can be sure that places such as Ombika will always be a magnet for both elephants and people.

Ombika waterhole in the moonlight is a rare experience. We once spent a night there with the park's wildlife veterinarian, Ian Hofmeyr, doing one of his regular black rhino counts to monitor the progress of translocated animals. The rhinos emerged into the clearing around the waterhole, like actors onto a silvery stage, alone – as is their cus-

Diminutive Damara dik-dik live in pairs in the thicketed country of northern Namibia. Their nearest relatives are found in Tanzania, 2 000 kilometres away.

tom – or, occasionally, a cow and calf together. They were usually suspicious, staring intently into the gloom through myopic eyes, ears cocked alertly, nostrils flared as they sought the scent which could tell them whether or not all was well. If disturbed, they would give a loud snort and dance around in agitation with an alarmed tail curled up over their backs. But if the wind was right and the observers still, they soon settled down, then walked slowly to the pool to quench their thirst. These rhinos, and the sight of a herd of elephants moving out across the moonlit calcrete, in single file, pale and silent as a troop of ghosts, are African memories to treasure.

The Benguela Current runs cold and deep – it comes from the southern end of the world, from the icy silence of Antarctica. The cold water wells up along the south-western coast of Africa creating a climate where it seldom rains. The coast of Namibia washed by this frigid current is barren, dry and dangerous, littered by shipwrecks, feared by mariners and known as the Skeleton Coast. Along this forbidding shore lies the oldest desert in the world – the Namib. Many strange creatures penetrate these desert wastes; but the most unexpected of all are the stately desert elephants of Kaokoland.

Along the western flank of Namibia, between the Cunene River which forms the border with Angola, and the Hoanib River to the south, lies the wilderness of western Kaokoland – a world of sand, gravel plains and dust, where the last 30 members of a once numerous population of elephants still roam. South of the Hoanib the gravel plains give way to a purple tinged landscape, even more rugged and harsh. Here amongst shattered and broken rock, isolated hills and flat-topped mountains – the lunar world of western Damaraland – another small population of about 40 elephants survives, scattered in small groups across the land.

These two regions together are known as the Kaokoveld. The elephants that live in this unforgiving country are true desert elephants and though not a separate race have adapted to their hostile environment. The elephant bulls of these areas and adjoining ranges are generally taller than others. The average shoulder height of big bulls in Etosha is 3,5 metres and record animals from southern Angola of 4,01 metres and 3,82 metres are known. Their ivory does not, however,

THE KAOKOVELD

NAMIBIA

(Above) *The handsome springbok is the only true gazelle in southern Africa. They congregate in herds of thousands, and where not enclosed by fences still migrate over great distances.*
(Right) *The tall desert elephants of the Kaokoveld wander across shifting sand dunes and stark gravel plains where the only sustenance is a living fossil – the strange* Welwitschia mirabilis.
(Hoanib area, Skeleton Coast Park, Namibia)

match their height and these bulls are usually characterized by short, thick, upturned and often broken tusks.

Food resources are thinly spread in the desert and the elephants must trek over great distances to get to the valleys where some stunted mopane (*Colophospermum mopane*) trees provide sustenance. The elephants' energy budget is critical, and in drought periods they are gaunt and thin, in poor condition. There is insufficient food for them to move from their feeding grounds to water and back again more than once every three or four days. The stress of trudging over the exposed plains under a burning desert sun also dictates that their journeys must largely be made at night. But when rain has fallen and there is food and water aplenty they drink daily, like elephants elsewhere, and indulge in a desert extravagance, a cooling shower or mud wallow.

The rivers of the arid Kaokoveld, such as the Hoanib, are born on the highlands – the western flank of the sub-continent – two hundred kilometres to the east. They wend their way down the escarpment, cutting through millions of years of rock, twisting and turning until they break free of the foothills and flow out across the gravel plains. Here their course is easy, almost relaxed, until the gentle meanders reach the coastal dunes which stretch uninterrupted to the central zone of the Namib, far to the south. In this sand desert the orange and yellow dunes, the highest on earth, curl and curve across the land, marching in parallel ranks. Across the mouth of the Kuiseb River, however, the gravel plains crowd them into a narrow coastal strip, seldom more than 30 kilometres wide. Here, the sand loses its rich

Despite heavy poaching, there is still a viable population of about 100 black rhino in the southern Kaokoveld. In the north only three remain.

tones and in Kaokoland, the northern reach of the Namib, it is pale grey to white.

Once every few years there is abundant rain in the hinterland and a flood of brown water rushes seawards. If strong, the flood breaches the dunes and breaks through to the Atlantic. More usually, however, the waters dam up between the dunes, forming short-lived lakes in the middle of the desert, which support a dense growth of tamarisk (*Tamarix usneoides*) trees and tall rank grasses such as sorghum (*Sorghum verticilliflorum*). After the flood the river bed, too, is green, and in this seeming paradox of luxuriant grass in the midst of a harsh desert the remnants of the western Kaokoland elephants still roam. Scarcely a decade ago they numbered 200, and are now whittled down by poaching to a scant thirty.

The deep silt of the river bed built up over aeons of time, is rich in minerals and nutrients washed down from the plateau, and deep below the dry sand and clay lies water. This water sustains trees – mopane, tall ana (*Acacia albida*), camelthorns (*A. erioloba*)

and leadwoods (*Combretum imberbe*) which reach into the desert on both banks of the river, seldom leaving its rich environs. The ana trees are in full leaf in the dry season when all others are bare and lifeless. When the short summer rains come, if they come at all, and life returns to the river, the mopane trees are in full foliage – their double-winged leaves like emerald butterflies. But the ana then loses its leaves and stands bare and wintry in the midst of summer greenery.

Away from the river beds, on the shallow gravel soils and barren hills, plants – many of them endemic – are more sparsely distributed. The plains are dotted with rounded yellow-green succulent *Euphorbia damarana* and the bleak and whitened stems of *Boscia albitrunca*. These plains are the only place on earth where one of the world's most ancient and primitive plant forms, *Welwitschia mirabilis*, still grows. This plant has a large underground stem, and only a small part of it appears above the ground. It produces only two thick, leathery, straplike leaves which grow from the base and die off at the apex throughout the life of the plant, which may be 2 000 years or more. The leaves are seldom more than three metres long and are torn and twisted by desert winds and occasionally also eaten by elephants.

Down the life-giving threads of greenery closer to the ground, made up of shrubs including *Salvadora persica*, *Salsola aphylla* and *Sueda plumosa*, move many small animals including the slender mongoose and the striped mouse which are found as far west as the sand dunes in the river bed – but not in the surrounding desert country.

To cope with a world in which trees and other food plants are scarce and widely dispersed, the desert elephants have learned to be frugal feeders, and by following and watching them one soon sees the necessity for their economy. Elephants in the lush tropics will demolish entire trees for no better reason than to get at a few leaves, but their desert counterparts seldom break down or push over trees. If they did, they would soon have nothing left to eat. Instead, every bit of greenery picked is eaten and we could scarcely find more than a few leaves trodden underfoot and wasted. To get to the more inaccessible food plants these elephants have become proficient rock climbers and they negotiate narrow ledges with dizzying drops of 150 metres or more to reach a single plant. As do elephants elsewhere they use the same paths when travelling, and in places the way is worn deeply and smoothly into the exposed rock surface – a sure sign that generations of elephants have wandered across these areas. Some gorges are so narrow that the rock walls on either side have been polished smooth by their passing bodies.

During one memorable visit to Damaraland, where rock shards and boulders often lie strewn across great plains, we sat no more than 20 metres away from feeding elephants, secure in the knowledge that they could not move faster than a slow shuffle across the rocks. For here they must pick their way, moving rocks aside with the gentle touch of a foot before settling their full weight. In so doing they have cleared paths which wind through otherwise formidable rock fields. Continual wear on the gravel and rock polishes the soles of the desert elephants' feet and from behind the smooth surfaces reflect light, flashing as the animals walk.

In the lower reaches of the Hoanib the desert crowds in on the river and here the elephants occasionally wander on the seashore and over the dunes where Paul and Clive Walker once followed them. Huge mounds of bare sand-blasted rock overlook the river bed. Among the iron-grey, acid brown rubble of the weathering boulders many species of herbs, some with delicate white flowers, bloom and live out their lives. Other plants like the succulent *Commiphora virgata* and *Aloe asperifolia* cling precariously to the bare rock, rootlets holding to every crack and fissure where water and dust collect to create an elemental soil. It seldom rains near the coast and for moisture most of these plants depend on the nightly fog from the sea which can reach 50 kilometres inland. It is cool near the sea, with a mean daily temperature of only 16,2°C throughout the year.

The flood water of the Hoanib is heavy with silt and when the pools form and dry, the silt settles. The heavier particles sink but the finer clay stays in suspension until the last drops of moisture evaporate. The clay then dries and cracks, each individual piece slowly parting from its fellows as the cracks widen and deepen to form a mosaic of Roman beauty. Then the ends start curling; and the layer of clay parts from the sandy material below. These clay beds preserve a record of wildlife of the river – the tracks of any animal walking across the wet clay are baked into its surface and stay there for months or years – until next it rains.

When it rains the desert lives. Ephemeral grasses such as *Stipagrostis hirtigluma* clothe the gravel plains and butterflies in their millions appear. Nomadic birds, including Stark's lark and the grey-backed finch-

When incubating, the drab-coloured female ostrich sits on the nest during the day and the jet-black male at night. This makes the best use of their colouring for camouflage and for heat absorption and reflection.

lark, which move eastwards during drought, pour into the desert and break the silence with their song. Black-shouldered kites – small raptors with delicate powder-grey upperparts and conspicuous black wing patches which are more commonly known from the better-watered savannas and woodlands of Africa – also move down the river and breed.

The elephants, and in particular the calves, also respond to the improved conditions, for during the dry years when the herds trek up to 70 kilometres overnight from feeding grounds to waterholes the calves suffer badly. In Addo only one calf in 15 dies in its first year, whereas in Kaokoveld only two out of five calves born in recent years have sur-

Wandering across the arid stretches of Kaokoland and Damaraland, the desert giraffes feed on the smallest shrubs and sparsest bushes.

With the skill of a master-swordsman, the gemsbok uses its rapier-like horns to ward off predators.

Hartmann's mountain zebra tend to keep to the escarpments that fringe the desert plains, but when rain has fallen they penetrate deeply into the desert and feast on the wiry annual grasses.

142

vived. But rain has fallen, the first in five years, and for the calves born after 1982 the prospects are improved immeasurably.

The desert elephants share their sere Kaokoland habitat with black rhino, whose very large posterior horns give them a characteristic heavy-snouted appearance. Though never abundant, these large, lumbering mammals now number no more than three – scarcely a viable breeding population – with a further 100 in Damaraland. They sometimes wander more than 100 kilometres in search of food, or after being disturbed, and drink regularly at fountains far apart. Their mainly solitary and nomadic lifestyle, the largest regular associations being no more than a cow and a calf, ensures that the scant food is well used, but not over-exploited. The Ovahimba pastoralists of Kaokaoland traditionally hunted the rhino, killing them with poisoned arrows. But while they were hunted only occasionally, and their competition with the Himba cattle for water was limited, they could survive. Now the balance has tipped against them and in the past two decades they have been exterminated in all the permanently settled areas of the eastern edge of Kaokoland and Damaraland and even pursued into the harsh western desert by poachers after rhino horn.

Giraffe, more at home in the acacia savannas of the higher rainfall areas, also penetrate the desert, living along the river beds but occasionally sallying forth to feed on the sparse trees inland. The Kaokoland giraffe are completely independent of free water and never drink, obtaining all their liquid requirements from their food. Much sought after for their hides and meat, they have been wiped out in all the settled areas, falling easy prey to poison-tipped arrows. Further south in barren and rocky Damaraland these remarkable animals climb to the summits of the most rugged mountains drawn there by the lightest of showers which cause the sparse trees to bud. During the short rainy season when food is temporarily abundant, the giraffes gather in somewhat larger groups, but when the dry season sets in they scatter to make better use of the available food sources.

The beautiful gemsbok (or Cape oryx) with its black and white marked face, rapier-like horns and long streaming tail is the antelope most at home in the desert. As with so many of the desert animals the gemsbok has developed a unique way of coping with the stress of the climate: instead of sweating to maintain an even body temperature and thereby losing a great amount of liquid, its physiology allows body heat to build up during the day and to be released during the chilly night.

The springbok can withstand extremes of heat and cold. It makes better use of the desert by migrating to more favourable areas when times are hard and by concentrating in herds of thousands when rain has produced a flush of plant material. The largest bird on earth, the ostrich, also wanders through the desert, in areas where there appears to be little to eat other than scattered small bushes. Lions, cheetah and leopard occur along the desert rivers, but the most common larger carnivore is the black-backed jackal. Its patient trot may take it kilometres along the seashore to feed on dead fish. It also frequents fur seal colonies to take dead pups – as does the brown hyaena – and thereby provides the spectacle of a terrestrial carnivore feeding on a marine carnivore.

Rainfall is the key to the movements of most of the desert animals. Thus the elephants concentrate on the river beds when it is dry; but disperse during the rains. On a larger scale, in times past when it rained in the western desert areas thousands of springbok, gemsbok, mountain zebra and others moved in to take advantage of the abundant grazing. In dry years the animals moved eastwards to the higher rainfall areas. But hundreds of kilometres of veterinary cordon fences have disrupted and blocked these ancient migration routes and most of this multitude of game has perished.

The finely balanced ecosystem of this harsh land has been irretrievably disrupted by modern man. Poaching, and other activities have wiped out the rhino and elephant from large areas and for a time only the efforts of Clive Walker and the Endangered Wildlife Trust stood between these animals and annihilation. The Ovahimba pastoralists have settled, thanks to boreholes, abandoning their former nomadic but ecologically viable lifestyle. Modern medicine has ensured an increase in the human population and the degradation of grazing land by too many domestic animals. The veterinary fences which destroyed the migratory system of the plains game now serve to separate man from the wilderness.

The desert elephants trek long distances from their feeding grounds to isolated water points, following age-old paths.

The slow attrition of the desert wildlife has been a conservation issue for some years. Because only these animals can use the desert efficiently, when they go, only silence and emptiness remain. The government of Namibia has recently taken charge of the Damaraland desert areas and, hopefully, will in time control Kaokoland as well. The conservation department has an excellent record, and the future of the desert elephants – for long so bleak – has now taken a decided turn for the better.

PILANESBERG NATIONAL PARK

BOPHUTHATSWANA

(Above) *A perfect blend of feline grace, stealth and power, the solitary leopard still survives in areas where man has long since eliminated the other large cats.*
(Left) *Elephant calves from Kruger soon joined up with two cows brought back from America to form the nucleus of a stable elephant herd in Pilanesberg.*
(Mankwe Valley, Pilanesberg National Park, Bophuthatswana)

The ragged grunting of a leopard, most graceful of the cats, the epitome of animal elegance, echoes against the low grey walls of the Mankwe valley. The Mankwe – 'place of the leopard' in the tongue of the Tswana people – rises in the heart of a long dead volcano. It cuts through the eroded walls of the old caldera and three more which lie in concentric circles around it, and within the narrow span of 20 kilometres breaks out on to a low, gently sloping plain. In the short course of its journey through the craters it passes from the heart of the Pilanesberg National Park on to the edge of the new town of Mogwase which is rapidly rising from the veld.

This journey of the Mankwe River epitomizes the dilemma of Africa – the span from wilderness to incipient urban modernity is small, the transition sudden. Yet it also holds the seeds of hope for conserving the African elephant and other large and spectacular mammals, for the catchment of the Mankwe, formerly developed and settled, has now been returned to the wild. Parts of the Pilanesberg National Park were for many years farms and cattle ranches. The northern crescent was tribal land settled by 90 families of the Bagatla tribe – 'the people of the monkey' – under their chieftain, Pilane. To the west were the Batloung, 'the people of the elephant' and to the south the Bakubung, 'the people of the hippo'. With the settlement of the Pilanesberg area, most of the large game was eliminated, as it has been or will be elsewhere in Africa. A few elusive species held their own, but in greatly reduced numbers. The grey duiker, steenbok, impala, greater kudu and mountain reedbuck survived heavy hunting. The area was large, and in parts the densely wooded mountain tops

145

The red hartebeest is the southernmost representative of an antelope that occurs throughout Africa in various forms.

and rugged gorges provided shelter for these animals. The stealthy and elusive leopard still preyed on antelopes and an occasional calf or sheep. The brown hyaena, the silent nocturnal scavenger, eked out a precarious living foraging off dead animals and occasionally catching small prey of its own. The transition of the Pilanesberg wilderness to tame and settled country was well advanced.

Then, scarcely a decade ago, a decision was taken to create a national park in the 50 000-hectare Pilanesberg area. The alkaline volcanic soils were not prime cropland, the high fluoride content of the water led to health problems, and the grazing was only of middling value to livestock. It would have seemed an improbable proposition, had the essential ingredients of political will and conviction not been present. The World Wide Fund for Nature, through an appeal by its local body the Southern African Nature Foundation, raised money for fencing, development and an ambitious restocking programme. The people and their 9 000 cattle were moved out to better land. Their houses,

shops and other buildings were demolished and the remains bulldozed into the ground.

Exotic *Eucalyptus* and other trees were felled; stock fences, livestock pens, telephone lines, power lines, and all the rubbish and rubble of civilization were broken down, gathered up and removed. A game-proof fence, strong enough to restrain elephants, was erected around the 110-kilometre perimeter. More than 6 000 animals including white and black rhino, hippo, buffalo, cheetah, giraffe, zebra, wildebeest, eland, gemsbok, springbok, kudu, impala, ostrich, waterbuck and red hartebeest were introduced. Virtually all the large mammal components of the original ecosystem being restored. And finally, the African elephant was re-established after an absence of about 150 years.

The return of the elephant to Pilanesberg was not without its share of tragedy and drama. The initial attempt was carried out prematurely when five young elephants from Addo were moved to Pilanesberg late in 1979. A young bull broke out of the park and set off in a southerly direction towards Addo. He travelled about 100 kilometres in four days, harassed by people and dogs along the way he killed an elderly farmer. This frightened, confused animal was then returned to Addo. Two of the remaining four elephants died tragically in the holding pen before release. The cause of their death has never been satisfactorily explained. Another bull died soon after. The sole survivor, a young bull, was left to a lonely existence.

In 1981, when the reserve was completely fenced, a successful translocation was carried out under the competent direction of Dr Jeremy Anderson, an old friend of ours.

Elephant calves translocated from Kruger, were cared for in bomas or stockades to acclimatize them to their new surroundings before their release into Pilanesberg.

The grass-eating white rhino is far more sociable than the browsing black rhino, and is often found in small groups.

When alarmed, warthogs run off with their tails held straight up in the air like cavalry pennants.

The handsome gemsbok, or Cape oryx, is one of the several species of antelope that were returned to Pilanesberg.

Eighteen young elephants between the ages of 18 months and three years were captured during culling operations in the Kruger National Park and moved to Pilanesberg. They arrived during the dry season and were kept in bomas (enclosures) until after the early summer rains had fallen and the greening grass was most palatable and nutritious. The youngsters stayed close to the release points and, except for the very smallest, were soon able to fend for themselves. It became obvious, however, that the strong sense of cohesiveness within an elephant herd or family group was lacking. The young elephants, seemingly lost and confused, wandered around in groups which split apart and formed up again at random. Perhaps this was to be expected: the entire capture and holding operation had been so traumatic that some of the animals had to be treated at Skukuza for stomach ulcers. They had been captured from different clans and groups in the wild and at the holding pens had been sorted into size classes to avoid competition at food troughs and to prevent bullying. Their social system, including a strong sense of hierarchy, had been destroyed. Four of the youngsters, not yet fully weaned, were unable to cope and died within a few months. The only solution was to catch larger animals but that entailed many technical and logistical problems.

But then help came from an unexpected quarter in the form of two tame African elephant cows, nearly full grown, called Durga and Owalla. These two animals and a bull named Tshombe were captured in the Kruger National Park in 1966 as youngsters and shipped to America. They were trained to perform in a circus and eventually ac-

quired by Randall Moore, who embraced the unusual mission of returning the elephants to Africa.

Moore found backers for his scheme and sailed to Kenya with the three animals. Initially the project went well, but it soon encountered difficulties. Tshombe died, and Randall and his two cows were deported. The news spread and a deal was made between Randall and new backers in terms of which the elephants were donated to the Pilanesberg National Park. However, the veterinary authorities intervened and the elephants were not allowed ashore in South Africa. They continued their journey to the United States where they were placed in quarantine for a year, and then once again crossed the Atlantic, for the fourth time, back to Africa. The new backers of the translocation to Pilanesberg included Randall Moore, ABC Sports (who filmed the operation) and Sun City, a casino and entertainment complex adjoining the park. Randall was given four months to habituate the elephants to the wild after which time he was to break contact with them.

To some conservationists there was simply too much razzmatazz about the operation – bikini-clad and sequined dancing girls atop the elephants did nothing to foster the image of a serious conservation venture. However, I was invited to Pilanesberg as a consultant during the final phase of the rehabilitation project. Randall and I tracked the elephants and established that they were feeding on a wide range of indigenous plants, had found the local waterholes, and made contact with the young elephants whose guardians they were to become.

Our last day with Durga and Owalla was

Seen in ancient hieroglyphics, the Egyptian goose occurs from the Nile to the Cape.

particularly rewarding. I was privileged to be taken for a ride on Owalla's back. Riding a soon-to-be-wild elephant through a tract of soon-to-be-wild Africa was a highlight of my long association with elephants. The rocking gait of the elephant, and having to duck and dodge overhanging branches as we progressed through the bush in search of the babies was an exciting experience.

Despite their long association with man, the elephants showed us two clear instances of purely elephant behaviour. One was when Durga noticed a bracelet made from elephant tail hairs which I habitually wear on my wrist. About a month before meeting her I had refurbished the bracelet with some whitish hairs taken from the tail of Shawu, the great Kruger bull who died in 1982. These pale hairs are held in high esteem by African hunters as a powerful talisman. Durga could presumably still smell elephant on the bracelet. Her trunk reached out purposefully and its sensitive fingers closed over my wrist, firmly holding me. Then she delicately

147

tried to grasp the strands of the bracelet, while sniffing all the while at the strange mixture of elephant and man scent. The bracelet was so absorbing that I had to hide it under my shirt sleeve to get her to leave me alone. The second incident was when we came across the remains of one of the young elephant calves that had died a few months before. The cows gently touched the hard, wrinkled, formless skin and delicately ran their trunks over the bleaching bones. One picked up a limb bone and weighed it carefully in her trunk, as though contemplating the ultimate fate of all elephants, and all men. We sat nearby, not wishing to disturb the cows, mindful of their potential sensitivities. There are few animals that respond like elephants to the bones of their own kind. We eventually withdrew from the scene, leaving Durga and Owalla standing next to the remains of the calf, quiet and still, perhaps gently mourning.

During the following year Jeremy Anderson and his staff wrought many more changes. The last of the exotic trees were felled. More animals were brought in, including sable and tsessebe, and others whose numbers had grown too rapidly, such as wildebeest, red hartebeest and impala, were culled or translocated. The carrying capacity of the park has been very carefully calculated and the animal populations will be kept within these limits. Another sensible innovation has been the zoning of a safari hunting area within the confines of the game fence. Here clients are taken out on trophy hunts by park staff. Included among the trophies on offer are southern white rhino, a rare contrast to the state of the northern white rhino which is on the brink of extinction. The safari hunting, predictably, earns far more revenue for the park than any other activity. Next in the ranking is the sale of live game, with tourism only a distant third but catching up fast.

The meat from the hunted animals is sold to local people, chiefly those who have been moved out of the park. This feedback to the community is only one of the means which the park management is exploring to make the park, and conservation, meaningful and relevant to its neighbours. Thus, provision is made in the Pilanesberg budget for community health and family planning projects. Conservation education, not only for the neighbours, has been pioneered by Pete Hancock, the park's education officer and his growing staff. Already 50 000 school children of Bophuthatswana have visited the park, or know its story. The Lengau Conservation Club, founded by the park staff, already has 2 000 members.

Another lesson learned at Pilanesberg is that the big carnivores, the animals at the top of the food pyramid, can be introduced only once all the other elements lower down are firmly in place. Cheetah were introduced too early, largely to satisfy the demand for game-viewing and partly to boost the local cheetah conservation effort. However, cheetah are abundant, and a pest, in the livestock ranching areas of Namibia and they can be purchased for as little as 150 US dollars. A sable antelope on the other hand costs 3 500 US dollars and a waterbuck 800 US dollars, and their calves are easy prey for cheetah. When one cheetah took two waterbuck calves in the space of a fortnight, the die was cast. Most of the cheetah were removed and no more will be reintroduced until the sable and other populations can stand the pressure of predation.

Nearly a year after their final contact with people, Paul and I visited Pilanesberg to find Durga and Owalla. They had been seen fairly regularly, and were usually accompanied by several of the young elephants. They had become wary, suspicious of people and avoided contact. We knew that it might be hard to find them but fortunately could rely on a radio collar fitted to Owalla to monitor her movements. On our first attempt we could not find the cows, but found instead a herd of seven youngsters and watched them for some time from the shelter of a clump of trees. When they started moving towards us, we withdrew ahead of them and took up our watch further on. The small group spread out, feeding until they reached the spot where we had been standing a few minutes earlier. Our scent must have hung there. One of the elephants put its trunk out to the exact spot where I had last stood and reared back

Sitting close behind Randall Moore, I rode the trained elephant cow Owalla at Pilanesberg on the day she and Durga were finally returned to the wild.

in alarm. Another trunk confirmed the smell of man and with a roar all the elephants turned and ran. It was reassuring to see how thoroughly wild these animals had become, because during the long quarantine period at Skukuza, up to four months for some of the animals, they had been handled and hand-fed and there were many pessimists who predicted that such familiarity with humans would lead to disaster. But the reactions which we witnessed indicated that these were thoroughly wild animals, and likely to remain so.

The following day we tracked Owalla into a dense thicket which we carefully entered. Broken and uprooted trees, piles of elephant dung, diggings and trampled shrubbery indicated a typically African thicket which was well used by elephants. Our cautious approach was just as well for we spotted a black rhino cow and small calf slowly moving through the thicket, idly browsing. It was a timely reminder that Pilanesberg was a 'real' African game reserve with dangerous beasts and the attendant risks. This thicket may have harboured cows and goats for a century, but now it had been returned to Africa of Yore. We retired to a high jumble of boulders on the hill slopes above the thicket. The canopy was a grey-green colour, with here and there a tall dark green candelabra tree or aloe standing taller. We saw a flicker of movement and the yellowish leaves of a tree shuddered

The rare Cape pangolin, or scaly anteater, has powerful claws for digging into termite mounds and ant nests. In defence it curls up into a tight armour-plated ball.

as an elephant broke a branch to feed. Soon we saw Durga, Owalla and three youngsters moving slowly through the thicket in our direction. They stopped at an excavation about 20 metres from us, and the two cows started throwing loose earth over their backs. One of them stooped down almost on her knees and dug a tusk into the ground to loosen more of the rich, deep red soil. We knew we were watching elephants that were as wild as any in Africa.

It is perhaps too early to make a final accounting of the reintroduction of elephants to Pilanesberg. But as things now stand, this project, like similar ones carried out in the Kagera National Park in Rwanda and Hluhluwe Game Reserve in Natal, can succeed. If suitable habitat is set aside for elephants and fenced to eliminate conflict with agricultural neighbours, there is every reason to believe that they can be successfully conserved. The rehabilitation of Durga and Owalla and the reintroduction of the youngsters from Kruger justifies the hopes of the far-sighted men who dream of recreating a tract of unspoiled Africa. For them, and for us, the ultimate success is the return of the African elephant, a species which more than any other epitomizes the remaining wilderness of this vast and restless continent.

KRUGER
NATIONAL
PARK

SOUTH AFRICA

(Above) *A male lion – his magnificent crown of shaggy hair glowing in the afternoon light – epitomizes regal dominance and is, like the rhino and the elephant, a symbol of Africa.*
(Left) *The new grass of summer is highly sought after by elephants. At this time the mopane trees* (Colophospermum mopane) *are clothed in gentle shades of lemon and yellow, soon to become emerald green.*
(Nkokodzi, Kruger National Park, South Africa)

Although in former days no doubt plentiful throughout the Lowveld, in 1902 the only indications of elephants in the present Kruger National Park were a few tracks in the neighbourhood of Olifants Gorge.

These were the disquieting words of Lieutenant Colonel James Stevenson-Hamilton, 'father' and first warden of the park, in his book *Wildlife in South Africa*. But the elephants which left their tracks – wrinkled, scuffed and cracked – on the sparse red earth in 1902 were not the last of their kind to roam the far places of the Kruger National Park. By 1905 some had returned, and in time new immigrants, steadily moving westwards from Moçambique, supplemented the small but growing population. By 1970, the park had nearly 9 000 elephants, more than could be supported, even though control measures had been instituted in 1967. Almost 13 000 elephants have since been culled in an ongoing programme to maintain the population at about 7 000. In the meantime to the east of the Lebombo mountains, events have come full circle. The only signs of elephants now in these parts are scattered piles of bleaching bones. No longer are there any tracks, for the elephants have been wiped out.

The recolonization of Kruger by elephants is a dynamic process, well documented in the reports of the wardens. Each prospective area was first visited by scouting parties of bulls. Sometimes their visits were seasonal, linked to the annual fruiting of the marula (*Sclerocarya caffra*), the sweet yellow fruits of which elephants crave. In time the bulls would settle and after a few years the first breeding herds would follow – adult cows,

151

Roan antelope, relatively rare in Kruger, are annually immunized against anthrax, a potential major cause of mortality.

immatures and calves. Younger bulls, either restless or pushed out, would then advance once more into unoccupied country and the process would be repeated. It took 30 years before the elephants had occupied the northern half of the park and nearly five decades later, in the extreme south-western corner – sparsely occupied by bulls and only one small breeding herd – we can see the culmination of the colonization process. As recently as the dry season of 1982, I recorded the first sightings of breeding herds at Shitlave dam near Pretoriuskop, an area from which they have been absent for about 150 years.

Paul's interest in the Kruger elephants initially centred on ivory – specifically the tusks of the great bull Mafunyane who died late in 1983. His tusks weighed 55,1 kilograms each; tapering slightly, they are beautifully matched, each 2,51 metres long. Like Ahmed

of Kenya and some of the other big tuskers of East Africa, Mafunyane was not very large. His shoulder height was only 3,27 metres, measured when he was darted to be fitted with a radio collar. By comparison the bull Shawu stood 3,4 metres at the shoulder. Shawu's long, relatively thin, sweeping tusks crossed over towards their tips, and so were not worn down by rubbing on the ground – a process which ensured that those of Mafunyane had bevelled tips, like gigantic chisels. At the time of his death in late 1982 Shawu's left tusk was 3,17 metres long and the right 3,06 metres. These slender tusks, 450 millimetres in circumference at the lip, weighed only 52,6 and 50,8 kilograms respectively. Only six African elephant tusks are known to be longer than Shawu's master tusk.

Shingwedzi, also one of the big Kruger bulls, had much shorter, but thicker and therefore heavier tusks. His master tusk was 2,64 metres long and weighed 58,1 kilograms, while the short servant tusk, broken by much labour and only 2,07 metres long nevertheless weighed a respectable 47,2 kilograms.

The quality, colour and size of ivory is determined by a combination of factors. Genetics and the environment – for example, the ratio of minerals in the diet – influence the rate of growth of the tusk, while the behaviour of the individual influences the rate of wear and breakage. A tusk which is more often used for fighting, is more prone to damage than one which is not used for anything more strenuous than stripping bark. Ivory needs time to grow and so, in general, large tuskers are older animals. Tusks are primarily weapons, and it is ironic that they are at their best when the old bull, virtually in re-

tirement, is unlikely to use them much for fighting. As the more aggressive bulls suffer greater breakage of their tusks, it is quite likely that the great tuskers which we admire so much are, in fact, the less successful animals. By avoiding fights, they have kept their tusks unscathed.

Serious fighting between bulls, as shown by their behaviour and the age of those killed, usually occurs between 25 and 40 years of age, when they regularly experience musth. The biological justification for larger ivory, age for age, may be the advantage which a tusker enjoys during a serious fight. Victory gives him a better chance to mate and leave offspring – the ultimate objective of life and the measure of biological success. The potential maximum length of tusks in African elephants is about five metres in bulls and four metres in cows. However, because individuals vary and some wear on the ivory is unavoidable so no such tusks are known.

From ivory to ecology the Kruger National Park features large in our experiences of elephants, and of Africa. For it is in this immense 20 000 km² wilderness that Paul and I have learned much of what we know of these great beasts. Here our perceptions have been formed, rough-hewn and polished, whether in a contemplative hour or two watching an elephant feeding and recording in minute detail every bite and every movement, the interest of an immobilization operation to mark an animal, the adrenalin-charged excitement of a close encounter with a bull in musth, or the numb and distracted horror of taking part in a culling operation which in minutes reduces a herd to ivory, skin, flesh, blood, guts and statistics.

The varied landscapes of the Kruger Na-

Head down, wings outstretched, balancing like the tightrope walker from which this eagle derives its name, the bateleur glides for hours over the wilder parts of Africa.

The beautifully mottled wild dog needs a huge hunting range and can therefore survive only in large conservation areas like Kruger.

Elephants carrying small radio-transmitters on collars can be tracked using a hand-held antenna from the roof of a Land Rover, the work-horse of Africa.

tional Park embrace vignettes of the entire southern savanna zone, a belt of semi-arid, drought-plagued country stretching from the fringe of the pro-Namib in Angola and Namibia clear across the continent to the arid hinterland of Moçambique. Here lies the transition between the more moist miombo woodlands to the north and the arid Kalahari and high, cool grasslands to the south. The entire zone, but particularly Kruger, is one of great biological diversity as it contains elements of all these neighbouring systems in the form of plants and animals more at home in the great swathes of country on either side of it.

The Lowveld – whose heartland is the Kruger Park – stretches through Swaziland and the eastern Transvaal province of South Africa, generally at an altitude of 250 - 500 metres. Its proximity to the coastal lowlands of Mocambique ensures a hot, humid summer with temperatures often well above 40°C and most rain falling from November to March. During the dry winter months it is much cooler, with day after day of almost cloudless blue sky. The vegetation is well adapted to this regime; most of the woody plants are deciduous, losing their leaves from about May onwards, but the exact timing depends on the species concerned and the effects of late summer rains. Along the river courses, however, the vegetation is usually evergreen, and this together with the staggered shedding of leaves of upland trees and scrub means that the larder for browsing herbivores is seldom completely bare. Most trees start the new season's growth as early as September with an offering of flowers, followed by leaves in October just before the rains break. These flowers are crucial to browsers like giraffe and kudu during dry years. Grazers must be more patient, however, as the grasses do not normally flourish until early November, after the first rains have fallen.

The graceful impala and the imposing greater kudu are integral elements of the African savanna. These species are abundant throughout Kruger in virtually all habitats from dense thickets to the open grasslands dotted with scrubby giraffe-browsed knobthorn (*Acacia nigrescens*) trees, to the dense mopane (*Colophospermum mopane*) forest of the Punda Maria wilderness.

Impala are medium-sized antelope, their rich, red-brown bodies reflecting the warm earth tones of Africa. When alarmed, or when simply light-hearted, they make spectacular leaps up to three metres and with a span of six. They are hardy, and can turn to grazing or browsing with equal facility. Rutting rams fight fiercely for control of a harem of 20-50 ewes and see rivals off with much clashing of their lyre-shaped horns, roaring that would do justice to a young lion, and flagging of the long, silky white hair on the short tail. At the end of November, during the early part of the southern summer most of the impala females give birth to their young within a short period of about three weeks. This abundant crop of youngsters provides a rich period of feasting for the carnivores, including the black-backed jackal, which is too small to tackle adults but is formidable against the lambs. The impala is the most numerous large mammal in the southern savanna – Kruger alone supports between 100 000 and 150 000 of these beautiful creatures – and is understandably the staple food of lion, leopard, cheetah, wild dog and spotted hyaena. To some extent, therefore, the impala is a buffer species, absorbing most

153

of the predation effort and thereby, perhaps, helping the less abundant antelopes such as roan, sable and tsessebe to survive.

The Lowveld is lion country. There are more lions per head of game in Kruger than anywhere else in Africa. But this was not always so, for in the early years lions and other predators were shot on sight in the belief that such action would give herbivores a better chance to increase. Later it was realized that in most cases the numbers of prey animals determined how many predators survive, and not the other way round.

The lion is the only social cat and each pride defends a territory within which there are adequate resources of food and water. The black, dark brown or ginger mane of the male lion is an impressive adornment serving to enhance his size – useful perhaps in dealing with unruly lionesses or for intimidating upstart youngsters. But this shaggy mat may have other purposes: it may serve as insulation against heat and as a shield against blows, for when males fight they swat at one another's heads and snarl, rather than bite.

Bird life in the southern savanna is similar to that of the arid thornbush country of East Africa, with many species occurring in these two regions but absent from a wide belt of intervening country. In the more developed countries – such as South Africa – there is little room for the large raptors outside the national parks, and the Kruger is therefore an important refuge. Viable populations of many of the larger birds of Southern Africa live here, including the beautiful bateleur, a superb glider rocking from side to side on its long pointed wings, its head hanging down to steady it as it scans the ground for food. This eagle's consummate skill and manoeu-

Baobab trees (Adansonia digitata) *live for well over a thousand years, their short stubby branches providing fruit and shade for generations of elephants.*

The winged seeds of the mountain mahogany (Entandrophragma caudatum) *break away from the central pillar or placenta of the fruit, which looks like a wooden banana, and drift away on the breeze.*

The great tuskers like João are living monuments to the success of elephant conservation in Kruger.

vrability in the air is a consequence of its aerodynamically unstable design, as it has almost no tail. It takes experience to fly as the adult bateleur does and young birds have longer tails which provide greater stability. After each moult the tail feathers are shorter, until as an adult at the age of seven years it is virtually rudderless, but flies with the panache of an aerial acrobat.

The baobab (*Adansonia digitata*) is as typical of the semi-arid savanna zones of Africa as are the flat topped acacias. Its strange, somewhat grotesque appearance – with huge bulbous stem and short, thick, stubby branches – has earned for it a place in African mythology as the tree planted upside down by an angry Creator. Baobabs, like termite mounds, are often the centre of small complex ecosystems which function in the midst of a greater scheme. The hollow stems hold water, equally useful to man and baboons for drinking and mosquitoes for breeding.

Cavernous trunks may shelter a poacher from a rain storm, or be home to a galago or a roost for bats. Small hollows provide nesting sites for birds such as ground hornbills, spotted eagle owls and spinetails. In the thick branches above, buffalo weavers and bateleurs build their nests. Bees also use baobabs for hives, and where the hollows occur at ground level porcupines, snakes, and even leopards may enter. The huge white flowers attract many unusual pollinators including fruit bats and galagos. The large fruits are food for man, chacma baboons and other animals. Elephants enjoy the fruit but also gouge the bark off the trees with their tusks and dig out the pulpy wood, creating holes which are often enlarged and used by other species. Occasionally elephants take to eating baobabs on such a scale that they eventually topple and almost completely devour them. Once felled, the soft fibrous wood quickly disintegrates and within three seasons there may be no sign of the tree left.

When long hours of association with elephants is part of one's life, one finds that individual animals have their own characteristics. They acquire an identity in the eye of the observer, and the dispassionate scientific view of animals is overwhelmed by the warmth and affection one develops for them.

The great Kruger bull Shingwedzi was one such animal. Although diffident towards humans he was approachable, and Paul and I knew him well in his last years. He died in a grove of huge yellow-stemmed sycamore figs (*Ficus sycomorus*) on the bank of the Shingwedzi River in January 1981. On Paul's first visit to the park after the death of Shingwedzi we went to pay our respects to the grand old elephant. By then the crocodiles and spotted hyaenas had demolished the carcass. There was only the odour of death, scattered bones, patches of skin, and the sad, rolled up soles of his feet. These are more durable than the rest of the skin, and are eventually eaten by the larvae of a highly specialized species of moth, *Ceratophaga vastella*.

Shingwedzi, because he was so easily identifiable, was one of the study animals who contributed to our understanding of the ranges over which individual elephants of different status roam. Other animals in the study were subjected to the indignity of immobilization and the fitting of a radio transmitter collar.

The darting of the elephant is done after a stalk on foot, a chase in a vehicle, or – most efficiently of all – from a helicopter. Using a 'chopper' ensures that the elephant can be guided to a suitable area for darting and kept there until it collapses. One of our pilots, Piet Otto, usually gets the almost immobile elephant to stand in the shade of a tree before it falls. This reduces the risk of overheating, and thereby subjects the animal to less stress. The helicopter also ensures a far less traumatic time for breeding herds, as a calf can be guided away from a darted cow and left in the care of the other animals.

On getting up after the marking operation, when the antidote to the immobilizing drug has been administered, a cow's first concern is to look for her calf. Some run in a circle searching for the scent of the herd and fol-

The chamaeleon plods patiently, hesitating at every step, while its turreted eyes swivel independently in all directions.

low them up immediately. On one memorable occasion a cow heard her calf bellow from a distance of almost a kilometre, and she rushed off roaring reassurance to her baby. Bulls, somewhat more nonchalant, wander off and rest in the shade of a convenient tree for some hours.

Using research tools such as immobilizing drugs and radio equipment, we have learned a great deal more about the African elephant. Yet our knowledge of elephant ecology, imperfect as it is, has served only to make us realize how complex is the elephant's role in African ecosystems and how far we are from understanding it all.

MAPUTO
ELEPHANT
RESERVE

MOÇAMBIQUE

TEMBE
ELEPHANT
PARK

KWAZULU, SOUTH AFRICA

(Above) *The thin, brightly coloured ears of the suni antelope are conspicuous when backlit – perhaps thereby providing a means of advertisement or communication.*
(Left) *Wandering young bulls from Moçambique kept the Tembe area as an elephant range for nearly forty years while breeding herds were absent.*
(Mozi, Tembe Elephant Park, South Africa)

Two hadeda ibis flapped out of a tree, screaming *ha haa, ha haah* as though their lives depended on it. Paul and I froze. If the elephant bull detected us, or took fright and turned in our direction we would be in trouble. The dense forest seemed to wait expectantly. A sombre bulbul called. It was early morning of an overcast day. We had tracked the old elephant bull for an hour through the thickets and forest of Sihangwane, and for the past ten minutes had been watching him, following his every move.

The old bull, sunken temples dusted with grey earth, took no notice of the birds and carried on drifting slowly from one bush to the next, taking a few bites and then moving on. His gait was slow, the steady plod of an old man. He lifted his feet one at a time, and then settled each one down silently on the sandy soil, always keeping three feet on the ground to carry his great weight. His huge head rocked slightly as he moved. With every step, his tail swung easily from side to side. Most of his tail hairs were lost and only a few short bristles remained. Occasionally the great tattered ears flapped forward and back, but neither far nor fast as it was cool and there was no need for vigorous ear flapping. As he walked, his relaxed trunk dangled, the tip curling up, back and sideways as though he were smelling out the path. Then the trunk swung up in a smooth, easy motion to grasp a bunch of leaves, crook them in its curl, grasp them firmly with the delicate fingers at the trunk tip and put them into his mouth. His eyes seemed to be half closed as he moved, seemingly deep in thought.

We were in an area known to us simply as the Central Pans, the heartland of the Sihangwane elephant range. Here were food

157

Striped, spotted and shaggy, with a brilliant white mane that can be raised in threat or display, the nyala male is one of the more striking of the southern antelopes.

and water for elephants, and the smell, the sound, the essence of wild Africa. Every pan lay in a deep basin, scooped and hollowed out over hundreds of years by animals. Every time an elephant wallowed or showered, it carried away a layer of mud on its skin, tusks and feet. The hollows grew deeper and be-

The rapid flicking of its conspicuous tail is a common signalling device used by the bush squirrel and its numerous relatives.

came small pans, coalescing into larger pans in time. The pans were surrounded by clumps of dense thicket, much of it deciduous, but with here and there the dark crown of an evergreen tree, or the yellow-green form of tall *Euphorbia ingens*. As it was July, the water levels in the pans were low. The water was either iron grey from the clay suspension, or a bright yellow-green from *Lemna minor*, a tiny flowering plant that floats on water and forms dense mats.

We stopped to rest at a pan where the grey-black mud had been trampled a thousand times by elephants' feet. The imprints had sunk up to 20 centimetres deep, some filled and others dry. The dry zone of trampled mud around the pan merged into paler sand, and a heavily grazed carpet of short, still faintly green *Cynodon* grass. A few scattered sedges (*Scirpus articulatus*) had their deep green stems splashed and speckled with mud by a passing giant. A tall *Acacia robusta* tree near the pan was bare underneath, the ele-

The leaves of the southern Ilala palm (Hyphaene natalensis) are coarse and fibrous. They are nevertheless chewed by elephants and then discarded.

phants having trampled the grass as they stood, occasionally shuffling, resting in the shade through the heat of day. The elephants had used this tree as a rubbing post – in places the bark was coated with a thick layer of mud, but elsewhere the tree was rubbed smooth by countless elephant shoulders and flanks, the wood polished so that the dark grain glowed. A nearby fallen tree, perhaps felled by an elephant for the same purpose, had also been buffed by thousands of feet, legs, bellies and chests. From this resting place, a well-used elephant path snaked off into the thicket, inviting us to follow it.

The thicket is a tangle of shrubs and trees with numerous climbing plants entwined in their branches. The sad call of the emerald-spotted wood dove, the rapid tapping of a bearded woodpecker, the regular gentle hammering of a tinker barbet are typical background sounds. Signs of elephants were everywhere – deep tracks in the mud, the wrinkled road maps of tracks on the path, scuffed trees, broken branches, their distinctive brown, khaki- and rust-coloured dung lay in piles, some opened up and scattered about by the busy pecking and scratching of crested francolins. The network of paths branched, looped, came together, and where a major path approached a large pan, it was covered by a layer of trampled dung.

The air of Africa hung heavy in the thicket. This place, and others like it, are a source of memories for Paul and me. It was to a place like this, in the Maputo Elephant Reserve, that Paul and Elaine first went when he gave up a career in advertising. Here they started their search for a corner of wild Africa where they could settle, away from the bustle of the city.

For me, Sihangwane held memories of numerous patrols with Bob Langeveld, a seasoned, grey-bearded hunter who had shot well over 2 000 elephants in various parts of Africa, mostly as part of the culling scheme in Luangwa. He taught me a great deal about hunting, and about men. This was also the place where I had courted a girl with long, blonde pigtails and a warm smile, who became my wife. In these dense thickets, Bob, Catherina, our Thonga tracker Jingo and I had tracked elephants for hours on end. We had often come suddenly on a bull, or group of bulls, at close quarters. The startled animals would burst into movement, heads high, great ears spread, tails up and held to the side, and then dash off and melt into the thicket. We were left, tightly clutching our rifles, ready to fire a warning shot or worse, exhilarated, delighted, relieved. We also stalked and watched bulls without their ever becoming aware of our presence, saw them feeding, drinking, showering and resting. One afternoon, on a day such as this, when hadedas flew up ahead of us and our tracker assured us an elephant was there, we carefully approached a pan and saw a wounded bull move his aching body slowly to the water to drink and then painfully make his way back into the sheltering forest.

During the summer months the vegetation is brilliant green, but as the dry season advances, many trees drop their leaves and their grey paleness is starkly etched against the darkness of the evergreen species. Driving north, up the deeply rutted sandy track from Sihangwane, one passes through tall, fairly dense woodland dominated by sand-loving species such as *Terminalia sericea* and *Strychnos madagascariensis*. The track

The deep orange blooms of the coral tree (Erythrina lysistemon) *add a touch of brightness to the veld and provide nectar for equally colourful sunbirds.*

winds around dense evergreen forest and thicket patches, home of the diminutive suni antelope, bushpigs, the four-toed elephant shrew and other seldom-seen creatures. Fires had been lit in the area by Thonga hunters just before our visit in July 1982. Consequently there was a mosaic of blackened, recently burnt areas, patches with a green flush of new grass, and the brown, wintry grass of unburnt areas. The older burns, already covered in a green flush, were sought after by the brown, white and black piebald and mottled Thonga cattle, grey duiker and reedbuck. Close to Bob's Hill, a high sand dune named after Bob Langeveld, the veld was still burning. The progress of the fire was marked by the snapping and crackling of the flames, the occasional whoosh and roar as the old, tinder-dry leaves of an Ilala palm (*Hyphaene natalensis*) ignited, and the fluttering flight of fork-tailed drongo and other birds, preying on the insects which were fleeing a fiery death.

There were also bright colours among the wintry browns and greys. Tall *Aloe marlo-*

thii, with succulent, spiny blue-grey leaves, put out tall branching candelabras of brilliant yellow and orange flowers. The smaller *A. parvi-bracteata*, which has a dark green stem stretching up a metre or more from a rosette of speckled and mottled leaves, is topped by branching inflorescences with red bell-like flowers. Hovering around these centres of brightness and colour were iridescent jewels, the emerald green, sulphurous yellow and carmine plumaged sunbirds of various species.

The view from Bob's Hill was unchanged. The grey-green canopy of the forests and woodlands stretched as far as the eye could see, dull under a heavy and lowering sky. Beacon Ridge, the long dune which runs parallel to Bob's Hill, was dark green, luxuriant with forest. Around us stood groves of pod mahogany, *Afzelia quanzensis*, the trees bare and grey, some still with large, dark pods hanging like bats, from their branches. From the hill, the track wound down the slope through thorny thickets to the Central Pans.

Maputaland, also known as Tongaland, lies on the south-east coast of Africa between the Lebombo Mountains and the sea. It stretches from Delagoa Bay, where Maputo, the capital of Moçambique, is situated, to Lake St Lucia in South Africa. It encompasses largely the tribal domain of the Thonga people which was divided between Britain and Portugal, so a modern political boundary cuts across this land from just north of Kosi Bay in the east to Swaziland in the west. This region is known physiographically as the Moçambique coastal plain, which used to lie under the sea. Over aeons of time, it was slowly lifted, but its coastal legacy lingers in beds of ammonites and other marine fossils, 159

Colonies of the cocktail ant (Crematogaster *sp.*) *fashion their arboreal nests from chewed plant fibres cemented together by secretions from their maxillary glands.*

After drinking his fill, an elephant bull wallows in the dark pool at Fomotini.

the poor sandy soils, and the long ridges of the sand dunes, now standing 50 kilometres or more from the sea.

Many small freshwater lakes, some in contact with the sea, others isolated, are scattered along the plain. The coastal dunes are covered in rich evergreen coastal forest; inland there is a complex mosaic of evergreen forest, groundwater forests, dry deciduous forest and thicket, savanna, swamps and sour alkaline grasslands, and *Acacia* savanna, which occurs on the richer soils on the slopes of the Lebombo. In the Maputo Re-

serve, flood plains and grasslands alternate with watercourses, lakes and pans.

Although the vegetation appears so rich and lush, the low soil fertility has ensured that only small populations of large mammals could be supported over most of the area. Nonetheless, there was a wide variety of mammals. The poor soils also could only support a fairly low human population and so this area has always been relatively underdeveloped. This is why elephants and some other larger mammals have survived.Those south of the international boundary were the only elephants left in South Africa outside of a protected area.

In Moçambique, the Maputo Elephant Reserve was created in 1932, protecting a small but viable population of about 300 animals. On the South African side of the border, there was more disturbance and the elephant breeding herds withdrew after 1945, remaining within the Maputo Reserve. Bulls still occupied a much larger range and some were permanently resident in the Sihangwane area of the Tembe tribal lands. During the late summer every year, the bulls moved southwards, raiding crops, trampling grain bins, and occasionally also killing people. The authorities regularly hunted down these marauders. When I worked in the area in 1975-76, I found that the pattern was continuing. It was significant that every one of eight bulls shot in three years had wounds of some kind – bullets, scrap iron from muzzle loaders or trunk tips amputated by snares. Some of the bulls were youngsters, confirming that they were still dispersing from the breeding herds at Maputo.

Because the Sihangwane area was so sparsely populated, Bob Langeveld and I ar-

gued in favour of a reserve for these persecuted elephants. The tribesmen would lose little in the way of natural resources if they chose to leave an area undisturbed in which the elephants could be confined so that their crops would be secure. The effectiveness of the elephant-proof fence of Addo had shown the way, but the costs would be high. The absence of females was a drawback to our schemes, but we reasoned that if the bulls could move into the area then cows would also do so in time.

But sanctuaries are not proclaimed overnight. The Tembe tribal lands are part of KwaZulu, a self-governing entity within South Africa. The KwaZulu government, quite rightly, was not prepared to proclaim a reserve on tribal land without the acquiescence of the people. The staff of the conservation service, who succeeded Bob and me, continued to press for the ideal, receiving help in an indirect way. The considerable disruption in Moçambique after independence resulted in, among other things, a lack of protection of the Maputo Elephant Reserve. Poaching increased dramatically and the reintroduced population of white rhino, which stood at about 50 in 1975, was whittled down to eight within seven years. Some elephant breeding herds, constantly harassed, left the reserve and moved south to the peace and quiet of Sihangwane. With a viable, resident elephant population, the case for an elephant reserve was much stronger. Chief Tembe and his tribal elders were convinced, and in 1984 the Tembe Elephant Reserve was proclaimed.

The eastern edge of the Sihangwane forest borders on a long, shallow depression, the Mozi Swamp, which is the Rio Futi, the lifeline of the elephant range. It is a swamp into which, for aeons, nutrients have drained from the higher ground. Reeds and sedges have grown and decayed, producing a rich, fertile strip of black mud. It holds water permanently and in places large pools of the darkly stained, peaty water have formed. One of these is called Fomotini Pan, its name echoing mfomothi, the Thonga name for the *Newtonia hildebrandtii* tree, which dominates the patches of dry forest. Fomotini is surrounded by beds of bulrushes (*Typha latifolia*) and reeds (*Phragmites mauritianus*). On the east bank are dense stands of Ilala palms and wild date palms (*Phoenix reclinata*), and on the higher ground, tall forest trees. Fomotini was an excellent place for waiting for the elephants to approach and drink.

Paul and I went to Fomotini and sat all day in a small hide built in a tall marula (*Sclerocarya caffra*) tree. At midmorning an elephant bull appeared. He was a specimen in his prime, about 40 years old, solid, muscular, his tusks not particularly big, but very white against his dark body. His hide was deeply wrinkled, his shoulders splattered with Mozi mud, dark blue-black. His ears were tattered at the edges, a legacy of a lifetime in the thorny thickets of Maputoland.

He drank his fill before moving off to feed on reeds and bulrushes at the edge of the pan. He then waded slowly and purposefully into the water, his wake eddying behind him and rocking the mounds of water lily leaves and stems which a jacana or lily-trotter had piled up for a nesting site. He drank again and then carried on into the pool until eventually only his head and the top of his shoulders rose up out of the dark peaty water. His trunk was held high above his head to breathe, but he exhaled under the water, sending up a white, frothy, churning mass of bubbles. On the east bank he drank again and then moved off slowly through a grove of palms towards the open grassland beyond. He disappeared as silently as he had arrived. We followed his tracks a little way and saw him emerge onto the open Mozi grassland. Perhaps we were incautious, for he suddenly became aware of us. Startled, he swung away, pacing quickly across the open country, heading for the distant dark line of a forested ridge.

We watched him until he faded from sight, knowing that his future depended upon the will of Chief Tembe's people to maintain this sanctuary in the face of their own ever-growing need for land. The right course has been charted, but for how long will they be able to keep to it?

The crested guinea fowl, with its elegant dark blue topknot and ruby-red eyes, is found in flocks in forest and thicket habitats throughout Africa.

In this land at the southern tip of the continent, the only two large African mammals to become extinct in historical times met their doom. The blue antelope and the quagga were wiped out by development, habitat change and hunting. Only at Addo, and only for the Addo elephants, was extinction decreed and paid for by the authorities. But the Addo bush, the dense thicket in which the elephants ranged, could protect its children, and the elephants were cunning. Major P. J. Pretorius, who found the German battle cruiser *Königsberg* in the Rufiji delta during the Great War, was as brave a hunter as any man. He devoted 11 months to his grisly and dangerous commission and shot 120 elephants. By the end of 1919 there were only 16 Addo elephants left. Sympathy swung away from the farmers whose crops had been ravaged to the embattled elephants, and the rifles were silenced.

The habitat of the Addo elephants, a dense low thicket of evergreen, succulent plants dominated by *Portulacaria afra, Schotia afra* and *Euclea undulata* lies between the Zuurberg Mountains, the Sundays River and Algoa Bay. It was avoided by settlers, both white and black, whose waves of expansion met here in the late eighteenth century. The elephants, the last Cape buffalo and other species of wildlife, held their own. Early in the twentieth century, after population increase, railways, roads, and modern farming practices came to the eastern Cape Province, the conflict between agriculturists and elephants intensified. Crop raiding by the elephants, confined to a small and waterless range impeded development. The extermination of the elephants was seen as the only solution, as also 50 years later in Rwanda

ADDO ELEPHANT NATIONAL PARK

SOUTH AFRICA

(Above) *A greater kudu bull, elegant and imposing, with long spiral horns and huge ears, is perfectly at home in the dense thickets of Addo.*
(Right) *The Addo elephants, having survived the slaughter in their steel-ringed fortress of greenery, now face the ultimate elephant problem: their growing numbers are stripping bare their beneficent range.*
(Gwarrie Pan, Addo Elephant National Park, South Africa)

when in 1973 the last two free-ranging populations were exterminated, and as it will be increasingly elsewhere in Africa over the next two decades.

With the hunt called off, the first requirement was to protect the surviving Addo elephants. This was done in 1931 by the proclamation of the Addo Elephant National Park. However, the park was small and the elephants could still raid neighbouring farms. Parallel situations exist today in other parks, such as Liwonde in Malaŵi, where elephants are shot if they cross the park boundary and raid crops. When Addo was proclaimed there were only 11 elephants, but by 1953 their numbers had grown to 17, the elephants' reproduction just keeping ahead of the rate at which they were shot. But between 1943 and 1953 eight calves were born and eight animals shot. The solution was to confine the elephants to the park – as achieved in 1954 by Graham Armstrong, who built a revolutionary elephant-proof fence of railway lines and cables around 2 200 hectares, finally ending the wanderings of his charges.

In their fenced-off sanctuary, the Addo elephants multiplied. When I first saw them in 1964 there were 35 of them. When I next saw them in 1976, as a newly-appointed research officer, they numbered 77. At that time they were left severely alone, but were fed oranges near the park headquarters to entice them out into the open so that visitors could see them. They charged vehicles on sight and were given a wide berth: the memory of local people killed by these animals was still fresh.

I went to Addo to study what were reputed to be the most dangerous elephants in Africa. My first few forays into their domain confirmed this reputation, at least in my mind, as I hurriedly gave way to a full charge of an entire herd of 21 elephants. However, I decided to call their bluff. Having once been hopelessly bogged down in mud in Malaŵi and repeatedly charged by an elephant that never pressed home its attack, I believed that the situation was not as bad as it seemed. I manoeuvred my Land Rover into a position where I invited a charge from a herd of nine elephants, led by a matriarch later named Pat-

sy. True to form, they screamed and charged *en masse*. At the last minute I roared away, the elephants in pursuit. Then, with the length of the vehicle between us, I stopped. The elephants halted in a cloud of dust and fury, close to the back of the Land Rover.

They threw earth and branches at me, roared, trumpeted and bellowed; I remained still. After a while they quitened down, began to shuffle and look around in embarrassment, not knowing what to make of the situation. A calf started to feed, and the others followed suit. The herd visibly relaxed and slowly dispersed, leaving me breathless, but exhilarated. I repeated the performance with Patsy's herd a few more times, and with every one of the seven other family groups in the park, and all the bulls. Within two months the Addo elephants were ignoring my vehicle. My work could progress.

In time I married. My wife Catherina joined in my studies and we came to know all the elephants individually and intimately. They allowed us to approach them closely, and to move among them. Some animals regularly came up to greet us, an outstretched

About ten days after death, sometimes sooner, elephant tusks can easily be drawn out of their sockets by hand.

An elephant calf, left behind by his mother, goes rushing after her, roaring in frustration, tail cocked in alarm and trunk swinging in agitation.

Eland numbers at Addo are carefully monitored and a regular cull of live animals is taken. These are moved to other reserves or sold to game ranchers.

164

trunk would touch an outstretched hand, developing a bond between us. We loved these animals, and they tolerated us. For nearly three years we had the Addo elephants to ourselves and could record their fascinating behaviour and ecology. Our lives were enriched by our close contact with these incredibly sentient creatures. But we knew that the park would have to be opened to tourists eventually and in 1979 it was. As the elephants were accustomed to people and vehicles by then, we thought it safe for visitors to drive through the area, provided they treated the elephants with due respect.

The dense Addo vegetation prevented us from following the elephants continuously. But whenever they were near paths, open areas or waterholes, we would watch them and record their activities. We saw them feeding, drinking, wallowing, dusting, swimming, playing, fighting, mating, and I once narrowly missed the birth of a calf. By the end of 1976 I realized that the Addo bulls were coming into musth fairly regularly. This condition is characterized by copious secretions from the temporal glands – which open just behind the eye and give a 'tear stain' appearance to the animal's face – and by a constant dribbling of fluid from the penis. At that time, musth was not recognized as occurring in the African elephant, as it was thought to be exclusive to the Asian elephant. However, Cynthia Moss subsequently came to the same conclusion about the regularity of musth in the elephant bulls she studied with Joyce Poole in Amboseli.

We found that some of the bulls, normally tolerant of us, would be very much more truculent when in musth. Our first intimation of this was when, during his first period of musth, one of our better known bulls, Oom Peet, did not greet our vehicle with his trunk outstretched as usual – instead he blocked our path, rested his tusks on the spare wheel, which is mounted flat on the bonnet of the Land Rover, and glared at us. The other bulls kept well clear of Peet when he was in musth, and for good reason. Peet was a killer. He dispatched a young bull during one bout of musth, breaking a tusk in the process. During his next musth period he broke off his other tusk while killing an old cow. During a third period of musth, with no tusks, he attacked another bull and was himself killed.

For adult elephants, death is usually a protracted business. There is no predator to make a quick kill, other than man. Elephants can live for 55 years, or a little longer. For bulls, their prime years from 25 to 40 – when musth-enraged fighting takes a heavy toll – are a dangerous time. If they survive this period, they also live to 55 years or more. By then, the last of the six sets of molar teeth will be worn away, making chewing difficult. The animal loses condition and eventually dies, perhaps as the direct result of some infection brought on by a generally poor physical condition. Elephants close to death usually stay near water to feed on the softer, succulent plants found there, and perhaps also to douse the raging fevers which seem to grip some dying animals as they stand gaunt and hollow-cheeked in their last days.

The cow that Peet killed was known to us as Catherine the Great. She was an old matriarch, one of the original 11 elephants when the park was proclaimed in 1931. She had only one tusk, the right one, and there was only one other cow of her vintage that also

Always green and succulent, the vegetation of Addo provides a productive and all but impenetrable elephant habitat.

had a tusk, a left one. Catherine had two female calves, each of which had two tusks, and the left-tusked cow had one female calf also with a left tusk. All the other Addo females were tuskless. In this respect, the Addo elephants are unique in Africa. There is probably a genetic basis for this condition, and perhaps there was also selection by ivory hunters which led to the extermination of tusked cows. All Addo bulls have tusks, although not particularly heavy ones. Provided that these young females produce tusked female calves, there is a chance of the cows, in time, becoming increasingly more like other elephant populations. If culling is done at Addo, it could be selective and the tusked cows could be given an advantage.

Early one morning Catherina and I saw a herd of Addo elephants near a waterhole. It was hot and the animals were on their way to drink and shower. Catherine the Great's little bull calf, scarcely 15 months old, was splattered by dark, dried blood and he was screaming and crying. It was the most pathetic, sad sound we had ever heard. His older sister,

165

Suricates – small social carnivores that live in packs – are found throughout the arid south-west of the continent.

Cheeky Chops, hurried along behind him, trying to caress him with her trunk. She also had bloodstains on her shoulders. We feared the worst, but it was not until late afternoon that we found the body of Catherine the Great. She had been tusked repeatedly in the shoulders and neck, and the stab wound that killed her had severed a jugular. Fragments of jagged ivory, broken off in the fury of the attack, were found in some of the wounds. We knew who had killed her, for we had seen Oom Peet that morning with his second tusk broken, but we would never know what had motivated him. While examining the body we heard elephants approaching, so quickly withdrew. The dead matriarch's herd filed out of the thicket and gathered around the carcass. They were silent, stood calmly, heads bowed, and reached out with their trunks to touch her. Some tried to lift her,

166 others simply laid their trunks on her stiffen-

ing body and grieved. Only the little bull calf still bellowed pathetically, tried to suckle, touched his mother, held her trunk and smelled the wounds. For an hour the elephants stood around; the grieving calf fell silent. Some of the adults threw dust, sand, leaves and branches over the carcass and then left quietly. The scientific explanation of what we saw would be inconclusive, but to us there was no doubt that we had witnessed an elephant wake.

The strange preoccupation of elephants with their dead has been observed by others. Iain and Oria Douglas-Hamilton described it in their book on the Manyara elephants. I have watched elephants pick up and carry the bones, skulls and tusks of their dead, and there are many similar accounts from other parts of Africa. In 1969 when I was living in Malawi, in the Kasungu National Park, we erected a small thatched pedestal on which we mounted an elephant skull with tusks. It was not long before a party of elephant bulls demolished the shack and carried the tusks off. We recovered them about 300 metres further. Elephants also sometimes heap branches on the bodies of people they have killed, much as we saw the Addo elephants covering their dead matriarch.

The Addo elephants were always more active during hot weather, and could be counted upon to emerge from the dense bush to drink and shower. On one such hot day in January 1982, when Catherina, Paul and I were on a return visit to Addo, we sat waiting for the elephants at a deep earth-walled dam in the middle of an open valley.

The first animals to burst from the dense thicket were two young calves, but hot on their heels came the rest of the group. As they

approached the water their pace quickened, as if each animal was afraid of being left behind or of losing its share of the water. Raising a cloud of dust, heads bobbing, ears flapping, trunks swinging amid a chorus of bellows, growls and screams, the phalanx of about 20 elephants skidded to a halt at the water's edge. The growls changed to purrs of delight as they dipped and lifted their trunks, pouring the cooling water down dry, thirsty throats. While the adults drank calmly, the youngsters tussled and battled with one another to improve their positions. Their thirst quenched, the adults rested contentedly, some showering. Several teenagers waded into the water, setting off a rush as others joined them, rolling, immersing themselves completely, splashing and squirting water from their trunks.

Paul and I crouched in dense bushes near the water's edge, knowing that we were safe because there were no crocodiles in Addo. We were close enough to feel as though we were participating in the elephants' activity. The water was churned up as splashing elephants sparred and butted, pushed and pulled, and tackled animals twice their size if they happened to be lying down. After half an hour the animals started to leave, their shiny wet skins soon drying to dark grey, contrasting with the red mud-covered animals that had not indulged in a dip. Slowly they moved away, spreading out to feed or to rest in small groups near stunted trees where the calves could find shade. Those who could not find any simply lay down under their mothers. We watched pensively as they departed, knowing that some of these animals, now so full of life, might soon be shot by the park authorities.

The Addo elephants have continued to increase in numbers, reaching 140 by 1988. Extending the elephant-proof fence became a full-time occupation for the park warden Pierre van Rooyen. He excelled at this task and the range of the elephants is now about 8 000 hectares. Sadly, it will not be enough to support the population. Our studies show that, even at present elephant densities, there will be a retrogression of the vegetation, several plant species will be eliminated, the thicket will be opened up, and plant height and density will decrease. Some of these changes are advantageous to buffalo and kudu, and the black rhino which were imported from Kenya in 1960. But, in the long term, the degrading trend must be stopped.

As the biologist most concerned with the Addo elephants, I know that it will devolve upon me to make the final recommendations concerning them. There are only two options – more land or fewer elephants. Addo is an island with shores ringed by steel. Within this small area, we must maintain viable populations of the Addo plant communities, elephants, buffalo, black rhino, the flightless dung beetle and a host of other creatures. The beetle is virtually confined to the park because it depends upon the coarse dung of wild animals, being unable to survive on the dung of cattle. Outside the park the Addo vegetation is threatened by cultivation, bush clearing and over-browsing by goats.

The caracal has become the scourge of small-stock farmers in southern Africa, where its competitors have largely been eliminated.

It is something of a Gordian knot. To leave the animals to themselves in some vain hope that Nature will sort it all out is a delusion. But land is expensive, so the most likely decision will be to cull the elephants, though there might also be a possibility of artificially controlling their fertility. These problems and realities, which we face at Addo today, will be the issues facing other Africans tomorrow, or the day after. If we make the right mix of choices we can, perhaps, show the way ahead.

167

BIOLOGICAL DATA ON AFRICAN ELEPHANTS

The following data have been derived from many sources, both published and unpublished. They are based on the savanna or bush elephant, *Loxodonta africana*, and are derived from studies in East and Southern Africa. Measurements given indicate the range that may be expected. Exact data are variable for different areas.

Weight and Measurements
Body weight:
Adult males 4 000 - 6 000 kg
Adult females 2 000 - 3 000 kg
Birth weight 100 - 120 kg
Tusk weight:
Adult males 10 - 60 kg (record 117 kg)
Adult females 4 - 8 kg
Tusk length:
Adult males 90 - 250 cm (record 345 cm)
Adult females 80 - 140 cm
Shoulder height:
Adult males 300 - 350 cm (record 401 cm)
Adult females 230 - 265 cm
Newborn calves 85 - 95 cm
Heart weight: 20 - 30 kg
Brain weight: 4 - 6 kg
Brain volume: 5 000 - 6 600 cc

Nutrition
Diet: Grass, herbs, branches and leaves, fruits, bark, wood, roots, bulbs and tubers.
Daily food intake: 150 - 200 kg (fresh weight)
Daily water intake: 180 - 220 ℓ
Daily dung production: 140 - 180 kg
Defecations per day: 10 - 17

Quick and intelligent, Cape clawless otters move with graceful ease.

Reproduction and longevity
Age at puberty: 10 - 13 years
Period of heat: 48 hours
Oestrous cycle: 2 - 3 weeks
Gestation period: 22 months (about 660 days)
Twins: rare occurrence; usually a single calf
Sex ratio at birth: 1:1
Suckling period: usually about 24 months
Calving interval: 3 - 4 years
Longevity: 60 years

Miscellaneous
Average walking speed: 6,5 km/h
Charging speed: 40 km/h
Body temperature: 36 - 37 °C
Teeth: 2 upper incisors (= tusks); 6 molars (upper and lower)
Maximum skin thickness: 2 - 3 cm
Length of tail hairs: 30 - 70 cm
Number of tail hairs: 500 - 700
Hooves (toenails): front 5, rear 4

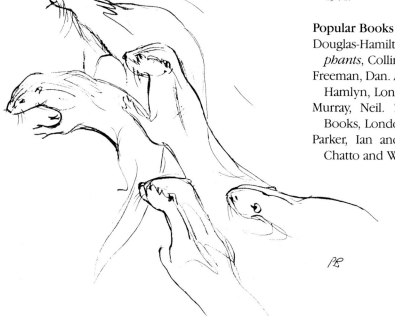

BIBLIOGRAPHY

Many books have been written about the African elephant. Some are technical, others make for easier reading. Only a few of the more important books are listed here, and are offered as a guide to further reading for anyone interested in these fascinating creatures.

Scientific Books
Eltringham, S. K. *Elephants* (Blandford Mammal Series), Blandford Press, Poole, 1982.
Hanks, John. *A Struggle for Survival – The Elephant Problem*, C. Struik, Cape Town, 1979.
Kingdon, Jonathan. *East African Mammals. An Atlas of Evolution in Africa*, Volume III Part B (Large Mammals) pp. 1-75, Academic Press, London, 1979.
Laws, R. M., Parker, I. S. C. and Johnstone, R. C. B. *Elephants and their Habitats – The Ecology of Elephants in North Bunyoro, Uganda*, Clarendon Press, Oxford, 1975.
Sikes, Sylvia K. *The Natural History of the African Elephant*, Weidenfeld and Nicolson, London, 1971.

Popular Books
Douglas-Hamilton, Iain and Oria. *Among the Elephants*, Collins, London, 1975.
Freeman, Dan. *Elephants – The Vanishing Giants*, Hamlyn, London, 1980.
Murray, Neil. *The Love of Elephants*, Octopus Books, London, 1976.
Parker, Ian and Amin, Mohamed. *Ivory Crisis*, Chatto and Windus, London, 1983.

CITES Convention on International Trade in Endangered Species of Wild Fauna and Flora (Washington Convention)
IUCN International Union for the Conservation of Nature and Natural Resources
IUCN/SSC Species Survival Commission of the IUCN
UNESCO United Nations Educational, Scientific and Cultural Organization
WWF World Wide Fund for Nature

The secretary bird, whose closest affinities may be with the eagles, bears the Arabic name saqr-et-tair *– the hunter bird.*

GLOSSARY

abiotic devoid of life; a term applied to the non-living elements of the environment, e.g. rocks, soil and climate.
arboreal living in trees or adapted to life in trees.
askaris young elephant bulls found in the company of old bulls, from the Swahili for soldier or guard.
biomass the total quantity of living organisms in a given area, expressed as weight per unit area (e.g. kg/ha).
biome a broad ecological unit distinguished by certain climax species of plant and animal life, e.g. desert.
biotic relating to life; a term applied to all living organisms, e.g. bacteria, animals and plants.
bush in Africa this commonly refers to a wilderness area of natural vegetation with wildlife, as opposed to settled areas.
canopy the upper zone or 'roof' of a forest, formed by the branches of neighbouring trees overlapping and touching.
carnivore an animal that eats flesh.
carrying capacity the largest number of individuals of a particular species that can be supported indefinitely in a particular area.
climax vegetation the permanent, mature, stable, equilibrium vegetation type in a particular environment. It is achieved as a result of the completion of plant succession.
community a naturally occurring assemblage of plants and animals living in the same environment and which are mutually interdependent.
conspecifics organisms belonging to the same species.
deciduous plants plants that seasonally drop and then replace their leaves.
density the size of a population relative to a definite unit of space.
ecology the scientific study of the interactions of animals or plants with their environment, both biotic and abiotic.
ecosystem all of the interacting organisms and elements, both biotic and abiotic, of a particular type of habitat (e.g. a forest).
ecotone the boundary zone where two disparate plant communities or types meet.

endemic species plants or animals found only in some limited area.
epiphyte a plant that grows on other plants but is not parasitic, e.g. orchids, ferns and moss.
evergreen plants plants that do not drop all their leaves seasonally.
flood plain the grass-covered, seasonally flooded and waterlogged low-lying regions alongside river courses.
flush seasonal new growth of vegetation, e.g. regrowth of grass after a burn, or new leaves of deciduous trees.
forest vegetation type consisting predominantly of stratified woody plants with a continuous canopy of trees, below which there are various strata of smaller trees or shrubs, grasses being virtually absent. Fire does not pass through forest.
gallery forest the band or zone of forest lining the banks of tropical rivers.
genus category of taxonomic classification higher than species (plural: genera).
gregarious animals animals that live together in an assemblage such as a colony, herd or troop.
habitat the locality or external environment – both living (e.g. plants) and non-living (e.g. soil) – in which an organism lives.
herbivore an animal that eats plants.
home range the area that an animal occupies and patrols regularly, but does not necessarily defend. The part of the home range that is defended constitutes the territory.
inselberg literally 'island mountain'; rocky, isolated outcrop or hill.
mangrove woody plants – characterized by aerial roots – that grow in waterlogged areas such as swamps, estuaries and lagoons.
migration a two-way seasonal movement of animals, involving a return to the area initially vacated.
montane occurring on mountains and areas above 1 500 m, usually in the eastern part of Africa.
niche the role or function of an organism in a particular habitat.
nomadic animals animals that move around irregularly in response to an environmental stimulus (e.g. rainfall), not necessarily returning to their point of departure.
oestrus the regularly occurring period during

Ever together, the members of an elephant herd or family group follow the matriach in aggression or flight, and to food, water, or a shady resting place.

which a female mammal is in heat, i.e. receptive to mating.

omnivore an animal that eats both plant and animal material.

organism any living creature.

pan a natural depression that retains water for some time after rain.

panga an African term for a machete.

population animals or plants of the same species occupying a clearly delimited area at a particular time.

precipitation rainfall and other sources of moisture (e.g. fog, mist, dew, snow or hail).

precocial animals animals that are born with their faculties well developed.

primary forest the natural climax vegetation in the forest zone, not showing the effects of man.

rain forest in Africa it is the evergreen, tropical lowland forest where the annual rainfall is at least 1 200 mm and with no more than two months receiving less than 50 mm of rain.

raptor a large bird of prey of the order Falconi-formes (e.g. eagles, hawks and vultures), which hunts other animals or birds or takes carrion.

ruminant a herbivorous mammal with a four-compartmented stomach, whose food is partly digested by bacterial fermentation, after which it is regurgitated, chewed and swallowed again, e.g. antelopes, buffalo and giraffe.

savanna vegetation type consisting predominantly of grasses with scattered trees and shrubs; it usually burns annually.

scavenger animal that eats dead organisms.

secondary forest forest that has been cut over, burnt or otherwise altered by man and is in a state of recovery (i.e. plant succession is moving back towards the climax forest type).

species the basic unit of taxonomic classification consisting of individuals or populations that are capable of freely interbreeding with one another (but not with other species under natural conditions) and producing fertile young.

subspecies a subdivision of a species; usually defined as a geographical race, which is a population differing genetically from other geographical races of the same species.

succession the stages of predictable change in the development of vegetation types or seres, from a pioneering stage on bare ground or water through various intermediate stages to the climax for that particular environment.

taxonomy scientific system of classifying and naming plants and animals.

terrestrial living on the ground.

territory an area occupied exclusively by an animal or group of animals and from which conspecifics are excluded by defence or display.

thermoregulation the action of regulating body temperature under different ambient temperatures.

thicket a very dense, almost impenetrable community of trees and/or large shrubs; it may be stratified like forest, with canopy and understory, or there may be no distinct stratification. Grass is discontinuous or absent. Fire may pass through deciduous thicket, but not through evergreen thicket.

type locality the place identified as the locality from which the type specimen was collected.

type specimen the specimen used for the original description of a species or subspecies.

understory the layer of shrubs and herbs close to the ground in multi-layered vegetation types.

veld word of South African origin meaning fairly open country, not under cultivation or forested; also used in the same sense as the American 'range'.

woodland vegetation type dominated by trees but with a major component of perennial grasses; trees are of moderate height, usually with canopies touching or overlapping. Fire usually occurs annually and is important in maintaining the balance between grasses and woody plants.

Lively and curious, elephant calves are alert to their surroundings and bravely charge at intruders – provided that mother is close by.
(Sanyati, Matusadona National Park, Zimbabwe)

INDEX

Numerals in **bold** type refer to captions to illustrations.

The great reach of an elephant bull ensures that he has access to titbits denied to other terrestrial browsers.

173

A solitary elephant bull paces steadily to a distant place, his journey determined by his own secret thoughts and age-old instincts.
(Letaba, Kruger National Park, South Africa)